SOCIAL WORK PRACTICE LEARNING

SOCIAL WORK PRACTICE LEARNING

A STUDENT GUIDE

DAVID EDMONDSON

Los Angeles | London | New Delhi
Singapore | Washington DC

Los Angeles | London | New Delhi
Singapore | Washington DC

SAGE Publications Ltd
1 Oliver's Yard
55 City Road
London EC1Y 1SP

SAGE Publications Inc.
2455 Teller Road
Thousand Oaks, California 91320

SAGE Publications India Pvt Ltd
B 1/I 1 Mohan Cooperative Industrial Area
Mathura Road
New Delhi 110 044

SAGE Publications Asia-Pacific Pte Ltd
3 Church Street
#10-04 Samsung Hub
Singapore 049483

Editor: Kate Wharton
Assistant editor: Emma Milman
Production editor: Katie Forsythe
Copyeditor: Jane Fricker
Indexer: Elske Janssen
Marketing manager: Tamara Navaratnam
Cover design: Lisa Harper
Typeset by: C&M Digitals (P) Ltd, Chennai, India
Printed and bound in Great Britain by Ashford
Colour Press Ltd

© David Edmondson 2014

Chapter 5 © Helen Mayall and Teresa O'Neill with Maureen
Ajayi, Shauna Crawley, Richard Hawkins (The Autistic
Organisation) and Melanie Metcalfe
First published 2014

Library of Congress Control Number: 2013946211

British Library Cataloguing in Publication data

A catalogue record for this book is available from
the British Library

ISBN 978-1-4462-0890-8
ISBN 978-1-4462-0891-5 (pbk)

MIX
Paper from
responsible sources
FSC® C011748
www.fsc.org

I would like to dedicate this book to the dear memory of my parents, Eric and Vera Edmondson. Much missed and much loved.

Contents

About the Author and Contributors

David Edmondson is a senior lecturer at Manchester Metropolitan University, registered social worker and is a founder member of SWIFT (Social Work in Film and Television) research network. He worked for many years as a qualified mental health social worker in the North West of England.

Helen Mayall is a senior lecturer at Manchester Metropolitan University. She teaches children's rights and children and families social work, often teaching alongside young service users. She is a registered social worker with experience of local authority social work with children and young people in North West England.

Donna O'Neill is a registered social worker working for Solihull MBC. Her current role focuses on the management and development of Practice Education within Local Authorities. She has worked for many years in Children and Families Teams and with young people looked after.

Teresa O'Neill is a senior lecturer at Manchester Metropolitan University. She is a registered social worker with over 20 years practice experience in children and families social work, specialising in fostering and adoption. Teresa's current research interests include services users' involvement in assessment of social work students.

Michaela Rogers is a registered social worker and lecturer at University of Salford. For over fifteen years she has worked with children and families in voluntary and statutory social work settings and she has expertise in domestic abuse work and foster care.

Dawn Whitaker is a lecturer at Lancaster University, and registered independent social worker. Dawn has worked for many years as a qualified mental health social worker in the North West of England, and continues to undertake independent best interest assessments / reports, for proceedings in the High Court / Court of Protection, instructed through the Official Solictor.

Introduction

The Purpose of this Book

A very warm welcome to *Social Work Practice Learning: A Student Guide*. This book aims to provide social work students with a quick and easy-to-access guide that can be used throughout the minimum 200 days of practice learning required to be completed as part of their professional social work training.

If you are a social work student entering professional social work training then this book is specifically designed for you. It incorporates all the new requirements for social work training and is written to help you successfully complete your social work placement(s) across a variety of contemporary fieldwork settings. The book is organised into 10 chapters, each focusing on key aspects of your practice-based learning:

- **Chapter 1** introduces you to the idea of social work and to the context, features and challenges facing social workers in practice today.
- **Chapter 2** introduces the new social work placement structure, the new Professional Capabilities Framework for Social Workers and the new revised placement structure.
- **Chapter 3** helps you prepare and plan for beginning your placement.
- **Chapter 4** looks at values and ethics in social work and working inclusively with service users and carers.
- **Chapter 5** focuses on applying values and ethics in practice, here in the context of working with young people.
- **Chapter 6** provides clear guidance about how your placements and practice will be assessed, and links your direct social work practice and activities with how to evidence your social work practice in order to pass your placement.
- **Chapter 7** introduces you to risk in the context of your practice learning and how you can work effectively to promote positive, safe and defensible practice.
- **Chapter 8** discusses the importance of supervision and reflective practice in social work.
- **Chapter 9** advises on trouble shooting and problem solving on placement.
- **Chapter 10** looks briefly at completing your social work training and preparing for professional practice.

All 10 chapters of the book are cross-referenced within the text to help you to integrate and consolidate your learning. The book uses a combination of features to promote flexible and blended learning, including:

- Resources and tips to inform your learning and development.
- Case studies and examples which are drawn from 'real-life' social work encounters, practice situations and dilemmas.
- Advice on working with diverse and different groups and communities.
- Reflections, views and tips from experienced social work practitioners.
- Reflections and opinions of service users, carers and others to ensure students gain insights into the views and perspectives of people experiencing social care services.
- The views, strategies and ideas of social work students who have recently completed their own social work placements.

This book is an introductory text and should be used as a foundation on which to build and develop your social work practice. Effective learning is both lifelong and collaborative, so if you have any ideas to add from your own experiences of placements and practice learning, it would be great to hear from you. If the ideas and tips are useful to share, these could be added to any forthcoming editions. You can contact me at the address below.

Finally, I hope you find the guide interesting and useful both as an introduction to social work and in helping you prepare for and hopefully enjoy your social work placement. Good luck!

David Edmondson
Manchester
April 2013

d.edmondson@mmu.ac.uk

The Features of the Book

The book includes the following useful features:

Placement Activities

These activities are designed to help you prepare for your placement. You are advised to try to complete all these activities and share your resulting answers, ideas and thoughts with other students and with your practice educator whilst on placement. The activities have been designed in conjunction with students, practice educators and others and draw on their collective experiences and ideas to help you to make the best of your placement.

> **PLACEMENT ACTIVITY**
> **The contribution and role of a social work student on placement**
>
> - What needs to be your commitment to making the placement a success?
> - What do you hope to have learned and achieved by the end of your placement?

e-Links

e-Links are provided to help you locate internet resources identified in the text.

→Signposts

These arrows signpost and cross-reference you to linked discussions across chapters of the book.

Points to Consider

The Points to Consider boxes prompt you to look at different aspects of social work and help you think about your practice learning.

Points to Consider

Thinking critically, having looked at the websites, reflect on:

- How easy are the websites to find and use?
- How accessible and usable are the websites for all users? Think about the typeface, font, colour and layout, etc.

Checklists

The Checklists offer a quick 'to do' list to help you in your preparation for placement.

Checklist

Before you go for your informal meeting, ask yourself the following:

- ☐ Do you know where you are meant to go for your informal meeting?
- ☐ What time is the meeting?
- ☐ How you will get to the meeting?
- ☐ How long will your journey take?

Information Points

The Information Points contain contextual and background information to help orientate you to particular features of social work.

The roots of social work

The 19th and early 20th centuries – moving away from the Poor Law and workhouse; advocates for reform and change; organised welfare provision

The organisations described below are included here as examples of emerging 19th-century charitable providers of social welfare in the UK. Contemporary charities are quite rightly proud of their origins, longevity and service. However, these histories also tell us about some deep-rooted ideas about welfare and those who receive welfare. However, these threads and ideas also help to explain the roots of social work and have also become part of the fabric of what we understand as social work today.

INFORMATION POINT

Social Work Comment

The contributions in italics included under this heading provide you with commentary from social work students, practice educators and others who draw on their own experiences and reflections to support you in preparing for your placement.

Acknowledgements

A genuine thanks to everyone who has made this book possible. I am particularly grateful to all the practitioners, educators, students and other people I have met over the years who have helped and guided me in my own social work practice and teaching. I have been very lucky in my career to have been able to work with so many truly great and inspiring social workers and local communities. Thanks are due to all the team at Sage for their continued support and encouragement. In producing this book I am especially indebted to Christine, who has helped me at every point and in every way and who along with Daniel has been so supportive over the many months of producing this book. Finally, I would also like to thank the following people who have contributed directly and significantly to the book:

Maureen Ajayi

Charlotte Ashworth

Philip Beattie

Shauna Crawley

Richard Hawkins

Christine Hayes

Emily Karlsson

Helen Mayall

Melanie Metcalfe

Pierre Nyongo

Michaela Rogers

Zoe Rogerson

Donna O'Neill

Teresa O'Neill

Ian Simpson

Dawn Whitaker

1

The Idea of Social Work: A Brief Introduction

Overview and Learning Outcomes

This chapter will cover:

- History, contexts and ideas about social work.
- Being and becoming a social worker.

By the end of Chapter 1 you will be able to:

- Offer an explanation to others of the roots and relevance of social work.
- Discuss the contemporary context of social work practice.
- Engage with debates about recent social work reforms.
- Make an effective contribution to debates about the purpose and future of social work.

Introduction to Chapter 1

This chapter seeks to orientate you to the practice of social work and to help you prepare for your forthcoming practice learning placement. It differs from the later parts of the book, where the focus is more on the placement itself and the skills, knowledge and values that are required to be successful in your practice and learning.

In this chapter, we deliberately take time to consider the context and history of social work to inform our thinking about what social work is and what it is for. In preparation for your forthcoming practice learning placement you should be able to explain your work and why social work is important. This last aspect tells us something about the current status and profile of social work, which has come under repeated public scrutiny and criticism in recent years, with some justification in certain regards. At your interview to be accepted onto a social work course you may well have been asked why you want to be a social worker. You possibly answered that you want to 'help' people. But what does this really mean and what does becoming a social worker really entail?

Students in training and experienced practitioners are often asked by service users, carers, other workers, critics and allies alike – *What is social work about? What do social workers do?* Whatever the quality of your answer, a supplementary question typically follows: *Why on earth do you want to be a social worker?* When you are out on placement, how are you going to reply?

It is important we consider these questions. After all, if we aren't clear about what we are doing and why, then not only will we not be able to do our job properly, we cannot reasonably expect others to accept or trust the services we offer.

So, when we say at our social work course interview that we want to help people, what are the things we may be thinking about? This question is further complicated, given social work and social workers frequently find themselves having to try to deal with very real and genuine crises in people's lives; severe needs and problems of daily living brought about by sudden illness, chronic health problems, family breakdown, domestic violence, neglect and abuse, loss and emotional distress. This list is by no means complete. Such events are perhaps among the most significant and life changing moments in people's lives. However, it is in just such circumstances we find social workers trying to do their work, often against a backdrop for individuals, families and groups of real poverty, neglected communities, health and social service cutbacks and experiences of inequality, discrimination and stigma. If we look back at the history of social work, it is exactly these social situations that gave rise to social work and gave purpose to our work. To be an accomplished social worker you need to be alive and alert to the broader context of your work and practice.

It is also important to note that today social work and social workers have a wide range of legislative and professional responsibilities which impose explicit duties and responsibilities on our practice (e.g. Children Act 1989, NHS and Community Care Act 1990, Human Rights Act 1998). You will undoubtedly look at human rights, law and policy in detail during your academic learning but it is important you are aware that significant areas of your practice are statute-led, whether this be in relation to social work in the areas of children and families, work with vulnerable adults or in specialist services and settings (e.g. community mental health work and specific duties located within mental health law). This aspect of social work practice is not only very challenging in itself, but frequently raises dilemmas for practitioners in terms of trying to balance respect for individual freedoms with responsibilities to the community and wider society which may involve intrusion into the private lives of people and aspects of 'social control' in our roles as 'agents' of the state.

Karen Broadhurst, writing about risk and social work, puts this challenge for social work elegantly by saying that the one of the key tasks of social work is providing effective risk management but trying to do this within the humane task of social work (Broadhurst et al. , 2010). These are not new tensions in social work and remain today. However, be assured, these are challenging dilemmas even for the most seasoned social work practitioner. Remember you are at the very beginning of your learning and career and your academic teaching and practice learning is provided to take you on the journey to be ready to begin your practice.

Contemporary Social Work in the Context of Reform

Social work in England today is once again facing major public scrutiny and review (DfE, 2011b, 2012; Social Work Reform Board [SWRB], 2010), driven most recently by public concerns following a series of high profile non-accidental child deaths and serious case reviews, perhaps marked most notably by the tragic death of 17-month-old Peter Connelly on 3 August 2007. The cumulative effect of these tragedies and reviews prompted the UK government to set up a comprehensive 'root and branch' reorganisation of social work. The Social Work Task Force, launched in 2009, was charged to drive and deliver social work reform and to improve frontline practice and management.

The Task Force quickly set out to examine and review the social work profession, ranging from social work management and casework, through to inter-agency working, administration and training and finally to change how social work is perceived by the public and reported in the media. The Task Force made 15 recommendations for a comprehensive reform programme and the Social Work Reform Board (SWRB, 2010) was set up to take forward the reforms. Alongside the Reform Board, the Munro Review of Child Protection was commissioned in 2010 by the Department for Education to provide an independent review of child protection in England. This review was published in three reports with the final report *The Munro Review of Child Protection: Final report: A child-centred system* being published in May 2011 (DfE, 2011b).

Reinforced by Eileen Munro's complementary *Review of Child Protection*, the Social Work Task Force identified several key issues faced by children's services and the wider social work profession. Particular attention was drawn to the organisational difficulties social workers face in their day-to-day work, notably in relation to over-bureaucratisation of child protection processes and procedures, inadequate leadership and management and too little professional development and support, particularly for recently qualified social workers (Edmondson et al., 2013).

The Task Force also critically commented on how inadequate social work has been at explaining its work to the public, and that the value and role of social workers in child protection work, arguably one of the most demanding and testing areas of social work practice today, are poorly understood and have failed to engage the public with the very real challenges and dilemmas facing many local authority social workers in their day-to-day practice. 'Damned if you do, damned if you don't' has become a commonly held view in social work team rooms about their likely treatment in the press in terms of the reporting of social work interventions where child protection is the main issue and removing a child may be necessary (*The Guardian*, 2012).

Commentaries about social work have reinforced the assertion that social work is again at a 'watershed' and a 'crossroads' in terms of its future and frequently questioned its ability to reform and change sufficiently to attain a new 'safe, confident' future (DCSF, 2009).

Later in the book, we will look at the implications of these reform programmes and particularly how these relate to your placements and practice learning.

INFORMATION POINT

Social work reform in the 21st century

Visit the e-links below to look at the work of the Task Force, Reform Board and the agencies relevant to the government's main social work reforms. Read about the Task Force and Reform Board recommendations for the future of social work and how the different agencies are involved in taking the reform programme forward.

The Social Work Task Force

In 2008 the Social Work Task Force (SWTF) was set up to improve the quality, status and public profile of social work, to reform social work education and training and also to review recruitment, training and retention of social workers.

   The Task Force produced its final report: *Building a Safe, Confident Future: The final report of the Social Work Task Force* in 2009, which made 15 key recommendations for the comprehensive reform of the social work profession (DCSF, 2009b).

The Social Work Reform Board

The Social Work Reform Board (SWRB) was established in 2010 to take forward the work of the Social Work Task Force.

The Munro Review of Child Protection

Alongside the Reform Board, the Munro Review of Child Protection had been commissioned in 2010 by the Department for Education to provide an independent review of child protection in England. The review was published in three reports with the final report, *The Munro Review of Child Protection: Final report: A child-centred system*, being published in May 2011 (DfE, 2011b).

The College of Social Work

The SWRB's recommendations were also supported by the creation of a new independent College of Social Work, primarily established to represent the social work profession and be responsible for upholding the agreed professional standards for social work. The College has a lead role in the development of professional standards for social work; represent the profession in national planning of services and improve the public profile of social work.

Figure 1.1

Have a good look around the College site and look at the useful student sections and news archive. Maybe sign up for the monthly e-bulletin or follow the College on Twitter.

Social Care Institute for Excellence

The Social Care Institute for Excellence (SCIE) was set up over a decade ago to promote and support the development and delivery of high quality social care for children and adults. SCIE is now considered an effective resource for people interested in social care and those delivering care.

Figure 1.2

Health and Care Professions Council

In July 2010, the government announced its intention to close the General Social Care Council (the previous regulatory body for social work), and transfer its regulatory functions to the Health Professions Council (HPC). In order to reflect this new remit, the HPC's name was changed in 2012 to the Health and Care Professions Council (HCPC). The HCPC is the main regulator for health and social care workers and has as its main remit the protection of the public.

Anyone wishing to use the title of social worker – which is protected in law – has to be registered with the HCPC and comply with the Standards of Proficiency for Social Workers in England (2012).

The Standards relate to proficiency and conduct rather than professional aspirations or expectations. There is a range of actions available to the Council including stopping people from practising. In terms of professional development, registered professional social workers are expected to be responsible for the 'scope' of their own practice and for meeting the professional requirements set out by the College of Social Work.

e-Links

www.hpc-uk.org/
www.education.gov.uk/swrb
www.collegeofsocialwork.org/
www.scie.org.uk/

The Idea of Social Work – Histories and Roots

It is generally agreed that social work finds its historical roots in charity and help for the poor. Malcolm Payne in his book *Origins of Social Work* (2005) argues that social work emerged in Britain from three distinct historical strands. These included the reorganisation and centralisation of poor relief; the development of the 'settlement' movement in the late 19th and early 20th centuries (as a response to increasing social problems and poverty created by rapid urbanisation); and perhaps most recognisably within contemporary constructions of social work, in the form of 'helping others' and the organisation and delivery of charitable 'good works'. In early social work, this typically included practical social support, 'friendly visiting' and the promotion of mutual help and 'betterment' through friendly societies, cooperative movements, guilds, etc.

In its history, social work has made claims to a philosophical tradition of egalitarianism and a belief and commitment to social justice, humane values and principles. Pat Higham (2006) argues that social work developed out of the 19th-century philanthropic tradition of charity and help, on the one hand, and the more punitive measures of the workhouse, control and coercive change as a means of social welfare, on the other. These strands of care and control are readily evident in contemporary debates about the purpose of social work. Think back to Karen Broadhurst's analysis of social work today and consider issues social workers face.

INFORMATION POINT

The roots of social work

The 19th and early 20th centuries – Moving away from the Poor Law and workhouse; advocates for reform and change; organised welfare provision

The organisations described below are included here as examples of emerging 19th-century charitable providers of social welfare in the UK. Contemporary charities are quite rightly proud of their origins, longevity and service. However, these histories also tell us about some deep-rooted ideas about welfare and those who receive welfare. These ideas and threads also help to explain the roots of social work and have become part of the fabric of what we today understand as social work.

There are many examples to choose from; consider the following:

- The Charity Organisation Society (COS) was founded in 1869. The COS is of profound importance in the development of modern welfare. The COS sought to actively bring local and independent services together in order to better organise delivery of more coordinated and effective services. The COS introduced an approach to welfare work which included a form of initial assessment, prioritisation of service provision and allocated 'case' work. However, the COS also codified 19th-century assumptions about welfare and help for the poor. Distribution of services and resources was focused very much around criteria based on those who were deemed most in need, or, more tellingly, most 'deserving' and 'undeserving'. Rather like today, in fact!

- The National Society for the Prevention of Cruelty to Children (NSPCC) was founded in 1884. Its development was informed in part by the example of the New York Society for the Prevention of Cruelty to Children.

- The National Children's Home and Orphanage was established in 1906/7. It was later renamed as NCH and then as Action for Children in 2008.

- Dr Barnardo opened his first home for boys in Stepney Causeway, London in 1870.

e-Links

www.infed.org/socialwork/charity_organization_society.htm
www.nspcc.org.uk/
www.actionforchildren.org.uk/
www.barnardos.org.uk/
www.workhouses.org.uk/

For an interesting history have a look at the History of Social Work website

www.historyofsocialwork.org/eng/index.php

In some respects, charitable organisations and welfare movements such as the ones above can be seen as a genuine and practical response to poverty, neglect and abuse but they are also important for our current discussion in demonstrating the influence and significance of shifting societal norms across the 19th and early 20th centuries. These ideas, particularly about what to do about 'the poor' and those in need, not only informed how these organisations were to emerge and develop but have also informed contemporary ideas about the provision and purpose of social welfare and in turn the development of 'social services' and social work.

Many charitable organisations were significantly informed by beliefs about those who are deemed 'deserving' and 'undeserving'; that there existed clear and definable religious and secular codes of morality and behaviour that could be instructively communicated to others and which should inform individual lifestyles and family life. There was also an acceptance that even in agencies driven by a commitment to religious and pastoral care, welfare provision and change could be organised and delivered within a secular moral framework of 'scientific charity'. This latter idea sought to apply a blend of science and business efficiency to dealing with the poor and also to addressing the perceived inefficiency and dependency creation of then charitable giving and charitable institutions. The development of 'the workhouse' in the 19th century as an organised and efficient way of addressing poverty was a typical manifestation of this idea.

Although such ideas about society have varied, modified and changed they are still relevant to our contemporary thinking about social welfare, social service and provision. These norms and ideas have strongly informed social service and social work as it has come to exist today and continue to inform the idea of professional social work and its purpose into the 21st century. If you listen to contemporary debates about welfare provision, much of the rhetoric clearly features ideas of deserving and undeserving, welfare to work rather than welfare as need or right; and mistrust and abhorrence of any accepted role for local councils or the state to provide welfare.

Higham's (2006) position reflects two contrasting approaches to social welfare that have vied for dominance during the early 20th century. The first approach considered the main cause of social problems as located within the individual, whereby change was directed at the personal level in order to remedy social problems; in contrast, the second approach considered the cause of social problems as located within societal structures, and intervention was directed mainly at the structural, cultural and sociopolitical level. This debate is reflected in the writing of several contemporary social work authors (Leskošek, 2009; McLaughlin, 2008; Pierson, 2011; Thompson, 2000).

Another noteworthy feature of welfare provision emerging from the 19th century was the development of the Settlement movement. This began in the 1880s in London in response to social problems and poverty created by rapid urbanisation, industrialisation and immigration. The idea quickly spread to other industrialised countries. A good early example of the Settlement movement in England can be found at Toynbee Hall, founded by a Church of England curate, Samuel Barnett, and his wife in the parish of St Jude's in the East End of London, one of the poorest areas of London. Through education and community development the Barnetts hoped to improve and change society.

The truly radical idea behind the social settlement was to invite individuals to come to live in the settlement. Settlement houses typically attracted well-educated, native-born, middle-class and upper-middle-class women and men, known as 'residents', to 'settle' and visit or less commonly reside for a period of time in poor districts and neighbourhoods. 'Settlers' were expected to provide education and support to local residents. Some settlements were linked to religious institutions, others to universities and secular groups.

INFORMATION POINT

The roots of social work

The development of settlements as a response to social need and a catalyst for social welfare, change and justice

The Settlement movement expanded rapidly both in the UK and internationally. Hull House in Chicago, founded by activist and social reformer Jane Addams, is a well-known example of a settlement in the USA. Many cities developed and still have similar schemes both in the UK (Manchester, Birmingham, London) and across the world (Chicago, New York). Have a look at the websites below for an interesting account of the roots of the settlement movements and examples of contemporary settlement projects and developments. The International Federation of Settlements and Neighbourhood Centres (IFS) connects global community organisations working for social justice. Have a look at their work.

Settlements are relevant to our understanding of modern ideas of welfare provision in that they were local, community-driven and practical responses to need and poverty which emphasised the importance of community and mutuality, the importance and benefits of education in promoting healthy and enriched lives, and the value of 'reaching in' to communities and drawing on the knowledge, skills and values of committed individuals with a desire to help others.

Toynbee Hall, London (UK)

Figure 1.3

Manchester Settlement (UK)

Figure 1.4

(Continued)

(Continued)

e-Links

www.toynbeehall.org.uk/
www.manchestersettlement.org.uk/
http://birminghamsettlement.org.uk/
www.ifsnetwork.org/

A further and distinct feature of social work we do need to note here has been the association of social work with a range of radical political movements and action across the 19th and 20th centuries which have sought to improve the living conditions of the poor, elderly and infirm and promote a more humane and just society.

The Toynbee Hall settlement, which opened its doors in the East End of London in 1884, included among its residents Clement Attlee and William Beveridge, both of whom maintained a life-long connection with Toynbee Hall. It is largely forgotten today that Clement Attlee, who as Labour Party leader in 1935 and then Prime Minister of the 1945–51 Labour government, oversaw and achieved the introduction of the welfare state, National Health Service and free, state secondary education, had previously worked as a practising social worker in London. In 1920, Attlee had written his first book, entitled *The Social Worker*. The book outlines Attlee's ideas about social reform and welfare with a key role identified for enlarged and organised social services. This took forward the ideas outlined in the Beveridge Report (1942) – produced by William Beveridge – which became the basis for the creation of the welfare state.

Attlee's experiences and writing in the early 20th century reflect this argument and for him the task of the social worker is of community worker, activist and advocate for social reform and social justice. The new political context and economy of welfare in post-Second World War Britain (1945 onwards) increased public awareness and scrutiny of state-sponsored support; it also signified increased centralised regulation, new organisational structures and the development of performance management, some of which remain in place today (Payne, 2005). At the time of Attlee's book in the 1920s, there was a small number of social work taught courses which could be described as training schemes for social service and social work. These were typically offered in urban areas such as London and Birmingham and were later to be developed into formal and recognised training and preparation for social work.

INFORMATION POINT

The roots of social work

Social work, political action and championing social justice

Look at the extract below from Attlee's book. Although, we may be forgiven for finding the language used in Attlee's book rather fusty today, I think he writes with honest purpose. In the best sense, I wonder if we can really say contemporary debates about welfare, poverty and helping the poor will really produce a *'better apportionment of all the things that make up a good life'*.

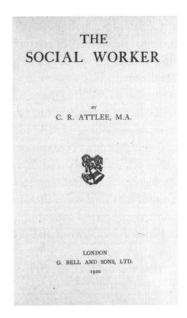

THE
SOCIAL WORKER

BY
C. R. ATTLEE, M.A.

LONDON
G. BELL AND SONS, LTD.
1920

Figure 1.5

Photograph © National Portrait Gallery, London

'Social workers,' someone will say rather pityingly, 'good people no doubt in their way, but very dull, forever fussing over their lame ducks; all very well, of course, for people who like that sort of thing, elderly spinsters and men with no settled occupation.' This or something like it is a not uncommon view, but it is, I believe, a profound misconception. The Social Service movement of modern times is not confined to any one class, nor is it the preserve of a particular section of dull and respectable people. It has arisen out of a deep discontent with society as at present constituted, and among its prophets have been the greatest spirits of our time. It is not a movement concerned alone with the material, with housing and drains, clinics and feeding centres, gas and water, but is the expression of the desire for social justice, for freedom and beauty, and for the better apportionment of all the things that make up a good life. It is the constructive side of the criticism passed by the reformer and the revolutionary on the failure of our industrialised society to provide a fit environment where a good life shall be possible for all. (Attlee, 1920: 2–3)

The place of values in the idea of social work

So far we have looked at the historical context of social work in the UK and notably the emergence of organised responses to poverty, need and welfare in the later 19th century with the establishment of the Charity Organisation Society, Settlements and the emergence of particular charitable welfare organisations (Barnardo's, NSPCC). Social welfare in this context was still rooted in Christian-based ethics and influenced by religious ideas of redemption and improving the moral wellbeing of the individual.

However, into the early 20th century, more secular and liberal foundations of social welfare were coming to the fore with a growing ethos towards recognising the value of the individual and less conditional welfare provision and social service. It has long been argued that social work is a value-based activity (Barnard, 2006).

Frederic G. Reamer has written extensively on social work values and ethics, notably in relation to social work in the USA, and has identified four overlapping key stages in the evolution and development of contemporary social work: '(1) the morality period, (2) the values period, (3) the ethical theory and decision-making period, and (4) the ethical standards and risk management period' (Reamer, 1998: 488). Drawing directly on Reamer, Table 1.1 below provides an overview of the development of values and ethics in social work; the features and changes that have occurred over time to bring us to this point; and the relationship between values and ethics in social work and prevailing ideas in society about welfare and the role and purpose of social work.

During what Reamer (1998, 2003) described as the values period in social work history, Reverend Felix Biestek, later to become Professor of Social Work at Loyola University in Chicago, wrote *The Casework Relationship* (1957). This book quickly became a landmark in social work writing, and in it Biestek set out what he called the seven principles for effective and positive social work practice and case-based work. These were:

1. Individualisation.
2. Purposeful expression of feeling.
3. Controlled emotional involvement.
4. Acceptance.
5. Non-judgemental attitude.
6. Client self-determination.
7. Confidentiality.

These principles were heavily influential in social work education and this book became a core text in many UK programmes. The set of principles was quite novel in that it was one of the early 'list' approaches to setting out principles for practice, required application and action on the part of the worker and was, as a list of statements to follow, relatively plain and unambiguous.

However, Biestek's work was to fall out of favour and was heavily criticised for its author's religious foundations and in focusing on individual working relationships without

Table 1.1   Values, ethics and the development of social work

	Period	Features
1. The morality period	Early 20th century	- Early emphasis on correcting and rescuing the moral wellbeing of individuals who were poor and in need - Paternalistic efforts to shift and rescue those who were deemed 'deserving' - The gradual move from 'cause' to 'case'
2. The values period	1950s–1970s	- Refocus of attention on the values and ethics of the social work profession - Focus on social justice, social reform, civil rights - Practice attentive to human rights, welfare rights, anti-discriminatory and anti-oppressive practice
3. The ethical theory and decision-making period	1980s	- Academic attention on new fields of applied and professional ethics and theories of ethics in social work and related professions, e.g. medicine and nursing - Debates emerge within social work of decision-making and dilemmas of practice, e.g. rights and duties; care and control; preventative work vs protection work
4. The ethical standards and risk management period	1990s onwards	- The provision of codified ethical guidelines which as well as providing guidance for practice also include statements of values and attention to direct practice issues, e.g. confidentiality, consent, distributing limited resources, reporting unethical conduct - Ongoing revision, updating and expansion of codes to contested and debated ideas about professional role; concern to set and maintain rigorous practice standards; legal issues and misconduct

Source: Reamer, 1998, 2003.

consideration of the wider political context of social work, notably in relation to structural oppression and discrimination as root causes of poverty and need.

Some decades later, Clark (2000) conducted a thorough analysis of ethical guidelines in social work, and identified eight value-led rules for good practice; these state that social workers should be 'respectful', 'honest and truthful', 'knowledgeable and skilful', 'careful and diligent', 'effective and helpful', 'legitimate and authorised', 'collaborative and accountable' and 'reputable and credible' (Clark, 2000: 49–62). From these Clark identified the following 'stocks' (Clark, 2000) of ethical social work practice as:

- Respect.
- Justice.
- Citizenship.
- Discipline.

Clark soundly argues that these principles cannot remain theoretical and abstract and 'have to be elaborated in the context of real lives in real communities' (Clark, 2000: 172). For our purposes here these translate into a model of 'real' practice which emphasises:

- the worth and uniqueness of every person;
- the rights and entitlement to justice;
- freedom; and
- the essentiality of community.

These last definitions are interesting in our contemporary practice as they explicitly link our professional values to broadly sociopolitical aspirations and ambitions for social work. They assert the role of social workers as active in promoting commitments to social justice, freedom and the importance of community. Implicit, therefore, is a call to actively challenge structures and systems which deny these goals, in particular, discrimination, oppression, social exclusion, poverty and need. Keep these principles at the forefront of your thinking and practice.
→ Look at: **Chapter 4 Understanding Values and Ethics**.

Social justice and a commitment to anti-oppressive and anti-discriminatory practice

Lena Dominelli (2009) argues that social justice refers to individuals, groups and communities having rights and entitlements based on the notions of equality of treatment, access and inclusion. Such commitments are core components of anti-oppressive social work practice which is founded upon 'social work's historical concern with the underdog' and shaped by 'struggles against structural inequalities like poverty, sexism, racism and disablism' (Dominelli, 2009: 50). In beginning your social work career you will have the opportunity to read about and discuss social work in relation to 'anti-oppressive practice' and also 'anti-discriminatory practice'. These terms tend to get used in social work regularly and interchangeably, so be aware of this in your reading.

Neil Thompson prefers to use anti-discriminatory practice, which he defines as:

> an attempt to eradicate discrimination and oppression from our own practice and challenge them in the practice of others and in the institutional structures in which we operate. (2006: 40–1)

Working with people to reduce and eradicate oppression is at the heart of social work practice. However, it is also important to acknowledge that as social workers we are an inherent part of society; and involved in personal, cultural and social interactions that create, and reinforce oppression.

Anti-discrimination legislation has been profoundly important in informing social work practice. This has historically included key legislation such as the Equal Pay Act 1970, Sex Discrimination

Act 1975, the Race Relations Act 1976 and Disability Discrimination Act 1995. The Equality Act which came into force on 1 October 2010 brought together these and other separate pieces of discrimination legislation into one single Act. As social workers, we are trained to be aware of our legal duties and also our legal obligation to adhere to the European Convention on Human Rights (ECHR), incorporated into UK law through the Human Rights Act (1998) and a professional obligation to work in accordance with the Universal Declaration of Human Rights (1948). It will be critical that you understand the legislative framework informing your practice. Ensure you read these key statements during practice learning. They will help you locate your work and the purpose of your work in promoting ethical and rights-based social work.

Anti-oppressive social work practice asserts a commitment to practising in a way that identifies and seeks to challenge and change legal and political systems, socioeconomic structures and interpersonal relations which impact negatively on the lives of those we work with.

However, Ruth Stark, writing for the International Federation of Social Workers (IFSW), acknowledges, in relation to social work:

> ... we have not yet reached that state where dignity and justice for all people is either recognised or practiced. The fact that we have not yet achieved that state in our societies is the reason why many people become social workers – to work with people for positive change in their lives. ... Where people are abused, harmed, discriminated against, commit violent acts against others; are confused, suffering from mental health issues; are deprived of basic life sources like food, water and shelter – you will find a role for social workers to help achieve social inclusion, social cohesion and social justice. (Stark, 2008)

Read this statement carefully. It sets out in clear terms how and why we should be helping people and about the idea of social work. As Neil Thompson asserts, for social work, there can be no middle ground; our interventions will either challenge inequality or reinforce it (Thompson, 2001). Consequently, as social workers we all need to adopt a questioning, critical approach to practice, otherwise we run the risk of unwittingly reinforcing existing social inequalities, social exclusion and the marginalisation of the individuals, groups and communities we claim we want to help.

Social work in the modern era

Into the 21st century Mark Lymbery (2005) has described the stages of the development of modern social work as characterised by models which emphasised 'individual casework' (drawing on the COS approach), 'social administration' (derived historically in the Poor Law, the COS and other larger scale welfare services) and finally 'social action' (identified with the Settlement movement and later politically active responses to need and poverty).

Malcolm Payne offers an alternative classification of the 'general perspectives' of social work which he classifies as: 'individualist-reformist', 'socialist-collectivist' and 'reflexive-therapeutic'

(Payne, 1996: 2). Lymbery (2005) suggests that the reflexive-therapeutic perspective was particularly powerful in the USA in the early part of the 20th century and in the UK in the 1950s onwards; that the socialist-collectivist perspective was prominent in the radical social work literature in the UK during the 1970s and early 1980s; and that the individualist-reformist perspective has tended to characterise the modern era of social work practice.

A response to the domination of the individual casework model outlined above was articulated in the late 1960s and early 1970s with the emergence of 'radical social work' which challenged the way casework was being used to target and pathologise the individual as the source and root of social problems and to ignore structural inequality or discrimination as causes of social need. In 1975, Roy Bailey and Mike Brake produced their classic edited book *Radical Social Work* (Bailey and Brake, 1975). Radical social work was defined as 'essentially understanding the position of the oppressed in the context of the social and economic structure they live in' (Bailey and Brake, 1975: 9) and emphasised the importance of sociological theories of community development to developing rights based social work practice.

However, Martin Davies has argued that UK social work falls largely within this individualist-reformist tradition and that although social workers have had recognisably differing roles over time, these can be 'all subsumed under a general theory of *maintenance*' (Davies, 1994: 57). Davies's emphasis here on the word maintenance is important as it critiques social work as ultimately accepting of both the basic structure of society and also of social work as a compliant profession which accepts imposed limits to its role and function. Within this maintenance model, varying beliefs and attitudes to social welfare and the purpose of welfare services can be identified, as can ideas about the 'deserving' and the 'undeserving' poor: a belief in the existence of a set of clear and definable religious and secular codes of morality and behaviour that should be used to inform and instruct individual lifestyles and family life, and revulsion at, and the rejection of, state-based welfare.

Thus, social work has to be interpreted and understood as a product not only of its history, but also of the prevailing political, social and economic philosophies of its time. It is important that as workers we are aware of the roots of social work, and how these influence the profession as it is practised today. However, it is also vitally important that we think critically about the social and political context of contemporary social work – as all these factors combine to influence what we consider to be the purpose of social work.

Consider for yourself the path being plotted out for social work in the following section, which looks at contemporary social work in our present era of welfare reform and 'fairness'. Is there a place for social work?

Contemporary Debates and Ideas about Social Work

In the plan *Building a Safe and Confident Future: Implementing the recommendations of the Social Work Task Force* (DCSF and DH, 2010) the government outlined the context to reform but also the purpose and value of social work:

The Task Force was established at a time of considerable public criticism of social workers. In response to concerns about low levels of understanding of the purpose and value of social work by the media and members of the public, the Task Force developed a clear and simple description of what social work is, and what social workers do:

Social work helps adults and children to be safe, so that they can cope and take control of their lives again.

Social workers [can] make life better for people in crisis who are struggling to cope, feel alone and cannot sort out their problems unaided.

This description makes a strong case for the value of the profession not only for the individuals who use social work services, but also for *the whole of society*. (DH, 2010b: 5)

The College of Social Work's ambition to offer a 'clear and simple' definition of social work as a springboard for supporting the profession in its current reforms and future direction (or some might argue its longer term rehabilitation) is worth noting here as this seems to acknowledge several features of the history of social work which have come to be played out in public debates about social work.

The first is the absence of a readily agreed definition of social work, both within academic social work but also across its different areas and settings of practice. As Vivienne Cree states:

… is almost impossible to find a simple definition of social work with which everyone is likely to agree. (Cree, 2003: 3)

This has not only hampered social work from being able to successfully explain its work in plain terms – unlike other professions such as medicine, nursing or teaching – but, it could be argued, has also undermined the ability of the profession, unlike those above, to elicit public support and respect for its work.

PLACEMENT ACTIVITY
Defining social work

Although defining social work is a challenge, it is important we try if we are to explain and justify our work to other people. Read the following definitions and highlight the key words and phrases which you think properly characterise social work.

Social work is a modern profession which forms part of a broad span of social care activities carried out by a huge workforce in the health and social care services. (Adams, 2010: 3)

Social workers work with people who experience complex problems that are multifaceted. They engage with the personal dimensions of multiple problems such as urban and rural squalor, deprivation and degradation in communities and societies, while attempting to empower and sometimes intervene. (Adams, 2007: 32–3)

Social work is what social workers do. (Thompson, 2000: 13)

(Continued)

(Continued)

The Department of Health and Department of Education and Skills' report *Options for Excellence: Building the social care workforce of the future* (2006) set out to define social work and offered the following:

The term 'social workers' refers to those workers trained to assess and respond to people with complex personal and social needs. ... Social Workers carry out a variety of tasks, including casework, acting as an advocate, risk assessment, and working as a care manager. As a profession, social work promotes social change, problem solving and human relationships and the empowerment and liberation of people to enhance wellbeing. (DH and DfES, 2006: 9)

Note down the key defining words and phrases in these statements which tell us something about the purpose of social work.
　Think about how you might use these terms during your social work placement to describe and explain what you do and why.

Defining Social Work

Possibly the best approximation of a definition which encapsulates contemporary social work is that of the 'International Definition of Social Work' as agreed by the International Federation of Social Workers (IFSW).

The social work profession promotes social change, problem solving in human relationships and the empowerment and liberation of people to enhance well-being. Utilising theories of human behaviour and social systems, social work intervenes at the points where people interact with their environments. Principles of human rights and social justice are fundamental to social work. (IFSW, 2000a)

The IFSW goes on to state that as an activity:

Social work in its various forms addresses the multiple, complex transactions between people and their environments. Its mission is to enable all people to develop their full potential, enrich their lives, and prevent dysfunction. Professional social work is focused on problem solving and change. As such, social workers are change agents in society and in the lives of the individuals, families and communities they serve. Social work is an interrelated system of values, theory and practice. (IFSW, 2000a)

The IFSW definition has now been adopted by over 90 member organisations (IFSW, 2013) including the UK's main social work and professional bodies such as the British Association of Social Workers (BASW).

Whose definition of social work?

The IFSW definition of social work emphasises a commitment for social workers to positive change, social justice and rights, empowerment and liberation. These are important principles and values for any social worker to be committed to and ought to be the foundation of your developing practice. This becomes even more important when we consider the contested nature of social work. As Vivienne Cree has stated:

Social work is always subject to competing claims of definition and practice, and cannot be separated from the society in which it is located. Rather social work has to be seen as a collection of competing and contradictory discourses that come together at a particular moment in time to frame the task of social work. (Cree, 2003: 4)

Further, Asquith cautions us to be aware that any discussion about defining social work has 'as much been about *whose* definition is seen as legitimate rather than *which* definition' (Asquith et al., 2005: 11). Asquith goes on to demonstrate this point:

What is seen to be valid knowledge or indeed the function of social work is defined by many others outwith the profession including academics, educators, professionals, administrators, politicians, users, carers and the media. There can be no doubt that within these different constituencies, there are very different views and assumptions about social work and its function, fuelled by vested interests and media representation. (Asquith et al., 2005: 11)

Thus, part of your introductory learning in any social work course has to consider not only the roots of social work as a way of understanding its historical threads, but also how contemporary political and socioeconomic discourses, as Cree puts it, 'frame the task of social work'. If we accept that social work is impacted on by contemporary ideas about welfare and welfare provision, then drawing on a clear set of values and ethical principles to direct and steer our practice becomes a key part of helping us work out how and why as social workers we go about our daily work.

For a comparative and international view of social work, look at the following national social work websites:

- Scotland: www.sssc.uk.com
- Australia: www.aasw.asn.au/
- Canada: www.casw-acts.ca/

INFORMATION POINT

Social Work Today

Debates about history and definition perhaps really reflect the view that activities that are traditionally described as 'social work' have been too many, too broad and too various to be easily consigned within the narrow strictures of an all-inclusive definition. It is arguable that we should simply ignore attempts at providing definitions altogether and instead focus on better describing and explaining social work activities which are meaningful and change lives. Contemporary discussion about social work too often emphasises the need to 're-image' or 're-brand' social work. Surveys and commentaries on public perceptions of social work in the UK have consistently evidenced the periodically difficult relationship between social work, the media and the public (Aldridge, 1994; Galilee, 2005). Social workers are 'routinely vilified in sections of the national press' (Brody, 2009) and frequently described or characterised in the media generally as either lazy, incompetent bureaucrats who are culpable in most welfare cases where things go wrong or, at best, well-meaning do-gooders. The association in various media of social workers as 'child snatchers' focuses almost exclusively on child protection, and the removal of children from families is a persistent and strong discourse of reporting, news and drama featuring social work and social workers (Edmondson and King, forthcoming).

Such portrayals of social work increasingly serve to encourage and reinforce an increasingly hostile and negative impression of social work and endorse particular neoliberal ideologies and discourses about welfare, social work and welfare provision in England (Carey and Foster, 2012; Garrett, 2012). Importantly, the Social Work Task Force was particularly critical about the inadequacy of social work in explaining its work to the public and the value and role of social workers in child protection work. Arguably child protection is one of the most demanding and testing areas of social work practice today, but remains poorly understood and has failed to engage the public with the very real challenges and dilemmas facing many local authority social workers in their day-to-day practice.

INFORMATION POINT

Contemporary examples of effective social work

1. 'Success story'

Professor Colin Pritchard has demonstrated that numbers of 'child abuse-related deaths' of children aged from birth to 14 years over the period 1974–2006 tell a relative 'success story' for England and Wales, where rates 'have never been lower since records began' and reflect positively on protection services for children. As Pritchard concluded, 'This should help to offset something of the media stereotypes and be a boost for the morale of front line staff of the CPS and the families whom they serve' (Pritchard and Williams, 2010: 1700).

2. FAST

Professor Lynn McDonald is the founder of Families and Schools Together (FAST), and the creator of the FAST family engagement model. Based on systems and ecological models of practice (you will study these during your course) and adopting task-centred social work principles (another social work approach you will become familiar with during your studies), FAST is now one of the highest rated evidence-based approaches to improving childhood success through supporting successful parenting.

The United Nations has recognised FAST as a leading evidence-based family skills programme. FAST has been implemented now in 13 different countries, including the USA, Australia, Austria, Canada, Germany, Russia, the Netherlands, Northern Ireland, Scotland, Wales, England, Tajikistan and Kazakhstan.

e-Link

www.familiesandschools.org/

3. Social work campaigners

Social workers as campaigners and reformers is not something confined to the past. Have a look at the links below, which also emphasise the importance of the role of women in social work history and in contemporary society.

There have been many links over the years between the Nobel Peace Prize and social work. Read for example about Jane Addams, Nobel Peace Prize winner in 1931, and her work as a social reformer in the USA. Read also about Liberian social worker Leymah Gbowee, awarded the Nobel Peace Prize in 2011 for her work in leading a women's movement to stop rape and the use of child soldiers in Liberia's civil war.

e-Links

www.nobelprize.org/nobel_prizes/peace/laureates/1931/addams-bio.html/
www.nobelprize.org/nobel_prizes/peace/articles/heroines/
www.socialworkersspeak.org/media/liberian-social-worker-wins-nobel-peace-prize.html

Summary

This introductory chapter has sought to trace the history of social work, raise discussion of how and why modern social work developed in the way that it did and to inform how we can engage with contemporary debates about the future of social work. In doing so, we briefly outlined historical developments in the late 19th and early 20th centuries which produced increasing centralisation and organisation of services to address poverty and provide welfare services based on assessment of need and casework. In addition, one can trace the influence and importance of the settlement movement in emphasising community action and models of welfare provision which sought to "reach in" and support communities in most need and at most peril. For social work, this placed emphasis on the importance of befriending, helping others and following principles of egalitarianism and social justice.

However, we have also seen social work has experienced internal debates about its location and involvement in processes which maintain inequality, discrimination and oppression. Into the 21st century, neoliberal ideas of welfare and the role of the state have challenged the worth and future of social work.

Perhaps the need in social work and for agencies supporting social work is more than merely re-imaging the profession, as has been suggested, and more about relocating and re-imagining the role of the profession its purpose.

Critical friends of social work, like Professor Bill Jordan (2004, 2006) and Dr Iain Ferguson and Rona Woodward (2009), are concerned for the future of social work in the face of drives to marginalise and exclude radical and empowering models of social work and corral it within tightly prescribed roles of assessment, administration and bureaucracy. Chris Jones has raised a challenge for social work by asserting that contemporary social workers: 'are often doing little more than supervising the deterioration of people's lives' (Jones et al., 2004). Some would argue this is a strong and emotive statement and not for the faint-hearted.

However whatever our personal perspectives on social work, a typical day in the world of the social worker will be likely to include having to weigh and balance:

- Choice, rights and duties.
- The needs of individuals and the needs of the community.
- Care and control.
- Risk and risk taking.
- Public services and private lives.

Social work remains, as it always has been, a contested profession. In reviewing a range of social work literature, Asquith identified a number of conceptions of the role of social workers (Asquith et al., 2005). These include the roles of:

- Counsellor (or caseworker).
- Advocate.
- Partner.
- Assessor (of risk or need).
- Care manager.
- Agent of social control.

The debate about what social work is meant to be, and do, will not cease. All we are saying at this point is that you need to be willing and prepared to engage with this debate. Without doubt, social work reform is going to be a close companion during your forthcoming training and practice learning and this will probably be the case through the course of your career. Rather than be disheartened by this you should be emboldened to seek to be the best worker you can.

Core to being a good and effective social worker is to locate your work in sound values and ethics. There is no substitute for this if you intend to practise well and be valued by the people you will be working with.

→ See what young people tell us about social work in **Chapter 5 Translating Values into Practice**.

The one sure thing about social work is that it is never dull and no day is ever the same. We hope this chapter helps you think harder about what social work is about and inspires you to begin to work out 'what' sort of social worker you want to be and 'how' you are going to achieve this.

2

The New Professional Capabilities Framework and Revised Placement Structure

Overview and Learning Outcomes

This chapter will cover:

● The new Professional Capabilities Framework for Social Workers.
● The new social work placement structure.

By the end of Chapter 2 you will be able to:

● Identify and begin to apply the new Professional Capabilities Framework for Social Workers to demonstrate and evidence your practice learning.
● Map and orientate the new social work placement structure.

Introduction to Chapter 2

Chapter 2 is designed to help you navigate through the new national social work placement structure in England and successfully complete the 200 days of practice learning required as part of your education and training (SWRB, 2010). The chapter will introduce you to the new social work practice learning structure, the new Professional Capabilities Framework for Social Workers, and outline the new 70-day first social work placement and 100-day second placement. The chapter will also introduce you to the 30 'Skills Development' days which form part of the new social work education curriculum.

The commentary running throughout Chapter 2 includes a range of activities and guidance, and signposts you to other parts of the book you should find useful during your placement and practice learning.

It is important to remember that social work courses do vary considerably in the detail of how placements are planned and delivered so you will need to adapt the advice and suggestions made in this book to your particular local circumstances.

Social Work Education and the Professional Capabilities Framework for Social Workers

In July 2012 the Social Work Reform Board (SWRB) made a set of recommendations to improve the quality of social work degree education. The SWRB and the College of Social Work (TCSW), which was established to represent and support professional social work, worked collaboratively on a range of areas for improvement in relation to degree courses. These included issuing guidance and frameworks on: selection and admissions to social work programmes; the social work curriculum; placements and the role of practice educators; and evaluating the impact of social work education on practice.

A key initiative by the College has been the development of the new Professional Capabilities Framework for Social Workers (PCF). The PCF was introduced in 2012 to direct and assist social workers to think about and plan their professional education, training and development. Figure 2.1 shows how the College sets out the PCF.

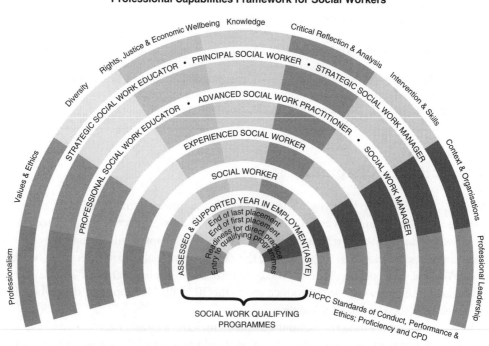

Professional Capabilities Framework for Social Workers

Figure 2.1　The Professional Capabilities Framework for Social Workers (TCSW, 2012a)

The PCF consists of nine 'capabilities' which are considered essential for any social worker to be able to demonstrate and apply in their social work practice.

Below are the PCF's nine 'capabilities' set out as a set of statements produced by the College of Social Work. The order of the capabilities follows the order they flow from left to right across the arc of the top of the PCF rainbow shown in Figure 2.1.

The nine domains of the social work PCF 'capabilities'

1. **Professionalism** – Identify and behave as a professional social worker, committed to professional development.

   Social workers are members of an internationally recognised profession, a title protected in UK law. Social workers demonstrate professional commitment by taking responsibility for their conduct, practice and learning, with support through supervision. As representatives of the social work profession they safeguard its reputation and are accountable to the professional regulator.

2. **Values and ethics** – Apply social work ethical principles and values to guide professional practice.

   Social workers have an obligation to conduct themselves ethically and to engage in ethical decision-making, including through partnership with people who use their services. Social workers are knowledgeable about the value-base of their profession, its ethical standards and relevant law.

3. **Diversity** – Recognise diversity and apply anti-discriminatory and anti-oppressive principles in practice.

   Social workers understand that diversity characterises and shapes human experience and is critical to the formation of identity. Diversity is multidimensional and includes race, disability, class, economic status, age, sexuality, gender and transgender, faith and belief. Social workers appreciate that, as a consequence of difference, a person's life experience may include oppression, marginalisation and alienation as well as privilege, power and acclaim, and are able to challenge appropriately.

4. **Rights, justice and economic wellbeing** – Advance human rights and promote social justice and economic wellbeing.

   Social workers recognise the fundamental principles of human rights and equality, and that these are protected in national and international law, conventions and policies. They ensure these principles underpin their practice. Social workers understand the importance of using and contributing to case law and applying these rights in their own practice. They understand the effects of oppression, discrimination and poverty.

5. **Knowledge** – Apply knowledge of social sciences, law and social work practice theory.

   Social workers understand psychological, social, cultural, spiritual and physical influences on people; human development throughout the life span and the legal framework for practice. They apply this knowledge in their work with individuals, families and communities. They know and use theories and methods of social work practice.

6. **Critical reflection and analysis** – Apply critical reflection and analysis to inform and provide a rationale for professional decision-making.

   Social workers are knowledgeable about and apply the principles of critical thinking and reasoned discernment. They identify, distinguish, evaluate and integrate multiple sources of knowledge and evidence. These include practice evidence, their own practice experience, service user and carer experience, together with research-based, organisational, policy and legal knowledge. They use critical thinking augmented by creativity and curiosity.

7. **Intervention and skills** – Use judgement and authority to intervene with individuals, families and communities to promote independence, provide support and prevent harm, neglect and abuse.

   Social workers engage with individuals, families, groups and communities, working alongside people to assess and intervene. They enable effective relationships and are effective communicators, using appropriate skills. Using their professional judgement, they employ a range of interventions: promoting independence, providing support and protection, taking preventative action and ensuring safety whilst balancing rights and risks. They understand and take account of differentials in power, and are able to use authority appropriately. They evaluate their own practice and the outcomes for those they work with.

8. **Context and organisations** – Engage with, inform and adapt to changing contexts that shape practice. Operate effectively within own organisational frameworks and contribute to the development of services and organisations. Operate effectively within multi-agency and inter-professional settings.

   Social workers are informed about and proactively responsive to the challenges and opportunities that come with changing social contexts and constructs. They fulfil this responsibility in accordance with their professional values and ethics, both as individual professionals and as members of the organisation in which they work. They collaborate, inform and are informed by their work with others, inter-professionally and with communities.

9. **Professional leadership** – Take responsibility for the professional learning and development of others through supervision, mentoring, assessing, research, teaching, leadership and management.

   The social work profession evolves through the contribution of its members in activities such as practice research, supervision, assessment of practice, teaching and management. An individual's contribution will gain influence when undertaken as part of a learning, practice-focused organisation. Learning may be facilitated with a wide range of people including social work colleagues, service users and carers, volunteers, foster carers and other professionals (TCSW, 2012a: 1–3).

At first these terms and statements may seem rather intimidating but over time and with careful thought and practice you will begin to find you can unlock what each capability means and, finally, how you can demonstrate and evidence these capabilities in your social work practice learning. At the beginning of your training you should take time to familiarise yourself with the PCF as this will be the key framework for the assessment of your progression through your practice learning and pre-qualifying course. We will look at these features in more detail later in the book. The PCF will also inform your post-qualifying training and professional development.

Points to Consider

Social work education – the PCF and the College of Social Work

Visit the College of Social Work website and take a careful look at all the different parts of the Framework. Although they will look rather abstract at the moment, by the time you begin your placement you will benefit greatly from being reasonably familiar with the Framework.

Also, take a look at: 'The College of Social Work: A Guide for Students' on the College website. This provides helpful information and guidance about the College, its role and services.

e-Links

www.tcsw.org.uk/home/
www.education.gov.uk/swrb/a0074240/professional-standards-for-social-workers-in-england.

Moving from 'Competence' to 'Capability'

Before we go on, let's explore what we mean in plain terms by 'capability' and how we might demonstrate and evidence capability in social work practice.

The term capability in an educational, training or work setting is often linked to discussions of whether someone is capable or able to do certain tasks and activities (e.g. *Nadeem is a very capable social worker*' or '*The course is within the capabilities of most people to pass*'). At an interview to be accepted onto a social work course, part of the assessment made by the interviewer includes consideration of what an applicant has already done, how they present on the day and also a predictive assessment of whether or not the interviewee will be able to develop the competencies and capabilities required of social workers.

Professional training programmes, including the new incoming educational programmes established for social work, are based on models and frameworks which include decisions about what practitioners need to know and what they ought be able to practise in order to be sound and effective in their work. In social work, the Professional Capabilities Framework for Social Workers (TCSW, 2012a) provides such a model with its set of nine capabilities, as identified above. In the recent past, social work education and professional development training have been heavily criticised for an over-reliance on a 'technical-rational' approach which tried to reduce social work to a list of defined tasks. Social workers in training were required to achieve a sufficient level of technical and administrative competence. Competence, here, emphasises what things people need to do in order to perform a job and sees social work as largely a set of tasks and outputs (completing an assessment form, keeping electronic records, etc.).

However, reducing social work to a list of largely visible tasks and actions is misleading. It's a bit like saying if we try to paint using a painting by numbers kit we will really be able to reproduce an exact copy of an original famous work of art. Using Leonardo da Vinci's *Mona Lisa* as an example, we can buy a painting by numbers canvas which in essence maps out for us different parts of the final painting. However, whatever the level of detail we are given, will it really capture the essence of the original painting? No! Not even close. The same applies to social work. It is more than merely the accumulation of a set of constituent parts.

In seeking to help others who face difficult social problems, social workers have to engage with a range of complex human relations, problems and dilemmas. As Donald Schön famously stated:

> In the varied topography of professional practice there is a high ground where practitioners can make effective use of research based theory and technique, and there is a swampy lowland where situations are confusing 'messes' incapable of technical solution. (Schön, 1983: 42)

For Schön, professional practice is about combining our theoretical knowledge and combining it with wisdom gained through reflecting and building on experiences. The best social workers not only have a solid grasp of theory and knowledge, but are also capable of being flexible and adaptable in the way they apply this in their work. Crucially, in addition, social workers must be able to think for themselves, to reflect on their practice skills in order to improve and use their professional values and ethics to guide how and why they practise in the way they do.

Finally, professional social workers have to be able to do all this in a world of fluctuating societal values and political discourses (e.g. ideas about who should receive welfare and support), changing economic conditions (most vividly in the contemporary context of providing welfare and care during a global recession) and operational settings and boundaries which in recent times have blurred and changed (e.g. the drive to multi-disciplinary and multi-agency working).

Thus, preparing trainee social workers for practice requires more than just basic tools to do the job but also the foundations for developing their practice. It will take you time to develop these advanced skills to help you and crucially the people with whom you work. We will look at this in later chapters.

Developing 'capability'

Before we go on, let's have a go at understanding 'competence' and 'capability' in some real-world situations.

Learning to drive – moving from competence to capability

At various points in our lives we are often judged as to our ability to do things. Learning to drive is now considered almost essential to many walks of working life, including getting a job in social work. In order to pass your driving test you need to pass a theory test (which includes assessment of knowledge of basic car mechanics, the highway code and rules, hazards and difficulties, etc.) and a practical test (the nerve-racking bit with the driving examiner observing you as you drive safely around a prescribed route which tests your ability in different driving situations). Passing your driving test indicates you have reached a competent, 'good enough' basic standard to legally drive a car.

However, being a good and effective driver requires more than merely mastering the mechanics of operating a motor vehicle. To be a competent and capable driver you in addition need to be able to demonstrate you can drive responsibly; apply the rules of the road which are set in place to govern how we should drive; respond and react intuitively to challenging conditions and situations. Good drivers also seek to build on their basic knowledge and skills in order to improve as a driver and as a shared road user with others. Thus, learning to drive requires you to acquire and develop knowledge and skills beyond passing a test which requires you to meet a basic standard of proficiency.

What do you think?

Produce a short list of the sorts of things you would expect someone who is learning to drive needs to know; what sorts of skills they must have; what sorts of values, attitudes and attributes promote good and safe driving. Here are some examples:

- Driving skills, e.g. operating the car as a machine; driving in busy traffic.
- Driving knowledge, e.g. knowing how a car works; the rules of the road; the challenges and risks of driving in wet conditions.
- Desirable driver values, attitudes and attributes, e.g. driving with respect and care for other road users; not being easily distracted when driving; being flexible to changing road conditions and situations.

Comment

If you are struggling with thinking of answers, just think of a good driver you know and also a rotten driver. The rest should be easy!

So, in summary, to be an able and capable driver seems to actually require a combination of interconnected skills, knowledge and values/attributes. Passing our driving test implies we have reached a basic standard of competence across a set of specific things we need to know (laws, speed limits, etc.); tasks we can perform (changing gear, parking, etc.); and advice about how to drive safely and effectively (e.g. to apply the Highway Code [DT, 2007]). Social work training introduces you to the key values, attributes, skills and knowledge essential for beginning professional practice – experience and practice wisdom comes with time.

Linking the Nine Domains of the PCF

It is important to note that although the nine PCF capabilities are set out as distinct domains or areas, the College of Social Work states:

> The nine capabilities should be seen as interdependent, not separate. As they interact in professional practice, so there are overlaps between the capabilities within the domains, and many issues will be relevant to more than one domain. Understanding of what a social worker does will only be complete by taking into account all nine capabilities. (TCSW, 2012a: 1)

The College of Social Work stresses that the PCF should be viewed as a 'living document', which may in part be 'organisational speak' for 'it will keep changing'. So, it is likely you will need to be vigilant and flexible learners as you train and as the PCF develops and changes.

However, what is clear is that the PCF is designed to be viewed 'holistically', and 'domains' are also meant to be viewed as both interdependent and interactive. There are inevitably overlaps between the capabilities within the domains and across your developing social work practice (social work skills, knowledge, values and attributes).

As the College states:

> Professionals and their practice will be assessed, by which we mean that throughout their careers, social work students and practitioners need to demonstrate integration of all aspects of learning, and provide a sufficiency of evidence across all nine domains. (TCSW, 2012a: 1)

As students you will be expected to be able to evidence your practice and learning during each of your placements. This will take time to develop but you will find you settle into this activity as your placements progress.

PLACEMENT ACTIVITY
Social work, linking the domains of the PCF and evidencing your practice

The PCF identifies nine capabilities considered essential to social work. We are going to look at PCFs 3, 4 and 5 and see if we can identify how we could demonstrate and evidence these.

Practice example

The Care Quality Commission (CQC) has found that workloads for social workers increased in 2012 as a result of clients having had their welfare benefits cut following a Department for Work and Pensions (DWP) Work Capacity Assessment; 38% of such decisions are overturned at appeal.

Mr Hussein, a client of yours with mental health problems, faces a benefit cut resulting from his own recent review. He does not know what to do, but is now very worried for the future. You suggest to Mr Hussein that he appeal the decision and want to help. How will you do this? How can you demonstrate through your actions and activities evidence for PCF 3, 4 and 5?

PCF 3. Diversity – Recognise diversity and apply anti-discriminatory and anti-oppressive principles in practice.

PCF 4. Rights, justice and economic wellbeing – Advance human rights and promote social justice and economic wellbeing.

PCF 5. Knowledge – Apply knowledge of social sciences, law and social work practice theory.

Note: for more detail of each PCF domain, see the nine social work PCF 'capabilities' outlined earlier in this chapter.

Compare your answers to the Year 1 classroom notes below produced by a group of social work students who looked at the case. The notes are headings the groups used to present their decisions to the class.

Year 1 Classroom Notes: Helping Mr Hussein

Demonstrating PCF 3, 4 and 5:

- Read the DWP's rules relating to the decision and see if there are grounds for appeal (PCF 4 and 5).
- Learn about the DWP's appeals procedures in order to help Mr Hussein prepare an appeal letter (PCF 4 and 5).
- Make Mr Hussein aware of his legal rights (PCF 4).
- Offer to accompany Mr Hussein to any review or appeal hearing (PCF 4).
- Be prepared to challenge any possible discriminatory attitudes regarding his health (PCF 3).
- Be aware of any possible written or spoken language difficulties for Mr Hussein (PCF 3).
- Apply your knowledge of mental health practice and approaches to offer support during this stressful time (PCF 5).

How do your own answers compare?

The PCF as a Ladder of Training and Professional Development

The PCF is made up of three progressing levels – beginning at the base with *students* and followed by *qualified social workers in practice* and then finally *advanced social work roles*. Thus, the PCF should be seen as the backdrop both to your initial social work education and to your Continuing Professional Development after qualification.

Have a look at the career points and the corresponding social work stages and roles in Table 2.1.

Table 2.1   Career points in social work and corresponding stages and roles

Career points	Stages and roles
Advanced social work roles	Principal social worker
	Advanced practitioner, professional educator, social work manager
	Experienced social worker
Qualified social workers in practice	Newly qualified social worker
	Assessed and Supported Year in Employment (ASYE)
Students	End of second placement
You are here	End of first placement
	Readiness for direct practice assessment
	Entry to qualifying programmes

As you can see, within the three career points there are differing stages and roles which relate to different points of professional development appropriate to the stage in your future social work career.

The PCF rainbow begins with you as trainee social worker and progresses through several stages, of qualified social workers in practice and advanced social work roles (see Figure 2.1).

Obviously, some of the more advanced roles may not be open or of interest to everyone. Not everyone can or wants to become a principal social worker or social work manager. Perhaps the core aspiration at this point, as you enter your course and professional training, is to ensure you progress from the first placement on to the end of your final placement, pass your course and qualify!

You will certainly meet practice educators during your placements and quite likely several advanced practitioners and social work managers.

As a trainee student social worker at the beginning of your training, you are at the 'initial qualification' stage of the PCF. As you can see this stage includes four progressive assessed sub-stages you will need to navigate. These are:

- Entry to qualifying programmes.
- Assessment of readiness for practice.
- End of first placement.
- End of final placement.

The College of Social Work has helpfully provided a narrative description of each PCF domain relating to the stages of initial qualification. These are paraphrased below.

Student qualifying programme

Point of entry

During their selection process prospective students will have demonstrated some awareness of the social context for social work practice for a qualifying programme and have suggested in their application they are capable of acquiring and developing the relevant skills, knowledge and values required for professional social work.

Readiness for direct practice

Students who have begun their course of training will be assessed as to their readiness for direct practice prior to their first placement. Students have to demonstrate basic communication skills, ability to engage with users, capacity to work as a member of an organisation, willingness to learn from feedback and supervision, and show basic social work skills, knowledge and values in order to be able to make effective use of their first practice placement.

End of the first placement

By the end of the first practice learning placement students should demonstrate effective use of knowledge, skills and commitment to core values in social work. They will have demonstrated capacity to work with people and with increasingly complex situations.

End of second placement and end of qualifying programme

In order to complete the second practice learning placement at the end of the qualifying programme, successful students who are becoming newly qualified social workers should have demonstrated the skills, knowledge and values to work with a range of user groups; the ability to undertake a range of tasks at a foundation level; and the capacity to work autonomously with more complex situations.

Newly qualified social workers

On completion of a qualifying programme of study, newly qualified social workers progress onto the new Assessed and Supported Year in Employment (ASYE).

Look at: **Chapter 10 Getting Ready for Professional Practice**.

$\rightarrow$

The New Social Work Placement Structure and the PCF

As a social work student, you will be required to complete a total of 200 days of practice-related learning as part of your professional social work training. This entails 170 days spent in placement with an additional 30 days devoted to skills development.

Developing skills for practice

A new addition to the revised programmes for social work training is that students are now required to complete 30 days of skills development during their programme of study. According to the College of Social Work the primary purpose of the skills development days is to help prepare students for their first placement. However, the organisation of these 30 days will vary from programme to programme and it is accepted that some days may be used later in your programme of study.

The skills days may take place in your academic setting or in the community. Some of the days will provide introduction to foundation skills which you can use in any placement, setting or service. These will be useful from the beginning of your training and career onwards. Others may be more relevant to your second and final placement.

PLACEMENT ACTIVITY
Developing skills for practice

Below are some of the activities you might experience as part of your skills for practice days. Make a note of how each of these activities could help you to develop your practice during placement:

- 'Shadowing' and observing qualified social workers and other practitioners, e.g. on a home visit.
- Observing individuals/families/groups in different settings, e.g. nurseries, day centres, lunch clubs, youth clubs, residential care settings.
- Role-play, e.g. acting out an interview.
- Meeting with service users and carers who may be willing to share their experiences, feelings and views, e.g. meeting with a group of young care leavers.
- Meeting with service users and carers who may be willing to share their experiences, feelings and views about what qualities good social workers need to possess, e.g. meeting with 'survivors' of abuse.
- Visiting specialist community-based agencies, e.g. a homeless project and meeting outreach workers.
- Skills days reserved for later in your training to develop more advanced skills.
- Role-play using specific social work skills, e.g. motivational interviewing techniques, using task-centred social work approaches.
- Interviewing skills, e.g. working with interpreters and translation services, undertaking grief work.
- Attending specific settings, e.g. courts, tribunals, case conferences.
- Discussing contemporary events that arise during the course, e.g. serious incidents in the news, publication of new policies and reports, local events.

These are just examples of the range of activities which you may find form part of your skills development days. You may have the opportunity to suggest your own ideas. Make a list of things you might be interested in learning more about.

Skills development is also about skills sharing. Are there particular skills or knowledge you have which could be shared with your fellow students? These could be based on your personal circumstances, education and training, work experience or something else. Make a list.

Features of the first and final social work placements

Your first placement is of 70 days' duration and the second and final social work placement is of 100 days. The social work placement is an important part of your social work training. For many students, the beginning of placement is an exciting, but also sometimes daunting experience, especially for students embarking on their first placement. Suddenly, all the teaching, seminars, group activities and assignments undertaken in the classroom become real as you find yourself in real service settings, meeting real people who are looking to you for help and advice. The importance of practice learning in social work is widely acknowledged:

> Practice activity is also a source of transferable learning in its own right. Such learning can transfer both from a practice setting to the 'classroom' and vice versa. (QAA, 2008: 7)

Placements provide an opportunity to put your academic learning into practice and to gain confidence and competence in understanding and applying social work values, skills and knowledge, safely and effectively, in work with service users and carers. In this way, placements are aimed at enabling you to 'bridge the gap' between *social work in theory* and *social work in practice* (Tilling, 2009: 358). During your placement you will be supported by your practice educator to understand the professional standards for practice.

Your placement aims to enable you to bring all these elements together, and understand how all the pieces of the social work learning jigsaw fit together. The better prepared you are, the more rewarding your practice experience will be; for most students it is the hands-on practice that *gives life* to academic study.

To be at your most effective in any social work placement you need to be aware of the aims of the typical social work placement and what opportunities and challenges the placement can present. During teaching, when I ask students about the aims of a social work placement they often say they would like to:

- Learn new skills on the job.
- Gain more social work experience.
- Observe and work alongside experienced qualified social workers to see how they work.
- Gain experience across different areas of practice and see if they like it.
- Meet and work with service users and carers in their communities.
- Experience a new area of practice.
- Importantly, put classroom learning and theory into practice and integrate a range of social work skills, knowledge, values and attributes into the practice of social work.

Let's try to translate these worthwhile ideals into some specific ideas and activities for *you* to apply to your own individual circumstances. Try the Placement Activity below.

PLACEMENT ACTIVITY
Identifying the aims of a social work placement

If we can clearly identify the aims and purpose of a social work placement, we should be better able to understand our roles on placement and how to get the best from experiential learning. Here are some examples offered by student social workers. Add your own notes to develop these for your own learning:

Gain social work experience

What sort of social work experiences do you want from your forthcoming placement?

1.
2.
3.

Develop new skills

What new skills do you want to develop in your placement?

1.
2.
3.

Observe and work alongside experienced qualified social workers

What could you learn from observing experienced qualified social workers?

1.
2.
3.

Meet service users and carers in their communities

Who would you be likely to meet? What could you learn from this?

1.
2.
3.

Put classroom learning and theory into practice

What could you use from your teaching? How could you apply this in practice?

1.
2.
3.

It is important that you plan for your placement and take responsibility for your learning on placement. As a professional social worker you will be expected to think about your learning and developmental needs throughout your career.

> Since 1 April 2005, the title 'social worker' has been protected in England by Section 61 of the Care Standards Act 2000. This may seem surprising, but prior to this date any person could describe themselves as a social worker, and some occasionally did.
>
> Today, when you have qualified you have to be registered with the Health and Care Professions Council (HCPC) to be entitled to use the title of 'social worker'.

INFORMATION POINT

The focus of learning in your placements

The College of Social Work, in its practice learning guidance, suggests students should normally have different experiences in their first and final placements. This means experiencing and working in different settings and with different service user groups across various ages.

The College of Social Work has set out that preparation for statutory social work in terms of practice-based learning should be defined by the tasks undertaken by students on placement (e.g. complex casework, risk assessment), rather than the setting (e.g. local authority) or type of placement (e.g. voluntary). This means, from the College's point of view, that students do not need to have a local authority 'statutory' placement in order to be able to satisfy requirements for social work training.

However, the College does make clear that despite flexibility about the type of placement, the location for second and final 100-day placement must prepare students for the more complex and statute-led aspects of a social worker's role by offering opportunities to demonstrate and evidence a range of tasks and activities. These would typically include:

- Formal assessment processes considering risk and /or safeguarding for children.
- Protection, for practice in mental health or with vulnerable adults (see PCF 7, 8).
- Opportunities to reflect on, discuss and analyse appropriate use of authority (see PCF 7, 6).
- Application and understanding of legal frameworks relevant for social work practice (see PCF 5, 8).
- Organisational policies and decisions and their impact on service delivery to service users (see PCF 8).
- The demands of a highly pressured environment, where time and competing interests have to be managed effectively (see PCF 1).
- Multi-agency working, including planning interventions with other agencies, and analysing and managing tensions (see PCF 7, 8).
- Presentation of outcomes of formal assessment processes, including analysis of risk/ recommendations in line with organisational policy/procedure at, e.g., panels/meetings/ courts (see PCF 6, 7, 8).
- Use of formal agency recording for assessment/risk (see PCF 1).

PCF domains – quick reference

1. **Professionalism** – Identify and behave as a professional social worker, committed to professional development.
2. **Values and ethics** – Apply social work ethical principles and values to guide professional practice.
3. **Diversity** – Recognise diversity and apply anti-discriminatory and anti-oppressive principles in practice.
4. **Rights, justice and economic wellbeing** – Advance human rights and promote social justice and economic wellbeing.
5. **Knowledge** – Apply knowledge of social sciences, law and social work practice theory
6. **Critical reflection and analysis** – Apply critical reflection and analysis to inform and provide a rationale for professional decision-making.
7. **Intervention and skills** – Use judgement and authority to intervene with individuals, families and communities to promote independence, provide support, and prevent harm, neglect and abuse.
8. **Contexts and organisations** – Engage with, inform and adapt to changing contexts that shape practice. Operate effectively within own organisational frameworks and contribute to the development of services and organisations. Operate effectively within multi-agency and inter-professional settings.
9. **Professional leadership** – Take responsibility for the professional learning and development of others through supervision, mentoring, assessing, research, teaching, leadership (TCSW, 2012a: 1–3).

It is important to note, before we get too anxious about what awaits us on placement, that the College of Social Work is clear that student experiences on placement should be on the basis that you will be working under the clear supervision and guidance of a practice educator and must be provided with appropriate levels of support, taking into account the challenging nature of the work and the individual needs of each student. So, the support you need to practice effectively and learn is part of the system of support you can expect on placement. Be reassured, practice educators want to help you.

Summary

This chapter has introduced you to the new PCF and to the placement structure which adds up to 200 days of practice learning. We will revisit both the PCF and the placements in the forthcoming chapters. Remember, it will take some time for you to become fully familiar with these aspects of your practice learning. Your course will carefully guide you through the placements and help you in making the most of your practice learning. In the next chapter we will be looking at preparing and beginning your placement and introducing some of the people you will be meeting.

3

Planning and Beginning your Placement

Overview and Learning Outcomes

This chapter will cover:

- Roles on placement.
- Preparing to visit your placement.

By the end of Chapter 3 you will be able to:

- Explain your role and the role of others during your placement.
- Confidently visit your placement and attend your informal meeting with the agency.

Introduction to Chapter 3

Having begun in the previous chapter to explore the PCF for Social Workers and new placement structure, Chapter 3 will now take you through preparing for the first placement in more detail. This will include exploring roles on placement and getting ready to visit the placement. It is increasingly common for agencies offering social work placements to invite prospective students to informally visit them to meet staff and others. This first visit is important as it is the first opportunity you will have to see your prospective placement and to find out more about its work.

Just as importantly, this visit also gives the agency the first opportunity to see you. Given other students may be competing for the placement, this visit is important. You need to think about how well you are going to present on the day. Are you going to give the agency any reason for second thoughts? Good planning and preparing for your placement will maximise your chances of success, so make sure you treat these visits seriously.

The commentary running throughout Chapter 3 includes a range of activities and guidance to help you plan and prepare and also signposts you to other parts of the book you should find useful during your placement and practice learning.

Key People during your Practice Learning

It is very important you have a clear understanding of your own role on placement and the roles of others who will have a part in your placement. All have a potential and important contribution to make to your practice learning and professional development. We will begin with three primary participants, who are:

- Your practice educator.
- Your tutor.
- You (the student).

Practice educator

This is the person in your placement who will take primary responsibility for supervising, managing and supporting you in your learning on placement, whilst also making a key contribution to your assessment.

The practice educator will typically work closely with you to help you develop. To do this, they will offer you regular supervision and contact throughout the placement in order to provide casework management, guidance and support. They will also provide opportunities to think about the role of the social worker; explore ways of applying relevant law and policy to social work practice; and how to integrate social work theory into practice. The practice educator will also help you explore your developmental needs in relation to further training and provide pastoral support to you during the placement period.

Importantly, it is also the practice educator who is going to write a placement report about your work and performance and assess whether you have met the requirements of your social work placement.

Sometimes, the practice educator is not based in your placement setting but will visit your placement setting on a regular basis to meet with you there. This is an increasingly common arrangement in recent years in social work placements. If you have a practice educator who is not based where you are on placement then an additional 'on-site supervisor' will be arranged.

The on-site workplace supervisor will work closely with your practice educator and you to ensure your agreed learning outcomes are met. In this situation, you would typically have supervision with both your workplace on-site supervisor and your off-site practice educator.

On-site supervisor or placement supervisor

This person usually works for the placement agency and will take management responsibility for your day-to-day work. The on-site supervisor or placement supervisor may or may not be a social worker but is someone who will allocate work and manage and support you in between meetings with your practice educator.

Where there is both a practice educator (sometimes described as an 'off-site' or 'long arm' practice educator) and an on-site supervisor, it is expected and typical that they will liaise periodically in order to ensure your work is properly allocated, organised and supported. You should always be involved in these arrangements and meetings and if properly managed this generally works well.

Tutor

Your course tutor typically has a central role in helping you to develop and integrate your academic learning during your course. The forum for this is usually through campus-based tutorials, assignment feedback and teaching. In the context of your placement your tutor provides a link between your educational course and your placement. The tutor will have periodic contact with you during the placement period and is generally involved in visiting the placement, offering advice and support from outside the university and in planning and reviewing your progress through the placement. The tutor can be a useful resource to improve the quality of your work and support the production of placement-related work. Your tutor is often involved in the periodic placement meetings you will experience during your placement, notably the pre-placement meeting and midway reviews which are typical of most programmes of learning. Keep in touch with your tutor during your placement as they will be interested in how things are going on placement and will want to support you.

You!

You have a very important contribution to make to the placement and to ensuring the placement is a successful and useful learning opportunity. But what is your contribution and role? Being clear about this at this point will help you plan and prepare for your placement but also help you think about your forthcoming placement visit. Have a go at the exercise below.

PLACEMENT ACTIVITY
The contribution and role of a social work student on placement

- What needs to be your commitment to making the placement a success?
- What do you hope to have learned and achieved by the end of your placement?

Social work comment

Top tips on getting the most from your placement:

Think about what the placement can offer you and what you can offer the placement. Reflect on the outcome/s you want to achieve by completing the placement.

Ensure that your knowledge is up-to-date regarding the legislation, policies and practice guidance in relation to the service user group you will be working with during your placement. What practice issues are there? What are the implications for the service user group?

Observe pieces of work undertaken by social workers in the team as much as possible and attend any training offered. (Emily, BA student)

Other participants in effective practice learning

In addition to your practice educator, tutor and you, there are several other important participants and contributors who are potentially valuable sources of information, guidance and feedback and who can help you maximise your learning and development on placement. These include:

- Service users and carers.
- Your placement organisation and team.
- Other agencies and services.
- Other professionals and workers.
- Other students.

This is by no means a complete list but should be used as a prompt to think about how you will utilise their feedback and contribution to your development as a reflective and professional social worker. As an active learner you should be keen to engage with and utilise the feedback from these people. Have a go at the Placement Activity below.

PLACEMENT ACTIVITY
Contributors to your practice learning

Make notes about the potential feedback and contribution of the people identified below to your practice learning.

Who	Potential feedback and contribution	How might you gather this feedback?
Practice educator		
Tutor		
Service users		
Carers		
The placement team and organisation		
Other agencies and services		
Other professionals and workers		
Other students		

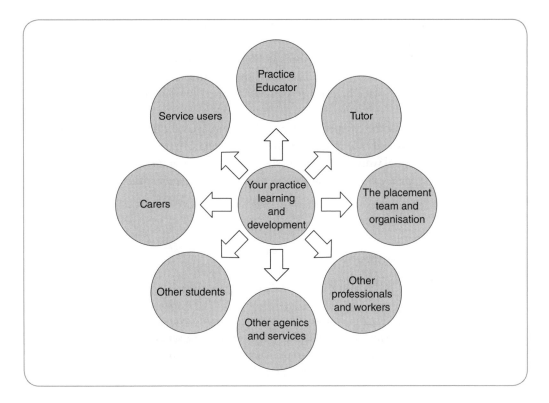

Preparing to Visit your Placement

So, we have begun to think about what a social work placement should do and the roles and contributions of different people in the placement process. By understanding the aims of the placement and your own role and contribution you should find yourself better prepared for your early social work placement related activities: notably, visiting your placement and also undertaking any 'shadowing' activity required as part of your preparation for practice.

Preparing for your 'informal' visit

It is common practice for agencies who wish to offer students a placement to invite them to come to the placement agency for an 'informal' meeting. This meeting typically takes place after the agency has received some basic information from your course programme about you as a prospective placement candidate. The key now is to not disappoint them and be at your best to secure the offer of a placement. Let's see how we can achieve this.

The meeting often involves your prospective practice educator and also possibly a senior practitioner or manager from within the service. This is often described as a way for the agency representatives to meet you and you to meet them. It also offers you an opportunity to have a look at the agency. The informal meeting is also likely to be the first time you will be meeting key people who will be involved in your prospective placement. Remember the old adage, first impressions count!

Although the meeting is often described as 'informal' and is generally conducted in a relaxed way, in many respects you should think of the meeting as akin to an informal interview, and, given this takes place before a placement is formally offered, how you present and behave is important.

Just to note, you may also be competing for the placement against other students. You need to take the meeting seriously and treat it as an opportunity to demonstrate your interest in the placement, commitment to social work and to emphasise your suitability and reliability as a prospective representative for the agency. So, how can you try to ensure the agency makes *you* that offer of a placement?

Social work comment

Getting ready for your informal visit:

> *Treat it as a job interview. This is important especially for the second placement. Placements expect students to be prepared and to be able to answer relevant questions about the organisation. Hence, research the placement, the service user group and what services the placement provides. And most importantly, be on time! (Emily, BA student)*

Research the placement agency and the community it serves

Make use of the time before placement to plan and prepare. The more you know, the better you will come across to your prospective placement. A good start in terms of preparing for your informal meeting is to do some research and profile the agency, its service user and carer focus and also the community in which it is set. There are also some practical things to consider, as we will see below.

Note that you will find over time that an essential currency of good social work is your local knowledge. This takes time to develop, but valued social workers are also resourceful and active learners who seek to develop their knowledge of local services and agencies as well as to cultivate useful contacts and engage with the community in which they work and operate. In this way, you should be well placed to support the people you work with and be a good resource to your future colleagues as well.

You should begin the practice of developing local knowledge early in your career and continue to develop, it. At this early stage of your training, some straightforward background work will help you perform better at your informal meeting. This will help you orientate yourself to your placement agency, develop your local knowledge of resources and ultimately enable you to be a better practitioner.

The agency and its setting

In preparing for your visit it is worthwhile to do plenty of 'agency-related' background reading. Many agencies have written documents which they produce as part of their normal business activities. It is often possible to obtain these documents via the internet. See if the placement agency has a website of its own – which is increasingly common – or if you can find information via a service-specific site (e.g. local mental health services in your area). Some agencies even produce booklets about how they offer and organise their social work placements. These are all potentially useful resources to read and to make sure you mention when you visit. At the very least this will impress the agency! So where could you look? Your background sources and reading may include:

- Annual reports.
- Project reports.
- Policy documents.
- Agency advertising, leaflets, etc.

As well as reading various agency reports and documents you might also find it useful to have a look at what is happening in the community where the placement is set. There are several possible sources you can use, including:

- Local newspapers and community newsletters.
- Libraries and community centres.
- The resources produced by other community and voluntary groups.
- Blogs and online forums.

Have a go at building up a community profile. If you look at local street maps and newspapers going back into the 19th and 20th centuries you can find out how local areas, and in turn their communities, have changed. Compare the areas then and now. Some older members of the community may well have lived through periods of great change which are important events in their lives. If you and some fellow students are likely to have placements near each other, maybe work collaboratively on this. You could even suggest this activity for one of your skills development days.

Getting to know the local 'patch': the community and its diversity

Where possible try to visit the local area where the placement agency is located and have a good look round. This is by far the best way of getting to know a neighbourhood or district, as well as ensuring you know where you will be going when you first visit. You will get a real sense of what the area looks like and how it feels. After all, this is where the people you will be working with probably live. Given we are interested in welfare issues, perhaps think about the profile of the community: its diversity; how affluent the area is; where the local health and social care services are located; how people get around; what transport services are available; whether there is adapted access to public buildings; the range of faith groups in the area, e.g. local churches, mosques, synagogues, etc.

Additionally, local streets, shops and services (or their absence) can be informative. What could these tell you about a local area?

Try creating a sketch map of the area and add to it. Your map could include many things:

- Local schools.
- Children's centres.
- Day centres.
- GP surgeries and health centres.
- Dentists.
- Laundrettes.
- Pawn shops.
- Betting shops.
- Local shops.

Not only is this good for getting to know a community, but it will give you something to talk to service users and carers about, which they may well be interested in and knowledgeable about. In addition, this work will also help you build up your own 'knowledge bank' in terms of resources and services and remind you about not just where people live but how they live.

Web resources and community mapping

As well as getting out and about locally, there are also a number of useful electronic resources which you can access and use to help you further. Using Wiki maps or any of the standard commercial search engines you can fairly speedily begin to profile an area or district relatively easily. Google Maps allows you to view pictures of roads and streets. Explore the area your placement is located. Visual images allow you to 'see' things we sometimes miss on the move.

With modest persistence you can locate not only your prospective placement but also nearby schools, GP surgeries, hospitals, community resources, etc. Enter the postcode or address of your prospective placement or district in the site search box and see what you can find.

Other sources: local, regional and national services and agencies

In conducting your own searches you need to make sure you look at services nearer and more relevant to you and in turn to your service users and their carers. The better your local knowledge, the more useful a social worker you are likely to be. The list below is by no means exhaustive, but is a useful starting point:

Adult social care

- Audit Commission.
- Care Quality Commission.
- Local authority websites.
- Local voluntary and non-statutory groups.

Children's services

- Ofsted.
- Safeguarding Children Boards.
- Regional and local branches of national charities and groups, e.g. NSPCC.

Other services

- NHS and GP surgeries.
- Police.
- Housing associations.
- Citizens Advice.

These are just examples, and many local and community groups are now running their own websites, blogs, etc. Try to find out more about other local community groups you have discovered or are familiar with. However, just as with any resource, take care to apply some critical awareness to the reliability and usefulness of any information you gather.

Points to Consider

Thinking critically, having looked at the websites, reflect on:

- How easy are the websites to find and use?
- How accessible and usable are the websites for all users? Think about the typeface, font, colour and layout, etc.
- How useful are the links provided? Do they give information clearly? Is the information up-to-date and how accurate is it?
- How could you help service users, carers and colleagues access and use the sites?

Before you go to your informal meeting

Just as it is important to research and do some background reading to help you prepare for your informal visit there are some practical things you may need to consider in getting ready for your visit. They may seem obvious but they are often missed, which can give a poor impression.

Checklist

Before you go for your informal meeting, ask yourself the following:

☐ Do you know where you are meant to go for your informal meeting?
☐ What time is the meeting?
☐ How will you get to the meeting?
☐ How long will your journey take?
☐ Who are you meeting?
☐ How do you intend to present yourself? Consider the importance of dress code in social work. What should inform your thinking about your visit? What factors do you need to consider? What is appropriate dress – where, when and why?
☐ What do you need to take with you?
☐ Consider whether you need to let the agency know about any issues relevant to your home, personal family circumstances.

During the informal visit

Prospective agencies will be concerned to know how interested you are in the area of work they may specialise in and your attitude to service users and carers. The way you present can tell practice educators and others quite a lot about you – your values and attitudes and your approach to social work as a profession. If you cannot show interest now, then a reasonable conclusion might be made about how you are going to work on placement and whether or not you will be an asset to the agency.

Checklist

Subjects you might consider asking about during your informal meeting:

☐ The work of the agency.
☐ The individuals and communities they work with.
☐ Service user and carer involvement in decision-making about the organisation.
☐ Recent projects they are involved in.
☐ How they are funded.
☐ What you might get involved in.
☐ The days/hours you will be expected to work (Monday–Friday, evenings, weekends?).
☐ Any specific educational or learning needs you may have (you may have a learning plan you can share).
☐ Is there a dress code or expectation about appearance you will need to follow?
☐ Do students have their own desk/phone?
☐ Transport arrangements/car parking and any associated charges.
☐ Whether any specific pre-placements tasks are recommended (e.g. reading a key service policy document).

PLACEMENT ACTIVITY
What you might be asked during your informal meeting?

- Make a list of possible questions and jot down notes of what you want to say.
- Keep thinking about this before you go, and perhaps ask other people who have had their visit already what they were asked.

Navigating the Social Work Placement

Commencing your placement

So, here we are at the beginning of your placement. You have successfully navigated the placement selection processes, impressed at your informal meeting and you are ready to go. As we have mentioned, your placement is often an exciting moment but also potentially a bit daunting as your teaching and assignment work is no longer your only focus.

However your own social work course is organised and delivered, the introduction of a practice learning placement adds a new element and new dimension to your learning. You will be moving from solely concentrating on your academic work to having to juggle course work with the demands and expectations of your placement. This section of the book is offered to orientate you to the placement process and to link its stages to other parts of the book, in order to integrate your skills, knowledge and development around the spine of your placement days.

It is usual to feel a range of emotions in the first few days. This is normal and, it is fine to share this with your practice educator. It would actually be quite odd if you did not have some emotional response to a new experience.

A key message to you is to take your time, try to enjoy your new experience and, as you start your induction period and begin to meet people, aim to remain interested and attentive to what is going on around you.

Points to Consider

Keep a reflective log of the placement

In Chapter 8, we recommend you keep a reflective log. Reflective thinking may help to reduce any anxieties that you experience prior to your placement commencing, and also into these early first days and weeks. Typical thoughts include:

- How do I feel about the prospect of beginning this placement?
- What am I most anxious about?

(Continued)

(Continued)

- Why does this make me feel anxious?
- What can I do to address my anxiety?
- How have I managed similar anxieties in the past?
- What do I feel good and/or confident about?

Make some notes about your reflections and ideas for solutions. Not only will this help you put your feelings into words but also help you make a plan to address your anxieties and concerns.

I am always surprised by the reluctance and sometimes the resistance of students to using a reflective log. After all, you can choose who you want to show the log to or keep it to yourself. Students who use a log certainly tend to say it is useful to write down how you feel.

The log will not only help you remember these first few days much later on when you are asked to record and reflect on your placement and your placement experience, but will also help you gauge and assess how your learning and development has changed during the course of the placement.

Developing your own CV

In addition to keeping a reflective log, consider designing your own curriculum vitae, or CV, as a way of building up a record of your education, training and experience for future jobs or courses. Numerous free templates can be found on the internet.

Remember, you are not expected to know 'everything' about social work before you commence your placement. Whatever your initial experience, you will have the support of your practice educator, and colleagues, who will want you to make the most of your placement experience. Your practice educator will discuss the production of work with you.

Don't be afraid to ask questions; it is expected that you will! However, check that people have time to talk before engaging them in long conversations. It may be more appropriate to arrange a time to talk. If you have a lot of questions, make a note and raise them with your practice educator.

Checklist

- ☐ Do you know where you are meant to be on your first day; at what time and who you are meeting?
- ☐ Does the agency have a dress code? What is appropriate dress?
- ☐ What do you need to take with you?
- ☐ Think about what you might be asked during the early part of your placement?
- ☐ Your notes.

🗨 Social work comment

Getting ready for your first day:

> *Buy a ring binder so that you can start collecting material for your placement straight away.*
> *(Emily, BA student)*

The Stages of a Typical Placement

We have already looked at the pre-placement meeting and learning agreement and spent some time looking at the first few days of placement. Before we go further, have a look at the flow-chart in Figure 3.1 which plots a typical placement pathway for a social work student.

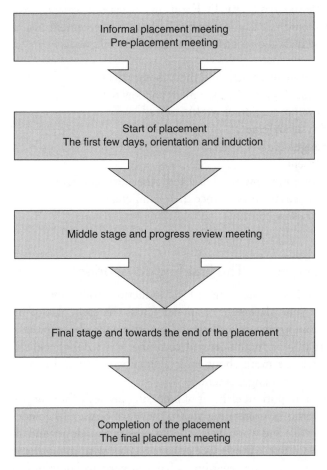

Figure 3.1 The placement stage by stage

The pre-placement meeting and learning agreement

At the start of your placement, you will spend time with your practice educator and tutor in order to complete a 'learning agreement' or contract. This sets out in writing the negotiated and agreed expectations of all parties involved.

The pre-placement meeting normally takes place prior to the commencement of your practice learning placement. The pre-placement meeting will vary from course to course but typically includes your practice educator, your tutor and you.

The pre-placement meeting is often chaired by the tutor. Its main purpose is to produce the practice learning agreement (or placement contract) for the placement and to ensure the placement offers an appropriate social work learning opportunity.

The learning agreement should also help you to clearly understand what you can expect from your placement, as well as what is likely to be expected of you. The learning agreement will celebrate your strengths and elaborate your learning needs; so perhaps begin to identify for yourself *how* these needs could be met. As part of this process you will explore how the work that you undertake on placement will enable you to meet the PCF and any associated assessment requirements.

The placement should not commence until a learning agreement has been completed and signed. The agreement should identify and consider the following:

- The key people in the placement and their contact details.
- The start and finish days for the placement and key dates within the placement (a date for a midpoint review; production of work).
- Health and safety arrangements.
- Supervision arrangements.
- Support arrangements.
- Learning opportunities; how the PCF and other key requirements will be met; how the student will demonstrate and evidence their competence.
- Mechanisms for raising concerns and managing disagreements.

The start of placement – The first few days, orientation and induction

Each placement will have some form of local induction. Inductions can be done in a block at the beginning of your placement or spread across the early part of the placement. This pattern will vary from agency to agency and practice educator to practice educator. However, it is likely that your induction will combine 'must do' checklists of practical tasks with activities which are more about inter-agency working and cooperation, knowledge exchange and professional engagement.

The induction is an important element of preparing properly for your placement. This is not only important in terms of orientating you to the work of the placement agency, its policies and procedures, your role and work; it also should explain your duties and obligations to others, notably to the people who use the service or have contact with it in other ways. The induction provides important information regarding what you need to know in order to work within your particular placement agency.

However, whatever the format, there are a number of features you will need to consider. The sorts of things you can typically expect to be part of your induction are:

- Welcome and introductions.
- A guided tour and building orientation.
- An explanation of general office procedures (e.g. petty cash, tea and coffee fund).
- Recording and record keeping.
- An introduction to office policies (lone worker policy, confidentiality, smoking, etc.).
- Health and safety guidance (fire safety, procedures for signing in and out).
- Provision of office equipment and property (keys, swipe cards, ID badge, phones).
- Visits to other agencies (if this is not pre-arranged perhaps take the initiative on this in consultation with your practice educator).
- Arrangements to shadow members of the team on visits.
- Getting to know the locality (walk around the area to get to know it well; 'tune in' to available local community resources).
- The office culture … or 'how we do things around here' (this is not written down or formally explained; it will take time to tune in to and understand office 'dos and don'ts'; be patient and observe).

Just to note, inductions are not necessarily the most exciting moment in preparing for your placement. I know, as I've attended, planned and delivered inductions over many years in a variety of different services and settings, so I can say this with some feeling! However, although you will not be expected to absorb every bit of information offered to you, it is a good idea to keep the information and know where to find it later on when you will undoubtedly need it. Not yawning, and staying awake during your induction is another good tip!

Using the induction to meet people and make useful contacts

Along with undertaking a number of practical tasks your induction is likely to offer you an opportunity to meet and engage with a range of people. These are people your practice educator thinks it is relevant for you to meet. Make sure you use this opportunity to build up a starter-list of useful contacts, telephone numbers and emails. Also collect relevant leaflets and information you may find useful.

Without doubt, some way into the placement, you will find you have a vague memory of someone you met at the induction who deals with just the thing you are now trying to sort out on day 67 at five minutes to five on a Friday afternoon. Keep your induction contact list handy.

Again, a social worker should be a walking resource in their own right. Good workers have a list of names and contacts of people who are good at their job and are helpful when approached. This can be a very valuable commodity in social work and in most aspects of social and health care. Make sure you keep your contact book up-to-date. Remember, good workers are good networkers!

Continue to consolidate and build on the information you gathered in preparing for your informal meeting. You may feel you are only a trainee at this point but don't undersell yourself.

Just as other people can be utilised as resources, don't forget you are also a resource in your own right and have personal and working experiences which give you certain unique insights, skills and knowledge that could be useful to other colleagues or to service users and carers.

As you travel through your induction, there are also other places to look to build up your knowledge. Have a look at:

- Internal, external and service directories.
- Intranet sources (where available).
- Reception and notice boards.
- Agency leaflets and policy documents.
- Resources identified and rated by colleagues.
- Resources identified and rated by service users and carers.

Also, when you are out and about, have a look at:

- Local libraries.
- Community groups you meet.
- Voluntary agencies and community centres you visit.
- GP and health settings you may find yourself in.
- Schools and children's centres you may have contact with.

The early stage of your placement

The early stage is an important part of your placement. The juggling of different demands (academic work, casework and practice evidence) can take some time to adjust to, but is a necessary and important part of your placement experience.

To demonstrate and evidence the best features of your practice, it is important to try to grasp what you will need to do as soon as you can and especially how and when work is required. With some investment in reading and understanding the placement procedures of your particular course, you will find things get clearer over time. Although 70 and 100 days seem a long time, they pass very quickly.

The early part of your placement is often used by practice educators to introduce you to the placement agency; how the agency functions and the rules and systems which should inform the way you will work and operate. Some of this will be covered in your formal induction. As well as an induction you will also meet with your practice educator early in the placement to catch up or have your first supervision meeting.

→ Look at: **Chapter 8 Using Supervision, Reflective Practice and Critical Thinking.**

The practice educator will use the early part of your placement to gradually expose you to the different work and activities of the service. This allows you time to get a sense of the agency, meet different staff and 'settle in'. Getting the balance just right between protecting you in the early days of your placement and letting you get 'stuck in' requires some management to give you time to get acclimatised and feel confident in your first pieces of direct work rather than throw you in at the deep end. You wouldn't thank your practice educator for this.

This 'settling in' period may typically include you accompanying and shadowing the practice educator as she/he undertakes home visits, attends multi-agency meetings, etc. As time goes on you may also be encouraged to go out with other staff as they do their work. Sometimes, some initial work which the practice educator deems appropriate may emerge from this early shadowing or observation.

Your practice educator should allocate work to you in a measured way with the intention of building up your casework over time. This is sensible, not just for you but also for the recipients of the service, who after all, ought to be the priority. Also, the type of work being allocated to you ought to be appropriate to your experience and level of training. Where possible, your allocated work should develop over time. Casework is not about numbers of cases but should be more about the complexity of work and incorporate sufficient additional time for you to plan and undertake interventions which allow you to reflect and learn. Remember, you are not just an extra pair of hands in the placement. You are in training and there to learn.

Checklist

Activities during the early stage of your placement:

☐ Complete Induction and shadowing.
☐ Prepare for early supervision meetings.
☐ Prepare for graduated allocation of casework.
☐ Acquaint yourself with the PCF.
☐ Start to gather evidence of your learning and development as required.
☐ Attend to your general coursework.
☐ Start your reflective log/diary.

Social work comment

I personally think that students can learn a lot from placements. Placements give you the opportunity to tackle the daily realities of social work practice and explore complex practice. For example, during my second placement involving advocacy work with service users, I noticed that understanding and interpretation of advocacy varied from one professional worker to another. I tried to understand the reasons behind these various views and approaches to inform my own practice. This, in turn, inspired my dissertation, which was focused on advocacy work. (Pierre, MA student)

The middle stage of your placement

As you progress from the early part of the placement, you will have hopefully settled and got a sense that a pattern of work is establishing itself. This will vary from placement to placement but you should by now be having regular and ongoing supervision meetings with your practice educator, getting to know the team better and gradually building up a caseload of work. You may still be doing several tasks for the first time and it probably feels as if there is still much more to learn (just in case you are in any doubt, there *is*) but also you are beginning to know where to find things and how to do things. There is an expectation you will be able to operate with more pace and do not need to have instructions and guidance repeated several times.

In addition, you should be identifying the tasks and activities you will be expected to have completed by the midway point of your placement. The midway or interim review usually has the same membership as the pre-placement meeting and again would normally be chaired by the tutor.

At this meeting, the tutor should ensure that the practice learning agreement is reviewed in order to assess progress towards completion of your placement and your placement portfolio.

The purpose of an interim meeting during your placement is to review your progress and prepare for the second half of the placement. This allows you, in collaboration with the other key members of your learning support team, to chart your progress, identify areas of achievement and also resolve any difficulties and plan or re-focus the remainder of your placement.

Checklist

Activities during the middle stage of your placement:

- ☐ Prepare for further allocation of more complex casework.
- ☐ Prepare for ongoing supervision meetings.
- ☐ Evidence your practice in relation to the PCF.
- ☐ Complete tasks as part of the action plan emerging out of your supervision meetings and progression to your midway review, e.g. direct observation of your practice.
- ☐ Attend to your general course work.
- ☐ Maintain your reflective log/diary.
- ☐ Organise your work diary with dates of key things to do.

The final stage of the placement

The midway review in some respects represents a plan and springboard for the remainder of the placement. Emerging from the midway review are placement tasks, dates and deadlines you will need to ensure are met and recorded, e.g. further direct observations need to be agreed, other elements of the placement portfolio need thinking about, and produced as evidence of your skills, knowledge and values.

In addition, in the second half and towards the final stage of your placement your casework may be continuing apace and even be increasing. Although it may not always feel it, this is actually a form of compliment in that your practice educator now is confident enough to give you more work and is possibly letting you work more autonomously.

A final placement meeting is common and should take place as close as reasonably possible to the end of the student's placement. Attendance should be the same as for the pre-placement meeting.

In most cases the final meeting is typically a forum in which to formally conclude the placement, hopefully celebrate the success of a placement and ensure the assessment process has been agreed, managed and completed. The final meeting also offers an opportunity to thank people involved in the placement.

Where you have experienced difficulties whilst on placement, this meeting could also be very useful in identifying the next steps to be taken to ensure issues are identified and addressed in future development. An added value of the final meeting, if managed properly, is that it may be taking place at a moment when the decision about whether you have passed or failed the placement has already been decided and communicated. As professional workers we have a duty to manage our professional working relationships, to try to reach some acknowledgement or resolution where there have been difficulties and to part in a professional manner.

Checklist

I'm leaving my placement, so I need to make sure I:

- ☐ Return keys.
- ☐ Return my ID card.
- ☐ Return any books or other items I have borrowed.
- ☐ *Note to self* – I should not be leaving with placement agency documents or records. Is there anything else I'm not sure I ought to have? I will check with my practice educator.

Endings and goodbyes

By the end date of your placement you will have completed all your required placement days and you should have produced all your evidence of work from the placement. However, these are only some of the tasks you need to attend to as the placement concludes. During the second half of your placement you should also be making plans for leaving and ending your working relationships with staff, service users and carers. Certainly you should make time to tell people you are leaving and say goodbye to placement staff. As a trainee one of the skills you should have had the opportunity to develop with service users and carers is how to effectively communicate with people and, in doing so, build up a rapport and engagement which help promote a sound, ethical and sustainable working relationship. Just as you have spent time and energy developing this relationship so you need to expend a similar effort in ensuring you give sufficient time and space to consider endings and how to transfer or close work appropriately with users and carers. It is courteous and proper to say goodbye and professional to ensure people know in sufficient time that you are leaving and what will be happening with their matters after you have gone. This is more than simply letting people know you are moving on and saying goodbye.

Points to Consider

As the placement concludes ensure you have made sufficient time for people to speak to you when you are preparing to leave. Most partings with service users and carers pass off amicably and without major comment, However, people do appreciate – and can nearly always accurately assess – the efforts of an honest, hardworking and diligent student. They may like the opportunity to tell you this in their own words and this can take a little extra time. Respect the people you have been working with enough to ensure you reserve time during your rounds of final contacts to accommodate this. Equally important, people may also want to take the opportunity to offer some critical feedback and negative comment. This feedback may not be comfortable or anticipated, but it is vital you provide time to listen to what people want to say. This is important: as learners we have to be committed to learn from all feedback, not just the comments we like; as practitioners, we should seek to be open and honest in our work and dealings. This includes knowing we can get things wrong or be misunderstood or misinterpreted. A good worker will want to correct this.

Having some extra time to draw on during your final round of visits or contacts will provide you with the opportunity to respond appropriately, acknowledge the spirit in which the comments are given and perhaps offer some form of resolution (e.g. I am sorry you feel this way; can I clarify things or suggest a way forward? Or, you may want to raise this formally with the agency).

Remember, despite you often feeling powerless as a student, as a student on placement, operating as the representative of an agency or organisation and as a trainee professional with potential access to resources, power dynamics with service users and carers are present and actively at work. As a trainee social worker, you are in a position of authority and power, whether you recognise this or not. You need to try to manage this responsibly. If you come away from a visit (any visit, at any time) feeling uncertain, talk to your practice educator. These things happen to most workers at moments in their training and career, but it is how we respond and deal with such things which counts.

You ought to discuss the final part of the placement and endings with your practice educator. They should help you to plan your work; agree which cases will be transferred to another worker and which will be closed; and identify when and how you will communicate this information to the individual service users and carers you have been working with.

The activity below is an introduction to some key points to consider when coming to the end of your working relationship with someone and the end of the placement. You can add to these points as you work through your placement, so revisit this exercise during your placements.

I think one of the most important foundations for promoting ethical and effective endings with service users and carers is in fact located in how we go about establishing sound beginnings.

A good healthy working relationship in social work is based on a clear, honest and ethical contract of how you will work with someone. For a student social worker, this contract should acknowledge you are only with the agency for a set time; everyone is clear about your role (as a social work student or trainee) and work (learning in practice towards your professional qualification). It is also important, as a social work student, to be transparent and consistent from the beginning that you will be leaving at some point; your working relationship with individuals will come to an end; after the placement ends you will not be stepping out of the professional boundaries you set at the beginning of the placement.

PLACEMENT ACTIVITY
Endings

As a developing professional practitioner, you have a professional duty to ensure you begin and end working relationships in an ethical and proper way. Consider the following in relation to endings and discuss your thoughts with your practice educator:

- *At the beginning of working with someone and agreeing a contract* – What will you need to include in your contract of work with an individual, family or group? Think about the importance of providing an outline of future work and setting boundaries; of being clear about how you will work with people and honest about what they can expect from you.

- *Revisiting and reminding service users and carers (and yourself) that there is an end date to your work and your placement* – Why may you need to repeat this? When would be a good time or moment to do this? How could you raise this?

- *During supervision* – Discuss with your practice educator which cases you have been working on should be transferred or closed. Think about how this will be decided and what you will need to do. Are there resource implications and referral procedures that need to be started so you don't delay or interrupt a service? Similarly, are there resource issues that may unduly influence the continuation of a service? You may need to make a case for some work to continue after you have left.

- *During reflection and supervision* – Think about and discuss how you feel about endings and saying goodbyes. How will these influence how you are likely to leave this placement?

- *During supervision* – Talk through and rehearse how should you end your work and contact with people? What form of communication should be used (e.g. verbal, letter, email, text). What do you want to communicate?

Remember to ensure you record the endings and goodbyes somewhere in your closing summary of work undertaken. This will be helpful for the next worker following you.

Summary

This chapter has introduced you to the people you will meet on placement and their roles and contribution to your practice learning. This should help you in getting to know who you will be working with during your placement. In addition, we have set out the basic stages of a typical social work placement. In the following chapters we will be using this framework of roles, contributors and stages to help you begin to develop your practice-based learning.

4

Understanding Values and Ethics

Overview and Learning Outcomes

This chapter will cover:

- Introducing values and ethics in the context of social work practice learning.
- Value-led approaches to practice.
- Applying values and ethics to promoting inclusive social work practice.

By the end of Chapter 4 you will be able to:

- Identify key social work values and ethics and be able to apply these to developing inclusive social work practice.

Introduction to Chapter 4

This chapter will begin by introducing and identifying values important in the context of your social work practice learning. You will examine these in much more detail during your taught course but an introduction at this point to this important feature of professional social work will help you to begin to think about the relevance and importance of developing and demonstrating practice which is value-informed and value-led. We will also look at representative features of codes of ethics used in social work and particularly how these will be relevant in your practice learning and demonstration of practice. Finally, the chapter concludes with an introduction to how values and ethics can and should inform our direct approach to social work practice and the promotion of inclusive and person-centred social work.

Values and Contemporary Social Work

It has long been argued that social work is a value-based activity (Barnard, 2006). Contemporary statements about social work emphasise the importance of values.

As the International Federation of Social Workers' definition affirms:

> Social work grew out of humanitarian and democratic ideals, and its values are based on respect for the equality, worth, and dignity of all people. Since its beginnings over a century ago, social work practice has focused on meeting human needs and developing human potential. Human rights and social justice serve as the motivation and justification for social work action. In solidarity with those who are disadvantaged, the profession strives to alleviate poverty and to liberate vulnerable and oppressed people in order to promote social inclusion. Social work values are embodied in the profession's national and international codes of ethics. (IFSW, 2000a)

Reading through this with care, we can identify a number of features of social work which readily locate values at the heart of good social work practice. As social workers in training, it is to be hoped the value-statements we can see above chime with your own personal values and beliefs. If they do not, then social work is definitely not a profession for you, as values should be the key drivers for our professional practice. Look at the words in the statement: 'respect', 'worth', 'dignity'. Are these ideas and principles you align yourself with? They ought to be!

Values help to inform and guide us as prospective professional social workers, both *how* and particularly *why* we should practise. Our professional ethics and codes stem from such sources. However, whereas codes of ethics and conduct are generally set out as the established or formalised rules of conduct, behaviour and actions for us to follow, social work values, by contrast, refer more directly to the underlying professional belief systems that guide us. However, just as we need to be aware of our professional values, so it is important to recognise that despite our best efforts to be vigilant and committed to the values of our profession, it is inevitable that our personal values and beliefs will also influence the way we approach work. The key message here is not to deny this but to see grappling with such tensions as part of our professional duty. This is why exploration of your personal beliefs and attitudes is part of the experience of placements and practice learning.

PLACEMENT ACTIVITY
How do our values and beliefs inform our practice?

1. What personal values informed your decision to become a social worker?
2. Using the statements offered earlier in the chapter, what do you think are the core values of social work?
3. In wanting to become a social worker, what area of practice are you most drawn to working in and why?
4. Which individuals, groups or communities of people would you prefer to work with? Why is this? Does this mean there may be groups or communities you do *not* want to work with? If so, is this defensible?

How will you ensure your beliefs, attitudes and preferences do not negatively impact on your practice and service delivery on placement? How well do your own values and beliefs reflect the values of social work, e.g. in valuing all people, accepting individuals for who they are, being non-judgemental.

Contemporary debates about social work values and ethics

In Chapter 1 we introduced you to the historical context of social work in the UK and notably the emergence of organised responses to poverty, need and welfare in the later 19th and early 20th century. We also set out debates about the values required for social work.

Look at: **Chapter 1 The Idea of Social Work: A Brief Introduction**.   →

As a social work student in training, you will be introduced to the Health and Care Professions Council's *Guidance on Conduct and Ethics for Students* (HCPC, 2012a), which is intended to inform your practice and conduct as a trainee social worker. We will refer you to the HCPC Guidance in the case examples we use across the chapters in this book, as it is this guidance you will be typically required to directly evidence during your practice learning. It is also important to note that you will find a distinct domain covering Values and Ethics embedded in the Professional Capabilities Framework for Social Workers (TCSW, 2012a) which you will be required to evidence and demonstrate in your practice learning.

> When qualified you will continue to use the PCF to inform and guide your professional practice as a registered social worker. This will take you through your career as a registered social worker. However, as part of your professional registration and regulation with the HCPC you will be required to adopt and adhere to the *HCPC's Standards of Proficiency for Social Workers in England* (2012b). Thus, you move from a statement of guidance (as a trainee) to a prescribed set of standards of future professional conduct and behaviour.

INFORMATION POINT

This book would recommend you make yourself familiar with all the HCPC's Guidance and also their Standards documents, which we will look at later in this chapter. These will be directly relevant to evidencing your practice on placement.

In addition, you are encouraged here to read the British Association of Social Workers' *Code of Ethics for Social Work* (BASW, 2012). BASW first adopted a code of ethics for social work in 1975 and its revised code of ethics in 2012 sets out in clear terms core values and principles for social work.

The British Association of Social Workers (BASW) is the largest independent professional association for social work in the UK. Visit their website to view their work, campaigns and range of interesting and useful publications and services. Students can join the association. BASW publishes the following:

- *The British Journal of Social Work.*
- *Practice: Social Work in Action.*
- *Professional Social Work.*
- *Rostrum* (focusing on social work in Scotland).

Download and read BASW's *Code of Ethics for Social Work* (2012).

e-Link

www.basw.co.uk/

The presence of a variety of sources in social work which emphasise the importance of values and ethics is a testament to their status and importance to the profession. However, it is reasonable to feel, from a student's point of view, that the presence of several guides and statements with overlapping and slightly differing statements and emphases is likely to be somewhat perplexing and intimidating. At the time of writing this book, the College of Social Work had also been looking at producing its own code of ethics. In the context of social work in England, the presence of differing documents produced by different organisations illustrates competing and contested debates and views about who should be driving the profession in terms of setting principles for practice.

As we suggested when we looked at the history and development of social work in Chapter 1, such tensions are not new. However, it is possible to identify and set out core values and principles of social work practice, and the remainder of this chapter will help you begin to look more directly about what we mean by values and ethics in social work.

Social Work Values

One of the distinguishing features of a profession is its set of principles which its members subscribe to and are committed to put into practice. For individual social workers, we can identify the following as key basic values:

- Respect.
- Acceptance.
- Individuality.
- Honesty and integrity.
- Equality.

PLACEMENT ACTIVITY
Translating social work values into everyday actions

Define and analyse each of the terms below. Use a dictionary if this helps. Try to identify some straightforward ways you could demonstrate these values in the way you approach and conduct yourself during your forthcoming placement. To complete this exercise does not require any specialist knowledge. However, it does require you to think about how to translate the words below into actions. Have a go and compare notes with another student on your course.

- Respect.
- Acceptance.
- Individuality.
- Honesty and integrity.
- Equality.

INFORMATION
POINT

International conventions relevant to social work values and ethics

As part of its Statement of Ethical Principles (2000b) the IFSW draws attention to the importance and relevance of international conventions to national social work practice.

International human rights declarations and conventions form common standards of achievement, and recognise rights that are accepted by the global community. Documents particularly relevant to social work practice and action are:

- The Universal Declaration of Human Rights.

- The International Covenant on Civil and Political Rights.

- The International Covenant on Economic, Social and Cultural Rights.

- The Convention on the Elimination of all Forms of Racial Discrimination.

- The Convention on the Elimination of All Forms of Discrimination against Women.

- The Convention on the Rights of the Child.

- Indigenous and Tribal Peoples Convention (ILO convention Number 169).

Take time to view these documents and inform your thinking and approach to ethical practice.

e-Link

http://ifsw.org/

Charles Levy's book *Social Work Ethics* (1976) identified three groups of values for social work, which we interpret here in light of some features of value-led practice:

1. Preferred conceptions of people.

Features of value-led practice:

- Recognises and emphasises the importance of human dignity and the inherent worth and uniqueness of individuals.
- A commitment to human rights and justice.
- Proposes the existence of common human needs and benefit in community and mutuality.
- The importance of diversity and difference.
- That people are capable of making constructive and positive change in their lives.

2. Preferred outcomes for people

Features of value-led practice:

- That individuals and groups should be enabled to achieve their full potential and enrich their lives.
- Social work should be committed to helping others to challenge and overcome the consequences of inequality, discrimination and oppression, e.g. poverty, racism, social stigma and exclusion.

3. Preferred instrumentalities for dealing with people

Features of value-led practice:

- People have rights and entitlements which we should uphold.
- People should be treated with respect and dignity.
- Our emphasis should be on problem solving and positive change.
- Social workers should be agents of change.

 Social work comment

Asserting a role for social work

> *I have been lucky enough to be able to work in a truly multi-disciplinary Community Mental Health Team that offers screening, assessment and interventions. What has been most encouraging is that in an environment where there is potential for the medical model to dominate, the social perspective on an individual's situation is seen as crucial and I have been able to do what I see as 'real' social work addressing issues of poverty and need in offering direct housing and benefits advice, employment support and also undertaking advocacy work.*
>
> *Being enthusiastic in seeking out and identifying social work tasks and interventions has enabled me to get the most out of the placement but also to get a solid understanding of, and champion, the crucial role a social worker can play in such teams.*
>
> *(Philip MA Student)*

Values and Debates in Social Work

David Howe (2009) describes how values are important in social work as they help guide actions. However, Howe suggests values are also sources of debate and tension. You may have already found in completing the first exercise in this chapter that your own personal beliefs and attitudes do not always easily knit together with the basic professional values of social work. I would suggest this would not be an untypical finding if you completed the exercise in an honest and diligent manner. We all have feelings and views of the world. These often change in intensity and influence over time, perhaps as a result of our personal life events or things we see and hear around us. For David Howe, the importance of 'emotional intelligence' is critical to how we understand and manage emotions for effective professional practice (2008).

Similarly, just as we can find tensions for us as individuals, as was asserted earlier in this chapter, debates about who 'owns' social work values seem to be generating tensions across the organisations that purport to be leading social work into the 21st century.

Given the nature of social work, it is also perhaps inherent in the practice of social work that social workers find themselves having to make difficult professional choices, often in difficult circumstances or situations. The IFSW acknowledges the complexity of integrating values in the 'real' world and encourages social workers to reflect on:

> … the challenges and dilemmas that face them and make ethically informed decisions about how to act in each particular case. Some of these problem areas include:
>
> - The fact that the loyalty of social workers is often in the middle of conflicting interests.
> - The fact that social workers function as both helpers and controllers.
> - The conflicts between the duty of social workers to protect the interests of the people with whom they work and societal demands for efficiency and utility.
> - The fact that resources in society are limited. (IFSW, 2000b)

These aspects of social work bring to our attention the tensions inherent in social work itself. For example:

- Care vs control.
- Freedom vs fairness.
- Individual rights vs societal rights.

Professional social work practice has increasingly found itself dealing with such dilemmas. As the College of Social Work has stated:

> Under Article 8 of the Human Rights Act, public authorities must respect families' rights to privacy unless there is an issue of public health or safety at stake. Social workers must therefore strike a difficult balance between investigating legitimate concerns, and prying needlessly into people's private lives. Striking this balance is complicated further by fluctuations in public attitudes. … In the aftermath of a tragedy such as Victoria Climbié or Baby P the pendulum swings towards greater vigilance. But the public also react strongly if they believe social workers are becoming overzealous. (TCSW, 2012f: Online)

Points to Consider

Wrestling with values and ethics in professional practice

Social workers face the challenge of balancing and reconciling competing duties, contradictory and conflicting rights, responsibilities and commitments.

Social workers are involved in a range of assessment tasks, such as reviewing funded packages of care provided under the NHS and Community Care Act 1990. Funding is limited so it is likely decisions you make in deciding who might get a service and who does not may be influenced by the size of your agency's budget for care. How do you balance your professional values and duty of care with the requirements of prioritising and perhaps in effect rationing services?

Achieving and maintaining value-led practice is no easy matter. In pledging ourselves to these values, your practice learning and future career requires you to:

- Commit to critically reflect – on an ongoing basis – on how your professional values are influenced by your personal values and beliefs and seek to manage this.
- Be aware and committed to social work as a value-led activity which is committed to social justice.
- Be prepared to question and challenge discrimination, oppression, social exclusion, poverty and need.

Let us now assess how our ethical codes can help guide us to be value-led in our practice.

Ethical Codes and Principles in Social Work

In essence, values refer to personal belief systems. Professional ethics stem from values and the sets of established rules or codes that guide or dictate conduct and actions for practice (essentially what we must do and what we must not do).

Sarah Banks (2001) conducted a survey of 15 IFSW affiliated codes of ethics, and in doing so uncovered a broad general consensus of four guiding ethical principles for social work practice; namely, 'respect for persons', 'user self-determination', 'social justice' and 'professional integrity' (Banks, 2001: 96).

PLACEMENT ACTIVITY
A commitment to good ethical practice

1. Identify some actions, activities or approaches which would meet the guiding principles Banks identified from her research on different national ethical codes (see Figure 4.2).

What does each principle mean to you?

- Respect for persons.
- User self-determination.
- Social justice.
- Professional integrity. (Banks, 2001: 96)

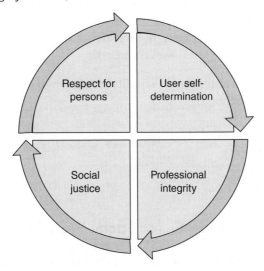

Figure 4.1 Banks's guiding principles

2. The Swedish ethics code includes the following:

There are other important personal qualities and abilities that are not foremost of an ethical character but that can harbour an ethical dimension and that link up with ethical traits of character. For example,

- Objectivity and clarity.
- Creativity.
- Social competence.
- The will to understand and the ability to cooperate.
- Independence.
- Humour. (Akademikerförbundet SSR, 2006: 11)

Reflect on how you rate yourself against these interesting criteria?

3. Ethics in other national settings

Having noted Banks's survey, have a look at the IFSW website, which includes different national codes of ethics provided by member organisations (including the UK).

- What are the key differences across codes?

e-Link

http://ifsw.org/

Social Work and Sound Ethical Traits

The revised BASW Code of Ethics (2012) and the IFSW Statement of Ethical Principles (2000b) are typical of many ethics codes in setting out sets of guides and rules for professional social work practice. However, they also stress what can be described as relevant 'ethical traits'. These are the characteristics and qualities seen as valuable in individual workers and which should be expressed and demonstrated in our manner of treating others. Typical examples of such ethical qualities expected in social workers include:

- An attitude of respect, friendliness and equality in relation to others.
- Tolerance/ broad-mindedness.
- Empathy/sensitivity.
- A sense of justice and balanced judgement.
- Integrity and responsibility.
- Critical self-insight.
- Courage/moral courage.

Ethical Codes and Standards for Social Work in England

At the time of writing this book, programmes of teaching are busy planning and preparing for the introduction of their new courses and the integration of the PCF – as the professional skills and knowledge relevant to practice – and the new codes of conduct and ethics. As with any new system, there is a period of bedding-in, integrating and making workable the different frameworks for integrating skills, knowledge, values and ethics. The work of knitting this into a coherent framework will take time and will change over time.

Table 4.1 Values and ethics for social workers in England – informing and guiding sources

Sources	Your status	Progress
	A student social worker in training ➡	A qualified and registered social worker ➡
Codes for values, ethics, conduct and behaviour	HCPC Guidance on Conduct and Ethics for Students (2012)	HCPC Standards of Proficiency for Social Workers in England (2012)
Practice framework promoting value-led and ethical practice	TCSW Professional Capabilities Framework for Social Workers (2012) – PCF 2 focuses on Value and Ethics (Note: for students in training)	TCSW Professional Capabilities Framework for Social Workers (2012) PCF 2 focuses on Value and Ethics (Note: now from your first year onwards as a registered social worker)
Relevant professional association and international codes	BASW Code of Ethics for Social Work (2012)	BASW Code of Ethics for Social Work (2012)
	IFSW Statement of Ethical Principles (2012)	IFSW Statement of Ethical Principles (2012)

BASW – British Association of Social Workers; HCPC – Health and Care Professions Council;
IFSW – International Federation of Social Workers; TCSW – The College of Social Work.

Progressing and developing as social workers in England – sources to inform and guide your values, ethics and practice

As a social worker in training you will find it necessary to be familiar with three key documents in relation to your social work training in order to demonstrate sound standards of ethical and professional practice. These are:

1. The Professional Capabilities Framework for Social Workers – PCF 2 'Values and Ethics' (TCSW, 2012a).

2. Guidance on Conduct and Ethics for Students (HCPC, 2012a).

And, relevant particularly later in your course, to help you prepare and be ready for professional practice:

3. The Standards of Proficiency for Social Workers in England (HCPC, 2012b).

Summaries of these statements are set out below and the relationship between the documents and the relevant point in your training is considered.

The Professional Capabilites Framework for Social Workers – Values and Ethics

1. PCF 2 'Values and ethics' – for students in training

This section is constructed from the 'PCF Search' facility on the TCSW website. It takes you through consideration of Values and Ethics from readiness for direct practice and the beginning of your first placement through to the end of your final placement.

Readiness for direct practice and the beginning of your first placement

Social workers have an obligation to conduct themselves ethically and to engage in ethical decision-making, including through partnership with people who use their services. Social workers are knowledgeable about the value-base of their profession, its ethical standards and relevant law.

- Understand the profession's ethical principles and their relevance to practice.
- Demonstrate awareness of own personal values and how these can impact on practice.

By the end of the first placement

Social workers have an obligation to conduct themselves ethically and to engage in ethical decision-making, including through partnership with people who use their services. Social workers are knowledgeable about the value-base of their profession, its ethical standards and relevant law.

- Understand and, with support, apply the profession's ethical principles.
- Recognise and, with support, manage the impact of own values on professional practice.
- Identify and, with guidance, manage potentially conflicting values and ethical dilemmas.
- Elicit and respect the needs and views of service users and carers and, with support, promote their participation in decision-making wherever possible.
- Recognise and, with support, promote individuals' rights to autonomy and self-determination.
- Promote and protect the privacy of individuals within and outside their families and networks, recognising the requirements of professional accountability and information sharing.

By the end of the final placement

Social workers have an obligation to conduct themselves ethically and to engage in ethical decision-making, including through partnership with people who use their services. Social workers are knowledgeable about the value-base of their profession, its ethical standards and relevant law.

- Understand and apply the profession's ethical principles and legislation, taking account of these in reaching decisions.
- Recognise and, with support, manage the impact of own values on professional practice.
- Manage potentially conflicting or competing values, and, with guidance, recognise, reflect on and work with ethical dilemmas.
- Demonstrate respectful partnership work with service users and carers, eliciting and respecting their needs and views, and promoting their participation in decision-making wherever possible.
- Recognise and promote individuals' rights to autonomy and self-determination.
- Promote and protect the privacy of individuals within and outside their families and networks, recognising the requirements of professional accountability and information sharing (TCSW, 2012a).

PLACEMENT ACTIVITY
Meeting PCF 2 'Values and ethics'

Consider the following case example and see if you can think of ways to evidence PCF 2 'Values and Ethics'. In this scenario, you are beginning your first placement. Read PCF2 relevant to the first placement and decide *how* these ethical standards could be demonstrated here.

You have visited a 45-year-old man (Martin) who is described as having a 'mild learning difficulty'. He lives with his mother who has recently suffered a stroke and been admitted to hospital. She is unlikely to return home soon. Martin is known to you as you have met him several times at a local community drop-in. He is always warm and friendly towards you. Martin has been referred to your agency for home support. When you arrive, Martin's sister (Alison) is in the house. Alison is insistent she is present during your visit and clearly expresses her view that Martin should move in with her for a time. Martin appears uncomfortable and is quiet during your visit. You are interested in hearing Alison's views, but you also want to ensure Martin can speak freely. What are your concerns here? How could you proceed? How could you demonstrate PCF2?

2. HCPC *Guidance on Conduct and Ethics for Students* (2012a)

The HCPC guidance sets out 13 guidance statements on conduct and ethics. The focus here is on your conduct and general behaviour as a student. Each guidance statement is supplemented by a set of additional guide notes, which seek to detail specific dos and don'ts of your practice development and learning.

The main headings of the guidance state:

1. You should always act in the best interests of your service users.
2. You should respect the confidentiality of your service users.
3. You should keep high standards of personal conduct.
4. You should provide any important information about your conduct, competence or health to your education provider.
5. You should limit your study or stop studying if your performance or judgement is affected by your health.
6. You should keep your professional knowledge and skills up-to-date.
7. You should act within the limits of your knowledge and skills.
8. You should communicate effectively with service users and your education provider and placement providers.
9. You should get informed consent to provide care or services (so far as possible).
10. You should keep accurate records on service users.
11. You should deal fairly and safely with the risks of infection.
12. You should behave honestly.
13. You should make sure that your behaviour does not damage public confidence in your profession.

You are encouraged to read the full HCPC guidance which can be found on the HCPC website. Each of the 13 statements has an accompanying set of elements. Read the full document to familiarise yourself with what is expected of you as a student social worker. As you can see, the guidance offers a set of dos and don'ts for you to follow. Most seem reasonable. However, as a document for social workers, the guidance reveals its legacy of being designed in an organisation which finds its historical roots in health (e.g. Guidance 11). Some course providers may review which points they wish to emphasise in their particular course as most relevant. As a social worker in training you need to be aware of the guidance document, which runs to several pages, but as the HCPC itself accepts:

The guidance does not provide answers to every situation you may face. However, we hope that it will help you and encourage you to ask for extra information from your education provider (if appropriate).

Education providers and those that provide practice placements often have their own policies and procedures which you should follow. (HCPC, 2012a: 6)

In terms of detailed, clear interpretation of the guidance and clarity about how to apply the guidance to your specific placement setting it is really important to seek advice from your practice educator and from your course programme.

PLACEMENT ACTIVITY
Meeting the HCPC Guidance on Conduct and Ethics for Students

Consider the following case example and see if you can think of ways to evidence HCPC Guidance – Statement 13 (about public confidence).

You have scheduled a home visit. However, the bus you are travelling on breaks down and you are asked to wait for a replacement. You are some way from the address you are visiting and will be late. You are aware another worker missed an appointment with this family last week. What should you ensure you do? How are you going to meet the HCPC Guidance 13?

---

3. HCPC *Standards of Proficiency for Social Workers in England* (2012b)

As well as using the HCPC guidance document being issued for students, during your course and practice learning you will also be introduced at some point to the HCPC's Standards of Proficiency for Social Workers in England (2012b). This document sets out the standards of conduct, performance and ethics required to be a registered social worker. This will become relevant when you come to register when you have qualified and so we have only included information on the standards to read, rather than offer a related placement activity. The focus for you at this point should be more centrally on meeting the requirements set out in the PCF and HCPC Guidance on Conduct and Ethics for Students.

HCPC Standards of Proficiency for Social Workers

Dos and don'ts – social workers seeking to register must be able to:

1. Practise safely and effectively within their scope of practice.
2. Practise within the legal and ethical boundaries of their profession.

3. Maintain fitness to practise.
4. Practise as an autonomous professional.
5. Be aware of the impact of culture, equality and diversit.
6. Practise in a non-discriminatory manner.
7. Maintain confidentiality.
8. Communicate effectively.
9. Work appropriately with others.
10. Maintain records appropriately.
11. Reflect on and review practice.
12. Assure the quality of their practice.
13. Understand the key concepts of the knowledge base relevant to their profession.
14. Draw on appropriate knowledge and skills to inform practice.
15. Establish and maintain a safe practice. (HCPC, 2012b)

Read the HCPC Standards document which can be viewed on the HCPC website.

e-Link
www.hpc-uk.org/

Be reassured, your local programme will no doubt spend considerable time taking you carefully through each document, explaining its content, purpose and how each relates to your course and practice learning. This task will made more achievable if you have first taken time to read each document yourself and at least have some basic familiarity with what each covers.

Summary

This chapter has introduced you to values and to value requirements in social work. We have then looked at ethical practice in social work; the relevance and importance of developing and demonstrating practice which is value-informed and value-led and the range of tensions and dilemmas which social work practitioners have to engage with on a daily basis. Dilemma is a good term here, as it captures some of the very difficult, problematic and challenging decisions social workers have to make between choices which may be undesirable, unfavourable and mutually incompatible with generating a satisfactory outcome for all. However, as a student in training you should not be asked to take the lead or sole responsibility for such decisions and, in being offered the opportunity to engage with these aspects of social work, you will have the support and guidance of your practice educator and tutor.

Look at: **Chapter 8 Using Supervision, Reflective Practice and Critical Thinking**. →

Also, be reassured that if your personal values reflect the values and principles you have been introduced to in the chapter here, then it is likely you will find social work rewarding and satisfying, despite the challenges and dilemmas that arise.

It is important to be aware that the documents relating to values, ethics and conduct in social work are relatively new, and likely to be the subject of revision and clarification over time.

In the following chapter, we put these regulatory elements to one side temporarily and return to practice, offering a very useful discussion (using the arena of social work with young people) of how it is possible to practise in a way which is value-informed, value-led and inclusive.

5

Translating Values and Ethics into Practice

By Helen Mayall and Teresa O'Neill. Additional contributions by Maureen Ajayi, Shauna Crawley, Richard Hawkins (The Autistic Organisation) and Melanie Metcalfe

---

Overview and Learning Outcomes

This chapter will cover:

- First meetings with young people.
- Empathy and managing feelings.
- Meeting places.
- Introductory meetings.
- Building trust.
- Overcoming barriers to building trust.
- Confidentiality and keeping records.
- Qualities young people look for in their social worker.

By the end of Chapter 5 you will be able to:

- Consider the current context for social work with young people.
- Identify some important areas to consider when preparing to work inclusively with young people.
- Reflect on the views of young people, who are experts by experience.
- Develop strategies for inclusive engagement with young people.

Introduction to Chapter 5

This chapter offers you an excellent example of applied values in social work which you will find helpful in helping you to work in a way that is inclusive and thoughtful. Although the example here focuses on working with young people, the principles underpinning this are founded on a value-led approach which would transfer to work with any service user or carer group and to any service or setting. We intend to use the term 'young people' in the way suggested by Thomas (2005), to include both children and young people, because 'even the smallest child is actually a young *person*' (Thomas, 2005: xv).

We have written this chapter in consultation with young people who have experience of using health and social care services, including social work services. The young people teach students on our social work programmes at Manchester Metropolitan University. This chapter is a further opportunity for the young people to share their experience with social work students and others. We have included anonymised quotations, with the young people's permission, in the hope that their words will help you prepare to work *with* young people in an inclusive way.

Why are Social Work Relationships with Young People Important?

First, social workers *do* make a difference to children's lives. Young people often want a good relationship with their social worker and some remember their social workers for a long time.

> *I had several social workers, growing up in the care system, and I can recall one good social worker, the things that she did personally for me, e.g. remembered my birthday every year, got me into therapeutic counselling when I lost my dad ... and ways of coping with it was writing, so my social worker got me a diary to write in, and I'm 22 now, and am now on my 10th diary. She helped me express my emotions by writing them, whether I was angry, sad, annoyed, worried, it still helps me now. She encouraged sibling contact, which was great, I was separated from my siblings and she helped get more contact for me, she listened to me and knew if I was having a bad day, she acknowledged it. (Young care leaver and student in higher education)*

Second, relationships with young people are central to safeguarding their welfare (Department for Education, 2013). Social workers do much that is successful in supporting and protecting children (Laming, 2009) and it is likely that effective social work has contributed to a steady decline in child-abuse related deaths in England and Wales since 1974 (Holland, 2011; Pritchard and Williams, 2010). Yet, in the hectic bustle of their work, social workers can sometimes lose their focus on the child, and therefore miss important, sometimes vital, information (Ferguson, 2011). Winter (2011) shows how the failure of the social worker–child relationship has been a feature of inquiries and serious case reviews since the death of Dennis O'Neill in 1945 (Home Department, 1945) to the present day (Laming, 2009):

The analysis of official inquiries and serious case reviews has shown that remarkably similar concerns have repeatedly been raised for over 50 years regarding the quality and nature of social worker relationships with young children. These concerns, located within the context of broader organisational failings, constitute significant shortcomings in social work practice. These include failures by social workers to: visit the children frequently; to engage and communicate with the children or to see them alone when visits did take place; to think through and articulate verbally or in records their concerns; to act decisively upon visible cumulative concerns especially children's weight loss, neglect, bruises and behavioural disturbance; and above all to make the child the focus of the intervention instead of focussing on the parents. (Winter, 2011: 23)

Third, successive government policy emphasises the importance of maintaining a focus on the child through the introduction of the Framework for the Assessment of Children in Need and their Families and the Practice Guidance (DH, 2000a, 2000b), the response to the Munro Review of Child Protection (DfE, 2011a) and Working Together to Safeguard Children (Department for Education, 2013).

The United Nations Convention on the Rights of the Child (UNCRC), Article 12, gives every child 'the right to say what they think in all matters affecting them, and to have their views taken seriously' (UNICEF, 2012). The UK signed the UNCRC in 1991 and, therefore, is required to implement its provisions, through legislative, administrative and other measures, and this includes social work with young people. However, because awareness of the UNCRC remains low both amongst professionals and the public, young people can be denied their rights (Children's Rights Alliance for England, 2013; United Nations Committee on the Rights of the Child, 2008).

Under the Children Act 1989, local authority social workers have specific duties to involve and consult looked after children and those children who could become looked after.

(4) Before making any decision with respect to a child whom they are looking after, or proposing to look after, a local authority shall, so far as is reasonably practicable, ascertain the wishes and feelings of –

(a) the child;

(b) his parents;

(c) any person who is not a parent of his but who has parental responsibility for him; and

(d) any other person whose wishes and feelings the authority consider to be relevant, regarding the matter to be decided.

(5) In making any such decision a local authority shall give due consideration –

(a) having regard to his age and understanding, to such wishes and feelings of the child as they have been able to ascertain;

(b) to such wishes and feelings of any person mentioned in subsection (4)(b) to (d) as they have been able to ascertain; and

(c) to the child's religious persuasion, racial origin and cultural and linguistic background. (Children Act 1989: Section 22)

The fourth reason is that often students come into the profession because they want to offer their help to people who need it (Stevens et al., 2012). You might already know that you want to work with young people, to spend time getting to know them and to make a difference to their lives.

Social workers working with children and families are busy with a range of activities, such as home visits, recording, supervision, attending meetings. About a quarter of social work time is spent in direct contact with service users, with just under three-quarters of social workers' time spent on other forms of 'client related work' (Baginsky et al., 2010). If you are to make the best use of the time you have with young people you will need to plan carefully and protect this precious time from competing pressures. This chapter has been written to help you think ahead and to draw your attention to what might help in developing positive relationships with young people.

First Meetings with Young People

As you begin your placement you might have little experience of working with young people, or you might have worked with young people before you started your course. Maybe you have children of your own, or younger siblings, and all of us have our own childhood behind us, so you could also draw on your life experience. Experience can help you develop the confidence to interact with young people but, as each child is unique, with their own unique experiences and personalities, it is important to keep an open mind (McLeod, 2008). Social workers need to be curious if they are to see things from a child's point of view (Morgan, 2011; DfE, 2011b).

PLACEMENT ACTIVITY
Thoughts on first meetings with young people

How do you feel about meeting a child or young person for the first time as a social work student?

- Take a few minutes to note down your thoughts about the experience and skills you bring to working with young people.
- What attitudes and values do you bring?
- What might you do to prepare yourself for meeting a child or young person for the first time, as a social work student?
- Where might be a suitable place to suggest for a first meeting?

Empathy and managing feelings

Meeting a child or young person for the first time can be a nervous occasion for both of you. Adults can feel anxious about these first meetings, perhaps because it is difficult to predict how things will go (McLeod, 2008). You might worry about whether the young person will respond to you and, if not, will you feel uncomfortable, silly, embarrassed (Howes, 2010)? However, young people can be anxious about these meetings too; strong feelings and fears about social workers are very common. It can help a young person settle and concentrate better on what you are saying if you can recognise and show that you accept their feelings.

Young people's reflections on first meetings

What might a young person think when they know a social worker is coming to see them?

Anything from anticipation to dread, depending on the person and the circumstance.

A young person's first assumption, if they are still living with their parents would be 'they're going to take me away from my family'.

They are coming to take me away from my home.

When a young person knows that a social worker is due to come and visit them they have a whole bunch of nerves and emotions going on inside them. They ask themselves questions, e.g. will I get good news or bad news? When is my next contact? What decisions have been made for me and my life now? When is the next review? What have I done now? They feel anxious, scared, nervous, lost, angry, sad, they want answers. They will be worried about family and siblings, etc.

Your practice educator will help you to prepare for these first meetings with young people and they might suggest that you anticipate and imagine how a child or young person might be feeling, as well as thinking through some of the more practical aspects of the meeting.

One of the first steps in working together with a child or young person is to put ourselves in their position and imagine their world. How would we feel in their situation? However, because we are not the same person, we need to check whether what we imagine is accurate. Empathy is therefore an active process of imagining, reflecting back and checking out (Healy, 2012; Trevithick, 2012) and it gives us a starting point to show that we are willing to work hard to see things from the child or young person's point of view. Empathetic statements are often tentative, and invite the child or young person to correct you on how they are feeling. It can be helpful to practise statements that start with:

I imagine that …

I am guessing that …

Let me check this out, you might be thinking that …

I wonder if you are thinking …

Meeting Places

Young people often have views about where they would like to meet their social worker. You might have thought of several possible options, but how do these compare with the young people's comments about venues below? For example, young people say that social workers frequently meet them in burger bars and fast food cafes. This could be a good venue for meeting some young people, sometimes, but remember these are public places and not suitable for private, personal conversations. If you are taking a young person out, you should check whether your placement agency has a policy or guidance that you should follow. Often you will visit young people where they live, but again, this might not offer sufficient privacy.

Young people's reflections on meeting places

... wherever they feel comfortable, depending on the young person. Some like it at home, some at school, some on a drive somewhere in the car, some like to go to the office, some fast food places, it all just depends on the young people. I hated fast food places, I felt it was embarrassing when staff wore their ID badges in public.

Cafés, youth centres, community centres, and at home. It all depends on the nature of the social work being done. For instance if working with somebody where confidentiality is important, e.g. closeted LGBT people, or those whose mental health issues stem from family disunity, it would be unwise for the sessions to take place at the home.

An office or small cramped room is one of the most uncomfortable places I have had to be when seeing my social worker; it made me feel like I didn't want to talk to her and I was, quite frankly, bored.

Introductory Meetings

Preparing yourself to make a good introduction will test your own understanding of your role, the purpose of the meeting and your early thinking about how best to communicate with the child or young person. However, young people can be forgiving of your mistakes, if they feel that you are genuinely trying to connect with them.

Young people's reflections on introductions

I think social workers should say their names and the reason they will be working with a young person. Most young people do not know why social workers get involved in their lives and professionals tend to talk about this, forgetting to tell the young person or child. ... Social workers have to be persistent. ... Sometimes young people are reticent and don't want to talk to someone they don't know, the relationship should, in time, develop, but sometimes, depending on the social worker, the connection is never there. If a social worker comes across as too pushy, or overfriendly to begin with, this may scare, or put off, young people from wanting to get to know them.

With a child, make sure to take into account they may be sensitive or shy. With a young person, don't underestimate their intelligence. Many young people who've gone through care have seen a lot and prefer it when things are straight up, honest and respectful rather than dictatorial.

As a young person that was in the care system, I feel that the best way that a social worker ever introduced themselves to me was when I was with someone I felt I was close to, so that I didn't feel like I was on my own with a stranger and also, asking the young person what they like to do? And introduce yourself whilst out doing an activity that they enjoy doing – a young person is more likely to take to you and open up to you if they feel like you know them and care about what they like doing!!

Prepare to explain clearly who you are and why you are there. Young people value your honesty and clarity about the reasons for your visit, but take into account the child's age and understanding. Try to imagine what the young person will hear when you speak your words. For example, the word 'assessment' has many different meanings and is notoriously confusing for children.

You might need to use creative ways of explaining to a child or young person who you are and what you do. Some young people will cope well with talking, but most will 'switch off' during long explanations, or might not understand you at all. It can be helpful to rehearse a couple of different ways to explain, and be prepared to use simple drawings. You might be able to ask if a child has their own favourite crayons, pencils or felt tip pens, and whether they would allow you to use them, but you should always have some age-appropriate drawing materials in your bag. Encourage the child or young person to join in the drawing as this shared activity can be helpful in beginning to develop a working relationship.

You may need help to communicate with a child or young person and to enable them to grasp the reasons for your visit; this could be due to a disability, their young age, or language differences. You need to consider who will be the best person to provide this support. In some situations this could be a family member, but you also need to arrange to see the child or young person alone (where and when appropriate), even if with an interpreter, or support worker (Department for Education, 2013). The timing for seeing a child or young person alone will depend on the circumstances, the reasons for the visit and whether there are concerns for their safety. Often this can be negotiated with the child or young person and their parents or carers.

You will already see that young people do not like to be rushed and the issue of time, or lack of time, is a prominent theme in young people's accounts of social work. First meetings can help you get off to a good start in your work with a child or young person so it is well worth investing the time to make a good first impression.

Building Trust

Many young people will expect you to know something about them when you first meet them. Social workers will usually read whatever relevant information is available before meeting a child or young person. There are some social workers who choose not to read the file for a looked after child until after their first meeting, to avoid pre-judging the young person, but this is less common practice. Young people who have had social workers before are likely to know that there is a file about them somewhere in the system.

How you use the pre-existing information about a child or young person could enhance or jeopardise your early work with them, as the following comments show.

Young people's reflections on reading their files

Always read the young person's file before meeting the young person then you will already know a bit about them and their life at that current time; try get background information, find out what's going on.

… too many times social workers label a young person or read up on the young person's files before they have even met the young person, so already have a bad outlook on the young person without even getting to know them first.

Given that you are likely to be asking a child or young person about their life and interests, it can help the process along if you are prepared to share something about your own hobbies and something about you as a person. There are professional boundaries to what you can disclose about yourself and your own life, but it is best to give this some thought and discuss it in supervision before you are caught by surprise. Young people are bound to be curious and social workers should be able to welcome and work with their curiosity.

A significant barrier for young people is 'too much seriousness and no fun'. So, if you can show an interest in the young person's hobbies and sometimes share activities, it can help to develop the relationship. If you are 'no good' at something (e.g. football, painting, modelling, beading, games, console games) this can be very helpful, as it enables the young person to take a lead and show you their expertise. Serious issues can be discussed during engaging and enjoyable activities (Thomas, 2005). Activities also enable the child or young person to be with you and have your attention, without feeling that they are under scrutiny. Sustained and frequent eye contact can be uncomfortable for young people so activities can help them, and you, to relax and engage in a more relaxed conversation.

Young people's reflections on sharing hobbies and interests

Most importantly, a social worker should share their hobbies and interests in their introduction. After all, you know most information about the young person or child and it's only fair that they know something about you too. This can be a way to break [down] barriers too … take time to know the child, and what's most important to them; sometimes this can be the only thing that puts a smile on their face.

A social worker can identify the child's hobbies, interests and likes and try and get involved with them in enjoying these, either by talking about it or taking part in them together. For example if a young person is into football, a social worker could talk about a match over the weekend that they know the young person will have watched. Doing activities and arts and crafts with young people can often get children interacting with you. … They are more likely to communicate with you if they feel relaxed and comfortable. It's all about going the extra mile, all the little things matter.

… find out their likes and dislikes, create conversation that doesn't involve their job, maybe talk about music, pets, ambitions and dreams, etc. … talk about something positive.

Social workers should show that they are not aliens, but are in fact the same species as the child they want to support.

Overcoming Barriers to Building Trust

A major barrier to developing trust between a young person and a social worker is previous experiences of being let down by other adults, sometimes by previous social workers. It takes time to build trust and even longer when there have been breaches of trust, so you will need to be patient. If you ask, a young person might tell you what would help them to trust you.

At the beginning of any professional relationship, it is important to negotiate the 'ground-rules', the expectations you have of each other and the behaviours you can reasonably expect. These rules can be renegotiated as circumstances change, but you should start out with a set of expectations that stand a good chance of being achievable, so that both you and the young person can begin with a degree of success.

In a busy week, being punctual can be difficult to achieve, but young people value it. It is always a good idea to make it clear how long you will have to spend with a young person, each time you meet and, if your time together is limited to a number of sessions, be open about it and remind them from time to time. Being reliable and predictable are characteristics that will help you, as will the ability to give a straightforward answer to a question, or at least a commitment to find out the answer.

Young people usually understand that there are limits to your availability, but they need to know how to contact you, when you will be available and how long they should expect to wait for you to reply to their messages. Remember to tell young people when you are on leave and who to contact in your absence.

Young people's reflections on overcoming barriers to building trust

Things that get in the way of that connection are giving false hopes, lying and not being honest and open, social workers not making time or hardly come and see you. They don't understand you or listen to you; they speak in alien language, changing the subject, when all you want is a straight answer. If a young person was to tell a social worker something and the social worker does not do anything.

Social workers should be genuine and have passion in working with the child or young person, without expecting much. Young people can always see these positive qualities in a social worker and it's that which is important in building the trust. Patience is also very important, not to give up on the child or young person. Children and young people that have involvement with social workers will have usually been let down by professionals, friends, family, so social workers need to realise and understand that it's a big expectation to want the child to be able to trust them.

Yes, [build trust] by being trustworthy. 'Building trust' alone is pointless if a child or young person feels that trust has been violated by the actions of a social worker or care provider. Honesty is the best policy when dealing with people who've likely dealt with heartbreak, lies or being moved around a lot in life.

It can be extremely difficult for a social worker to connect with a young person who has had so many people in their life that have let them down and they therefore have no, or little, trust in adults. A social worker would be able to tackle this by proving that they are reliable and by always attending meetings or catch-ups with young people and by keeping in contact with the young person outside of these visits, obviously within working hours.

Give [young people] several options to be able to present their thoughts and feelings. Text messages, phone calls, somewhere to post their thoughts. Having said that, the social worker needs to be available when [the] young person or child may wish to talk to them, if not, at least try and get in touch following a message received. Have a non-judgemental attitude this will allow the child or young person feel free to express their feelings.

The behaviours that demonstrate the respectful and helpful approach necessary for engaging service users can be summarised as follows:

- Punctuality.
- Reliability.
- Courteousness.
- Clear (jargon free) communication.
- Clarify your social work role and negotiate ground-rules.
- Be yourself, with limited self-disclosure, compassion and maintaining professional boundaries (Healy, 2012).

Confidentiality and Keeping Records

It is likely that young people will be concerned about confidentiality and how information will be recorded, shared and kept safe. Young people often want to know who else could read information about them and under what circumstances you would share information with other agencies.

Young people's reflections on confidentiality

Confidentiality is extremely important. Children and young people should be able to feel comfortable to express anything in confidence; if confidentiality cannot be maintained it will impact on the child and worker's relationship because the child will not be able to speak freely, and the social worker will never find out what it is the child wants or thinks or is experiencing.

Confidentiality is very important. Young people have to trust social workers with everything from abuse, violence, secrets, embarrassing, naughty things, etc. and don't expect it to be broadcast to everyone.

It depends on the situation. Obviously if somebody is at risk, breaking confidentiality should be a no-brainer as their safety is the most important thing. On the other hand, if it's more of an emotional issue, then if they connect with somebody they can talk about things with and attempt to find a resolution to a problem, then confidentiality can help that process.

It is therefore wise to clarify what will happen to personal information about the child or young person early in the relationship-building process. A lack of clarity, or avoidance, is likely to result in people being more guarded in their conversations with you and could seriously damage your relationship with a young person. It is usually helpful to come to a shared understanding about confidentiality, including the limits of confidentiality, as part of clarifying your role and establishing the ground-rules. Even if a young person has had social workers before, it is still crucial that you are both clear about what will happen to their information.

The Data Protection Act 1998 gives young people under 18 the right to see information held about them, if they have sufficient understanding, and unless it is thought this would harm them. Most local authorities, independent and voluntary organisations have leaflets and online information that will help you explain how young people can access information held about them in their files. Ultimately, a student social worker's responsibilities, both to keep records and maintain confidentiality, are included in the *HCPC's Guidance on Conduct and Ethics* (2012a).

Many social work agencies encourage social workers to share their recordings with the children and families they work with and young people generally welcome this way of working.

Young people's reflections on recording practices

> *... the opinions of those that are cared for should form an important part of the reviewing of social work.*

> *Keeping records of young people's lives should be written as if the young person is stood behind them, looking over at what is being written and checking with young people, if they agree with what was written, as one day that young person will read them. Make sure it's factual and backed up with evidence, no assumptions or opinions. Never leave a young person's work out for all to see. It's confidential.*

It can improve the quality of a recording to expect the young person to read it. This tends to concentrate the mind on whether you can justify what you have written. Have you recorded information correctly? If you include opinion, can you support it with evidence? Have you taken care to include positive information as well as recording problems and difficulties? Records are kept for a long time after young people have moved on in their lives: for looked after children records are kept until the person is 75 years old.

PLACEMENT ACTIVITY
Recording

During the early part of their placement, usually during the induction period, students are often introduced to agency policy on confidentiality, recording and information sharing.

- Make a note of any questions you might have for your practice educator about this area of practice.
- Once on placement, look for any leaflets produced by your agency that might help you explain agency practices and young people's rights concerning confidentiality and record keeping.

Young people's reflections on best social work practice

Empathy is important, remember you were a child or a young person once yourself. The best way to make a difference is to treat people with respect and encourage a friendly dialogue in the social work process.

Remember that what you're communicating to a young person may sound different to them, so be sure to repeat what it is you have said and clarify that they understand.

You have to be a good listener as well as communicator; it's not just all about the talking.

Try to understand what the child has been through, and be sensitive /cautious about what words you use when talking to them.

Be reliable and just show them that you care and are there to help. Social workers to go that extra mile.

My ideal social worker would be calm and cool. They would be understanding, patient, caring and have a passion to help me repair my family.

They would treat those they worked with as human beings, and understand that each person is different. They'd work with their co-workers, children and young people in a considerate manner. One cannot call oneself a social worker if they are not truly social.

Summary

This chapter aimed to introduce you to some issues to consider when preparing to work with young people. The different sections of the chapter give priority to aspects of practice identified by young people as the most important to them. We hope you have enjoyed hearing the views expressed and that these have inspired you to develop your thinking and skills further.

6

Assessment and Evidencing your Practice Learning

Overview and Learning Outcomes

This chapter will cover:

- Assessment of your social work practice learning on placement.
- Direct work in social work practice relevant to beginning your practice learning.
- Evidencing your social work practice learning and development.

By the end of Chapter 6 you will be able to:

- Identify the key features of assessment in relation to your practice learning.
- Describe some key features of direct work in social work relevant to beginning your placement.
- Evidence your practice learning and development.

Introduction to Chapter 6

This chapter is designed to help you better understand the assessment requirements of your social work placement and to help you to begin to demonstrate and then evidence your social work practice and development.

The goal here is to introduce the sorts of activities typically expected of student social workers in their placements; how you might evidence this work, and of course to help you to pass your placement. Too often students who have a real talent in terms of their social work practice on placement do not always evidence their skills and knowledge in a way which demonstrates their full potential. This leaves your practice and effort sold short and does not do justice to you, your practice educator and all the other people who helped you learn and develop (notably, service users, carers, other workers). If you read and use the information set out in the chapter you should be better able to show everyone how good a worker you can be (i.e. that you are a capable practitioner).

Assessment of your Practice Learning on Placement

As we discussed earlier in this book, in October 2011, the College of Social Work (TCSW) became responsible for implementing the reforms from the Social Work Reform Board (SWRB). In the TCSW's document *Reforming Social Work Qualifying Education* (2012b), practice placements are seen as critical to raising standards in social work and the Professional Capabilities Framework for Social Workers (PCF) is a key framework for the holistic assessment of students on placement.

As identified in Chapter 2, the PCF 'rainbow' sets out the profession's expectations of what social workers should be able to do at each stage of their career and professional development, ranging from being a social worker in training through to their early career and beyond. We also drew your attention to the parts of the PCF relevant for your entry and progression through your social work education and training. I hope you have taken the time to become more familiar with the PCF. If not, my strong advice is to go back and look again. This task will help you be prepared for evidencing your practice and learning from the beginning of the placement. This may seem an obvious point, but is often missed by students, who rely on working out what is expected of them on placement as they go along. This does not work well, and the more familiar you are with the PCF the more thorough and reliable will be your ability to evidence your work.

The College of Social Work argues that there are: 'a number of benefits in using the PCF to underpin the assessment of students' (TCSW, 2012b: 55). As the College's *Reforming Social Work Qualifying Education* (2012b) states, these include:

- Giving more scope to the judgement of the practice educator about a student's suitability to practice.
- Providing clearer shared national standards about what is expected of students at different points in their programme, highlighting the elements of progression that are significant (e.g. confidence, ability to work more autonomously, professional decision-making, engagement in more complex situations, use of authority).
- Enabling clearer identification by the practice educator of the areas that students need to work on to demonstrate their practice.
- Introducing students to the framework for professional development that will be used throughout their career as a social worker. (TCSW, 2012b: 55)

The College of Social Work emphasises *two* key principles in relation to student assessment during placement:

- Practice educators should make overarching judgements about the quality of a student's practice and assess a student's overall capability to work at the level required for the placement concerned based on clear evidence.
- The criteria for passing the first and last placement should be clearly linked to the student's progression in meeting the PCF as a whole, through other assessed work at an appropriate level. At the point of qualification, this means that passing the final placement should form a substantial part of the final assessment but will not be the only expectation that has to be met. (TCSW, 2012b: 56)

So, we can see from these principles that your practice educator (we discussed their role in Chapter 2) is the *key* figure in the assessment of your practice and performance on placement. It is the practice educator who will support you during your practice learning and will ultimately assess your practice making a judgement about whether you pass or fail the placement.

Look at: **Chapter 2 The New Professional Capabilities Framework and Revised Placement →
Structure**.

Also, the College's statement of principle tells us that assessment of your practice on placement (demonstrated and evidenced in meeting the requirements of the PCF) will be a *key* element in deciding whether you progress through your course. You will need to pass each of your placements in order to be able to become a qualified social worker.

The College of Social Work has stated that each social work programme should determine how the capability statements are used locally to translate the PCF into assessment criteria (TCSW, 2012b). Thus it is essential you make yourself familiar with the requirements of your own programme of study and use this book as a complementary source in your learning.

The PCF and gathering evidence of your practice learning

If you think of the PCF as a map with directions for your journey through your qualifying programme and placement, then in order to arrive safely and on time at your final destination (passing the placement and the course) you need to be familiar with the route before you start your journey and keep looking, checking it throughout.

Checklist

Gathering evidence of your practice learning during placement – knowing the PCF:

☐ Read all the PCF documents and make sure you know what you will need to evidence in order to pass first and second placement.

☐ Be clear, before you begin work on placement, what evidence you will need to produce in order to pass your placement. In this way, when you begin your direct work with service users, carers and others you will be able to think about what you have done, collect and collate your evidence and then report this.

☐ In making yourself familiar with the PCF, be able and willing to discuss the PCF during supervision and elsewhere (and impress your practice educator along the way ... a very good idea!).

☐ Use your reflective log or diary to record your daily work and reflections as you go along, rather than rely on memory. Remember, placements will typically get busier and busier. You will almost certainly forget some of the things you have done several weeks ago.

☐ Start collecting evidence of your performance in relation to the PCF from the beginning of your placement, rather than just before being asked to produce a piece of work by your practice educator. This will increase your choice of evidence and help you be clear about what you have evidenced already and what still needs to be identified. Put yourself in a position to be able to select the best evidence from the full range of your practice learning rather than just what you can remember.

'Holistic assessment' and social work

The term 'holistic assessment' is emphasised in social work practice learning. The College of Social Work has commented that:

> Social work practice is a complex activity, requiring an interplay of knowledge, skills and values. ... Within this, the nine capabilities should be seen as interdependent, not separate: they interact in professional practice, so there are overlaps between the capabilities, and many issues will be relevant to more than one capability. Moreover, understanding what a social worker does can only be complete by taking into account all nine capabilities. Assessing learning, performance and progression in relation to the PCF therefore requires an approach congruent with this framework. 'Holistic assessment' is a recognised approach for assessing in such circumstances. (TCSW, 2012a: 1)

Evidencing your social work practice and development

Although you will be guided about what your local programme requires and you may or may not be asked to formally submit a portfolio of your work, you certainly will be asked to provide work in order for your practice educator to make their assessment. Make sure you understand what your own programme expects to be covered in your placement. Whether you are formally required or not to submit a portfolio of your placement work, it is recommended you keep a file or folder in order to store all your documentation together and in turn help you produce the best evidence you can of your practice. The practice educator will draw on a range of your placement-related tasks, activities and written evidence in order to make a comprehensive assessment of your practice. These items may vary but would typically include:

- An analysis of one or more specific pieces of work you undertook, consisting of a case summary, reflection on practice, cross-referenced to PCF domains.
- A case study of a piece of work, including a commentary from you about what this demonstrates about your performance in relation to a specific PCF domain (e.g. PCF 7: 'Intervention and skills').
- Reports of direct observation of your practice (these may be based on observations by your practice educator and /or others as appropriate).
- Examples and commentary on your use of supervision over the period of the placement.
- Feedback from your practice educator from supervision records.
- General observation and feedback from service users and carers, from other staff and peers.
- Attendance and feedback from training events, development days and other forums.
- Other documents as appropriate, such as items produced by you on placement, e.g. an information leaflet produced for the agency, presentation to the team, a piece of research undertaken and reported on, an example of good practice.

The practice educator may also draw on other placement-related documents:

- The initial placement planning meeting /contract.
- Midpoint review meeting.

- Final placement meeting.
- Attendance records.
- Consent and confidentiality statements.

The practice educator's report

The College of Social Work has outlined the practice educator's role in student assessment. The practice educator's assessment report is organised into two parts: first, 'development of holistic practice' (an overall assessment of the student's progress on placement), and second, 'development of a specific capability' (e.g. focusing on say PCF 7: 'Intervention and skills' and HCPC Guidance on Conduct and Ethics for Students).

The practice educator will be expected to report on a student's ability to practise effectively drawing principally on: the student's case study and commentary; the practice educator's observations of the student in practice; discussions in supervision; agency records/reports on the casework undertaken by the student.

To promote fair, just and trustworthy assessment, the practice educator is expected to draw on a range of sources in order to assess and judge a student's practice.

The College suggests a practice educator should make use of observations of several 'slices of practice' in different settings and at different times; by different observers; made by those *capable* of making judgements; made with reference to known and agreed criteria or standards (Knight, 2006, in TCSW, 2012d: 3).

PLACEMENT ACTIVITY
Sources of holistic assessment

Name as many different practical activities (e.g. interviewing), thinking work (e.g. the quality of your analysis of information) and other sources of evidence (e.g. observing you) your practice educator could draw on to make a holistic assessment of your work.

Summary

This section has introduced you to assessment on your placement; what form the assessment of your practice and learning may take and some initial thoughts about possible sources of evidence.

The next section is designed to help you orientate to social work as a practice process, and to some of the direct work and key features of social work practice which will help you in your practice learning. You may well not use all these features in your placement and this will vary from placement to placement and from programme to programme. However, they are extremely useful to introduce and explore as you enter your training. If you learn to use them well – and remember you are at the very beginning of your professional career so this will take time and effort – you will be a better social work practitioner, provide a better service to the people you work with and be far happier in your work

An Introduction to Social Work Process

In Chapter 1 we discussed what it means to be a social worker and how we can begin to construct what being a social worker entails. What we do know is that social work is a complex business and so it is important we try to think about how to make sense of the day-to-day work we do and the different activities, processes and stages of the work we undertake.

An understanding of 'social work process' will also help us to orientate and locate ourselves during our practice. But what is it?

Gaining social work experience – 'Social work process'

Social work process can be identified as generally having five distinct but interrelated and interdependent stages. These stages feature:

1. **An initial referral** (a presenting difficulty or problem).
2. **An assessment** (collecting information and making sense of the resulting data).
3. **Planning and delivering a response** (producing a plan of care and delivering a social work intervention).
4. **Producing specific outputs** (e.g. practical services or equipment) **or other outcomes** (e.g. effective risk management, change and improvement).
5. **Review and evaluation**.

> **AS**sessment > **P**lanning > **I**ntervention > **R**eview & **E**valuation

Sutton (1999) suggests the mnemonic **ASPIRE** to help us remember the process of:

AS – Assessment

P – Planning

I – Intervention

RE – Review and Evaluation

ASPIRE is not the only way of presenting this sort of way of seeing social work practice but it is rather handy and easy to remember if you get stuck. It is just one of many examples of process you will come across in the course of your study and practice and although some of the terms and stages differ, the general principles remain the same.

The idea of describing and presenting social work practice as a process which includes stages comprising initial presentation/referral → assessment → planning → review is now a generally accepted template across a range of community health and social care services and settings. For example, we can identify this basic model in care management within adult social care services;

in the Care Programme Approach used in mental health services; the procedural models used by agencies such as Connexions in their work with 13- to 19-year-olds.

Although we often tend to think of a 'process' as linear and sequential – just as it is being described above – it is actually much more useful in the context of social work to think of social work process as circular and cyclical in motion and action.

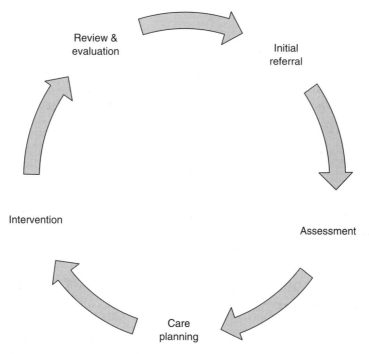

Figure 6.1   Social work process

Figure 6.1 plots social work practice as a cyclical process. The cycle begins with the referral or presenting problem and concludes with a review and evaluation of the process. However, as frequently is the case in social work practice, the cycle needs to be flexible enough to enable any stage to be undertaken independently or for particular stages to be revisited several times in order to accommodate and respond effectively to changes in circumstances, environments and risk issues. For example, a crisis situation relating to the protection of a child may require a rapid intervention with only a limited opportunity available for initial assessment and planning.

Being familiar with 'social work process' will help you understand and make sense of:

- What you are doing at a particular point in your work (e.g. assessing, planning, reviewing).
- Explaining your work to others (notably to service users and carers).

- Locating where you are in the cycle of social work process in relation to other interconnected activities (e.g. assessing in preparation for producing a plan; reviewing your intervention; getting ready to re-assess and re-plan, etc.).

Locating and understanding your role and contribution to social work process is a key part of beginning to understand your role as an effective practitioner. The cycle of the process is similar to the reflective practitioner cycle and the supervision and risk cycles described elsewhere in this book.

→ Look at: **Chapter 7 Introducing Risk.**

Similarly, it is important to remember that each stage of the process may come to influence and impact on any subsequent part. A number of internal and external variables and factors can impact on the social work process in this regard. Such factors could include:

- Risk.
- Time.
- Resources.
- Priorities.
- Changes in circumstances.
- Other participants.
- Other agencies … and more … including you!

This is why supervision with an experienced practice educator will be a real asset. You will have dedicated time in supervision to talk through all these complex matters. Use the time well!

As a result, for social workers, alertness, vigilance and a willingness to revise and update our information, plans and interventions are key attributes of good social work practice (and effective and positive risk management). Good quality social work is certainly value-led but it is also characterised by attributes of tenacity, resilience and commitment if we are to maximise the possibility of positive and safe outcomes in our practice. These attributes tend to be underplayed in academic social work literature but are essential assets you will find useful in your practice. Ask practitioners and see what they say!

Assessment: The Beginning of Social Work Process

As we suggested earlier, it is quite typical that following on from your induction and the early days of your placement you will be asked to undertake a piece of direct social work with a service user or carer. This may result from a new referral or you may be asked to pick up or review some existing piece of work. Whatever the referral or reason for you becoming involved, the foundation to ensuring your intervention is effective is a good quality assessment.

The importance of assessment in social work

Watson and West (2006) argue that at the heart of good quality social work practice is good quality assessment. Assessment informs our evaluation and judgements and in turn our plans, priorities and decisions as professional workers.

Crisp et al. (2003) assert that assessment involves collecting and analysing information about people with the aim of understanding their situation and determining recommendations for any further professional intervention. As you will learn during your teaching and in placement there are many types and forms of assessment in social work. Try the exercise below.

PLACEMENT ACTIVITY
Assessment

Name as many different types of assessment as you can in social work. Crisp's description above of assessment helps social workers to think about a possible structure for assessment. This involves:

- Collecting and analysing information about people.
- Understanding their situation.
- Determining recommendations for any further professional intervention.

Make a list of what sort of information you might want to collect as part of a social work assessment.

The purpose of assessment

In contemporary social work in England it is probably fair to say that much of social work practice, particularly in local authority settings, is driven by statutory duties and powers. This is reflected in the varying range, types and purpose of assessments typically undertaken by social workers. For example:

- A children and families social worker may be called upon to investigate and assess concerns about potential significant harm to a child under Section 47 of the 1989 Children Act.
- In youth justice and youth offending settings work a social worker may be asked to produce a pre-sentence report under the Criminal Justice Act 2003.
- In adult services a social worker may be required to assess an individual's care needs under Section 47 of the NHS and Community Care Act 1990.
- Carer needs assessments can be located in legislation, notably the Carers (Recognition and Services) Act 1995, Carers and Disabled Children's Act 2000 and Carers (Equal Opportunities) Act 2004.
- The Mental Health Act 1983 amended by the Mental Health Act 2007 includes specific roles and duties of assessment (possibly leading to compulsory hospital admission and detention) involving mental health social workers in their capacity as trained Approved Mental Health Professionals (AMHPs).

Definitions of an assessment

The following definitions of assessment will help us think about the meaning of assessment:

> ... an ongoing process in which the client or service user participates, the purpose of which is to assist the social worker to understand people in relation to their environment. Assessment is also a basis for planning what needs to be done to maintain, improve or bring about change in the person, the environment or both. (Coulshed and Orme, 2006: 24)

> Assessment is a key element of social work practice because without it workers would be left to react to events and intervene in an unplanned way. (Milner and O'Byrne, 2002: 8)

> Assessment is at the heart of all good social work practice. It covers a spectrum of activities, from observation and judgments made within the context of an initial encounter through to more formal and complex frameworks. (Watson and West, 2006: 30)

Points to Consider

Service users' views

Whittington (2007) has summarised research undertaken for the Social Care Institute for Excellence (SCIE) on assessment by Shardlow et al. (2005). In the research, adult service users were asked for their views about what was important to them in terms of social work and in particular social work relating to assessment. Service users emphasised:

- A desire for dependability.
- A desire for strong advocacy on the service user's behalf.
- The need for clarity both about the social work role and also the meaning of 'assessment'.
- The need for plain English to be used in assessments (and that professionals tended, albeit unconsciously, to use jargon).
- The importance of trained, independent interpreters and the need for social workers to be educated in the use of interpreters and the inherent risks in using family members, particularly children, as interpreters when making an assessment.

Value-led approaches to promote anti-oppressive social work practice

Jan Fook (2002) asserts the need for social workers to be critically aware of their roles and activities in the context of a professional commitment which emphasises social justice, rights and empowerment. Fook has focused particular attention with regard to the way we practise on how we begin our work with others and how we approach our very first point of contact with service users and carers (in gathering information and make an initial assessment of a presenting problem or difficulty someone is facing). Fook set out that both the criteria and process of assessment in social work are:

> Integral to the process of defining service users in disempowered ways, and of defining problems as the responsibility of disempowered rather than dominant groups; and of defining those with problems as separate from or different to dominant groups who do not have problems. … Assessment discourses [are thereby] integral to the process and structures which preserve dominant power relations. (Fook, 2002: 117)

Fook and Gardner (2007) say social work can help to guard against oppressive and disempowering practice by considering and valuing the following ideas:

- Problematic situations involve complex, competing and contradictory factors which need to be carefully weighed.
- The service user's own narrative and problem identification should be encouraged and supported, valued and considered.
- Existing and imposed labels or descriptions need to be treated with caution and questioned, resisted and rejected where necessary.
- Hierarchies of 'social problems' need to be evaluated in terms of the social constructions and political discourses which influence the context and direction of social work.
- Social workers need to use reflection and reflexivity to understand our motivations and decision-making.
- People are capable of change.

PLACEMENT ACTIVITY
Anti-oppressive practice and social work students' portfolios

Stewart Collins and Lynne Wilkie (2010) examined placement portfolios produced by social work students undertaking their final social work placements. They found that students gave positive attention to issues of power, empowerment and partnership. However, they also noted an 'apparent general acceptance of agency policies, procedures, and wider structural oppression. Also, some aspects of social divisions and forms of oppression such as gender, age, disability and language received considerable attention while others such as "race", class, sexuality and religion received less attention' (2010: 760).

What do you need to consider when thinking about anti-oppressive practice on placement and how might *you* provide evidence of this?

PLACEMENT ACTIVITY
Defining assessment

Using the definitions above, list some of the key words and phrases which help us understand what assessment is. If you can undertake and produce a good and comprehensive assessment you will be able to:

- Promote and accentuate the importance of the 'social' in any service or setting. Why is this important?
- Be clearer about what is going on and what needs addressing first. Why is this important?
- Clarify previous records and views. Why is this important?
- Advocate for others and signpost people to other services. Why is this important?
- Offer a good quality social service! Why is this important?

Features of a social work assessment

Ruben Martin (2010) outlines the features of assessment by suggesting this involves:

1. Gathering and assembling full and accurate information about a service user's circumstances and how these came about.
2. Objectively analysing information, making professional judgements and coming to accurate conclusions.
3. Participation by service users and others (e.g. family) to identify issues and how they might be addressed.
4. Assessing eligibility for services and level of need.
5. Gathering and exchanging information with others.
6. Recording data and information accurately.

This is an extremely useful development of not only the features of assessment but also its purpose. It also leads us to consider the importance of information gathering and being capable of producing a social history. However, as well as a commitment to efficiency, Martin (2010) suggests that we can build on these ideas in a social work context by recognising that:

- Assessment is fluid and dynamic and is part of an overall and ongoing social work process.
- Full participation of service users and carers is important.
- Social work should be value-led.
- Social work should be humane.

Have a go at the exercise opposite.

PLACEMENT ACTIVITY
The importance of accuracy – Information gathering as part of an initial social work assessment

Read the following case information – which is drawn from an adapted real case – and then answer the questions below. You are a mental health social worker and have recently been allocated this case.

Summary of information.

Marcia is a 28-year-old mother with two children (Joel 5, Carrie 9). Her mother, Lillian – who is Marcia's main and consistent support – is concerned Marcia is 'not coping with the kids' and 'stressed out'. Lillian is going to Antigua in a week to attend a family wedding and will be away for four to six weeks.

Lillian has tried to persuade Marcia to come to your office. Lillian reports that Marcia says she will ask for help when she needs it but not before.

Marcia recently separated from Patrick, her long-term partner and the father of Joel and Carrie. Patrick is described as a heavy 'social drinker'. There have been difficulties and domestic violence within the relationship. There are concerns about the finances of the family. However, at other times when Patrick is settled, he has helped at home.

Marcia has a history of mental health problems (described as a 'bipolar illness' in case records). In the past, Marcia has self-harmed by cutting herself on her upper arms and has also made a suicide/para-suicide attempt using gas from a domestic gas fire in her home.

Marcia was 'admitted informally' for psychiatric treatment approximately 18 months ago. There is no recent record of contact with mental health services.

School rang services about three weeks ago to pass on concerns about Joel and Carrie's progress. Both are coming to school late in the mornings and Joel has been quite disruptive in class. It was commented on that Marcia had been tearful a couple of times when bringing Joel and Carrie to school. You learn Joel and Carrie have been off school for the past fortnight.

Consider:

- What are the presenting issues, support needs and concerns you need to consider in relation to this case?
- What additional information might you need in order to help you complete your assessment?
- Where might you seek further information?
- What actions – if any – would you consider it appropriate to take?
- What strengths and assets can we identify?

The social worker's reflections

As the new social worker in the case I made contact with the school and the family. Both were concerned for Marcia's health and for the wellbeing of the children. Patrick could not be contacted. I also liaised with the mental health team who had previously been working with Marcia and was told she was fine, had medication and was compliant with her treatment. This information from mental health services later proved to be incomplete, not current and in some parts plain wrong. So, I would say take care when you are gathering

(Continued)

(Continued)

information and don't be over-influenced by reports. You must be alert and vigilant and be prepared to check and re-check your sources.

Note: you are at the very beginning of your training. The case above is quite complex and throws up lots of incomplete details, unanswered questions and areas you may or may not feel you know enough about at this time. All these feelings and responses are normal, legitimate and proper. Remember, you will have plenty of chance to hone your skills of assessment during your placements and practice learning. The task here is to begin thinking about the sort of information you will require in order to start a full assessment.

Points to Consider

In answering the above placement activity about Marcia above:

- How did you consider the relevance of culture or ethnicity?
- Why might Marcia be reluctant to access your support?

Approaches to Assessment and Information Gathering

Smale et al. (2000) argue that assessment in social work is important as it is the starting point – formally or informally – for plans and interventions which aim to:

- Provide *new resources* for individuals, families or communities.
- Bring about change in the *patterns of relationships* which have created or perpetuate problems.
- Provide a *combination* of the above.

However, the style of our assessment and how we undertake it can be crucial to what, how and why we practise. According to Smale et al. (2000) three approaches to assessment can be identified:

- The worker takes the role of the expert coming in from outside with a ready-made framework to understand the service user, his or her problems and the best option(s) for action.
- The worker takes a questioning role using a ready-made assessment framework (usually using an agency proforma designed for the purpose of assessment).
- The worker operates alongside the person and significant other people to arrive at a mutual understanding of the problem and negotiate who does what.

A key difference between the three approaches lies in the location of power and service user and carer involvement. It could be argued that power resides with:

- The worker in the first model.
- With the agency in the second model.
- In the third model it is more diffused and perhaps shared amongst the worker, the service user(s) and whoever else may be involved in the discussion.

Smale et al. (2000) see the interaction between assessor and assessed as fitting one of three models:

The questioning model

- The assessor sets the agenda and is seen as the 'expert'.
- The use of questions is the dominant behavioural tool used by the worker.
- Needs are quite standardised and the assessor uses expertise and knowledge gained through the process.
- Closed questions predominate.

The administrative (procedural) model

- Applies a rigid system to the assessment process.
- Typified by a large number of forms to be completed.
- Tends to be a one-way process in order to satisfy worker and agency needs.
- Gaining information is the main priority.
- Closed questions predominate.

The exchange model

- Both worker and service user construct their own agenda.
- Information sharing is important.
- Participation in the decision-making process is important.
- Holistic assessments and the exploration of problems and differing perceptions are valued.
- The individual is respected as the expert on his/her own situation.

The *exchange model* is commended by Smale et al. (2000) as the model which enables stereotypes to be avoided and strengths and needs properly acknowledged. In social work, you ought to be trying to practise using the exchange model. This complements the values of social work.

When you are on placement you will be encountering assessment in real time, so thinking about these models will be important and should help you in delivering practice, reflecting about practice, and improving practice.

Points to Consider

Your assessment is out of date the minute it is finished so make sure you keep revisiting your assessment to refresh and update your information. Be vigilant and alert!

Information gathering as part of assessment

Gathering information is absolutely critical to developing a good social work plan and intervention.

In order to inform a good quality assessment you ought to consider a range of potential sources of information in order to maximise the amount of data on which you are going to base your assessment. There is a simple formula to remember here: the more information the better your assessment is likely to be. The more thorough you are in gathering information, the more thorough the assessment.

Points to Consider

It is no exaggeration to say you will come across heaps of assessment tools and forms in your social work training and career. They are especially useful in helping us to think about what needs to be covered about a particular matter (e.g. community care assessment, carer assessment, risk assessment, needs assessment and so on). An assessment tool can also help order the work and provide a useful prompt list of what we need to pay attention to and prioritise. By completing an assessment form fully and comprehensively you will have gathered specific information for a specific task.

In beginning our practice learning, being able to draw on an assessment tool or form feels immensely helpful. However, it is important we do not as social workers see our professional task as simply filling in forms. Contemporary social work practice seems to feature an almost ceaseless compulsion towards the completion of forms as a goal in itself. However we must not forget that assessment tools are just that, tools. Supporting positive change in people's lives should be our goal, based on rights, justice and respect.

Beginning an assessment

Often a good place to start when undertaking an assessment is to check what – if any – information and reports have already been produced and recorded in relation to your piece of work. This is potentially valuable information. It can help you to produce information quickly and to make a good start on your assessment. It can also provide basic factual information (e.g. family members, agency contacts, a chronology of contacts) which means you don't have to take a service user or carer through basic information they have already given to services, possibly several times already (a frequent complaint from service users and carers).

PLACEMENT ACTIVITY
Information gathering: some initial sources

Consider the usefulness of the following potential sources of information:

- Records and reports.
- Colleagues.

- Other departments of your placement agency.
- Outside agencies.

What sorts of valuable information can these sources provide?

What might the problems be with this sort of information?

Summary

This section has introduced you to social work process and to assessment, which marks the beginning of social work process. Armed with your thoughts and ideas from Chapter 1 about what we mean by social work and what social workers need to have as their purpose, social work process provides a practice pathway which you can use to navigate any allocated work in any type of practice placement and in any setting.

Demonstrating and Evidencing your Practice Learning

This part of the chapter looks at several different social work tasks and activities which you may find you are using in your work on placement. These have been highlighted by the College of Social Work as suitable sources to demonstrate your practice and also as evidence of your practice learning. They include:

- Producing a case summary.
- Producing a case study.
- Observing and shadowing others.
- Direct observation of your practice.
- Training and development days, professional forums, presentations and other events.

We will look at these in turn.

Evidencing your Work: Producing a Case Summary

Whether you are asked formally or informally by your practice educator to summarise your work as part of your supervision or review of learning, being able to prepare, present and evaluate your work in the form of a case summary will be very helpful. A good case summary uses the framework of social work process to set out concisely and clearly what you have done. This is very useful as the basis of further analysis of your work, such as assessing outcomes for your work, reviewing and updating your plan of work and future interventions.

Use Table 6.1 to compare and then link social work process to mapping your work as a case summary.

Table 6.1   Linking social work process to your case summary

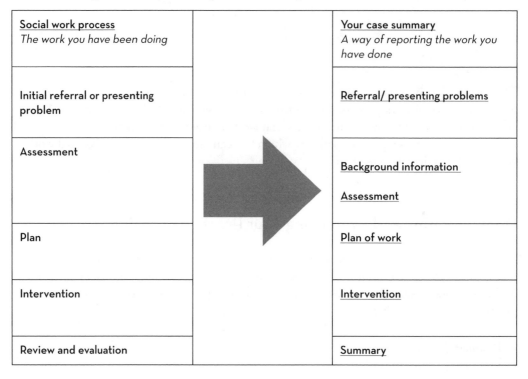

Social work process *The work you have been doing*		Your case summary *A way of reporting the work you have done*
Initial referral or presenting problem		Referral/ presenting problems
Assessment		Background information Assessment
Plan		Plan of work
Intervention		Intervention
Review and evaluation		Summary

The contents of your case summary

The case summary can be designed in various forms but a typical model might look like the outline below.

- Referral/presenting problem.

The reasons for the referral to your agency and the basis for this being allocated to you.

- Background information.

Individual circumstances, accommodation, income, social and economic factors, family and supports, etc.

- Assessment.

Your assessment of the presenting problems and prioritisation of the key risks and needs that have to be addressed. Also include the possible strengths and assets which can be drawn on, as well as other services involved.

- Plan.

A brief outline of your intended work and interventions. What you intended to do; what you managed to do and in what order of priority.

- Intervention.

A short summary, review and evaluation of your actions in terms of both outputs (what you did) and outcomes (the consequences and changes you may have been able to support or bring about).

- Summary.

This section concisely summarises the work you did; assessing what went well; what went less well; the next actions, interventions or piece of work which may be required.

Note: with this case summary outline it also becomes relatively straightforward to:

- Link your work and actions with specific PCF domains.
- You can also review and evaluate your work and actions against the HCPC *Guidance on Conduct and Ethics for Students* (2012a).
- You can reflect on your practice in supervision.
- You can also relate things you have done to a particular aspect of practice you are interested in (e.g. risk, anti-oppressive practice, service user involvement).

Evidencing your Work: Producing a Case Study

You may also be asked to produce a 'case study' as part of your portfolio of evidence. Social work practice learning programmes typically use the term 'case study' to refer to a student report produced for their placement portfolio. This is usually based on a single case or activity which occurred during the placement and in which the student took the lead or had a major role.

The case study is a valuable way of analysing your work, demonstrating your practice and evidencing your learning and development. It is also a source of evidence your practice educator can draw on in their report to comment on your practice learning. Thus, the case study merits sufficient care, time and attention if you are to produce a good piece of work which reflects the complexity of the case, and to offer a fair and just account of what has happened and a consideration of how and why things occurred.

From a learning and developmental point of view, the case study is also an excellent opportunity to research and critically analyse in some depth the complexity of your social work casework and your practice. Thus, the case study, when well done, is a valuable source of new knowledge and learning.

Helen Simons (2009) has reviewed case study research and examined differing definitions of case study. She concludes that what seems to be a common theme is a commitment to studying the complexity and uniqueness of 'a particular project, policy, institution, program or system in a "real life" context' (2009: 21). Approaches, methods and techniques of 'case study' work vary considerably. Thus case study work focuses on what is to be studied, rather than rigidly bound to a particular method, and is eclectic in the way it analyses what has happened, how and why.

Typically, case studies incorporate focus (on the case) but also flexibility (on how the case is studied). Gary Thomas (2011) suggests that a case study must have two key elements:

1. A 'practical, historical unity,' which I shall call the subject of the case study, and

2. An analytical or theoretical frame, which I shall call the object of the study.

Taking account of this, the definition of case study that I shall adopt for the typology I develop here is as follows:

Case studies are analyses of persons, events, decisions, periods, projects, policies, institutions, or other systems that are studied holistically by one or more methods. (Thomas, 2011: 513)

As we have said above, it is quite possible you will be prescribed a way of presenting your case study report and your course programme may give you a pre-set template to this end. However, as the Thomas definition suggests, you will still have to find yourself (with the advice and guidance of your practice educator) a '*subject*' for the case study.

Selecting a suitable 'case' for study

Your practice educator may advise you that the case which she or he recommends to be the subject of the case study may not be the case which in your view results in a clear, positive outcome (what you might describe as a 'success', whatever we think that means). This can sometimes feel quite uncomfortable from your point of view as you are all too aware (and often have this at the forefront of your thinking through your placement) that you are being assessed as to your suitability for professional social work. Thus, you would naturally like to select a case where you look as if you have achieved something tangible; feel something has changed or improved; most importantly you have done well.

However, your practice educator may suggest a case for study where outcomes are not necessarily clear-cut. Social work is actually frequently like this, as the work is often complex, complicated and, in terms of outcomes, difficult to capture or measure. Social work is a profession where the purpose of our work has to be considered against sometimes seemingly contradictory frames of reference (e.g. the need to balance care and control in relation to child protection) and which present dilemmas and challenges for practitioners. Similarly, social work may be taking place in contexts where prescribed service outcomes can be shifting or contested. For example, agencies may have deadlines and thresholds to meet about carer assessments which take resources away from other work for a time; or funding panels which approve commissioning of services run out of money near the end of the financial year and service provision is affected.

Your practice educator may identify a case to use as your case study where the focus is less on an explicit outcome in the time you have been involved and more about analysing a piece of complex casework where the *object* of the selected case study may not rely on a clear tangible resolution or change.

By contrast, your practice educator may see a more useful case study for learning as one which:

- Is complex.
- Offers the opportunity for a holistic, in-depth investigation of the case.
- Facilitates analysis of a range of factors and features social work should see as important, e.g. people's social circumstances, applied law and policy, local services and conditions, the experiences and feelings of individuals, communities, families and others.
- Can be used to involve service users and carers directly in order to bring out the details of the case from the viewpoint of them as key participants (we have a lot we can learn from this approach).
- Enables detailed analysis of the case study evidence.
- Allows us to reflect on our own work and the implications of our interventions, values and feelings.
- Enables us to apply different theories, models and approaches used in social work.
- We can use to try to develop and offer some tentative conclusions and recommendations.
- Identifies sources of good evidence of PCF and HCPC requirements.

Selecting your case study carefully can pay dividends in terms of evidencing your engagement with complex and demanding casework. Discuss this with your practice educator.

The usefulness of the case study approach to learning

Case study analysis has become increasingly used in instructive forms of learning and development. Robert Yin (2009) has described three different types of case study work: descriptive, exploratory and explanatory, indicating that a well-crafted case study will have elements of all three types.

Robert Stake (1995) offers a further description by identifying intrinsic case studies (where the researcher has a direct interest in the case under scrutiny), instrumental (where the case is selected in order to look beyond the obvious or at least what is initially obvious to the observer) and collective case studies (where several cases are examined). It is unlikely you will be asked to undertake a collective approach at this stage in your learning. However, it is likely you will be involved in both intrinsic and instrumental case study work, as your examination will not only involve an in-depth investigation of a case, but it will be a case where you will also have been an actor in the case (along with service users and carers) and our goal will be to try go beyond low level description (the obvious) and try to untangle and better understand the complexities of a typical social work case.

Yin (1994, 2009) suggests case studies have at least four applications and tasks. These are to:

- Describe the real-life context within which an intervention has occurred.
- Describe the intervention itself.
- Try to explain complex causal links between features and interventions described in the case study.
- Explore and better understand the situations in which the intervention being evaluated has no clear set of outcomes.

Stake (1995) argues that the goals of case study work should centre on producing intuitive and 'naturalistic' conclusions which resonate with the experiences of its intended readers and audience (here, your practice educator and perhaps colleagues, service users and others). Stake goes on, that by aiming to develop a more harmonious relationship between author and reader we can collectively generate greater understanding of the cases we are involved in.

Social work has been remiss as a profession in not working harder to collate the results of the best examples of case study to help explain its work to its professional and wider public. Done well, the case study facilitates the application and assessment of applicable social work theory, methods and approaches in practice. It explores values and ethics and practice dilemmas in a way that can teach us about our own work and in turn how to explain and discuss social work with some important people, notably service users, carers, colleagues and the wider public. Sharing and exchanging learning and knowledge from case studies is an excellent tool for professional development. Try it!

Sources for your case study analysis

Yin (1994, 2009) identifies six primary sources of evidence for case study research. Not all are absolutely essential in every case study, but the importance of multiple sources to the ultimate reliability of this type of study is well established (Stake, 1995; Thomas, 2011). The six sources are:

- Documentation.
- Archival records.
- Interviews.
- Direct observation.
- Participant observation.
- Physical artefacts.

Table 6.2 below is adapted from Yin (2009: 102) to include social work examples of sources and opportunities for collecting data for analysis.

Table 6.2 Possible sources of social work evidence in case study work

Source of evidence	Social work examples	Strengths	Weaknesses
Documentation	Previous case records, reports and previous case studies Letters, emails, notes, etc.	Stable – can be reviewed repeatedly Unobtrusive – not created as a result of the case study Exact – contains exact names, references and details of an event Broad coverage – long span of time, many events and many settings	Retrievability – can be difficult to find Biased selectivity, if collection is incomplete Reporting bias – reflects (unknown) bias of author Access – may be deliberately withheld
Archival records	Public files such as annual reports, agency documents, accounts, surveys, etc.	Same as those for documentation Precise and usually quantitative	Same as those for documentation Accessibility due to privacy reasons
Interviews	One-to-one interviews, surveys, feedback, etc.	Targeted – focuses directly on case study topics Insightful – provides perceived causal inferences and explanations	Bias due to poorly articulated questions Response bias Inaccuracies due to poor recall Reflexivity – interviewee gives what interviewer wants to hear
Direct observation	Your observations of participants involved in the case study, perhaps arising from home visits, meetings, case presentations, etc.	Reality – covers events in real time Contextual – covers context of 'case'	Time-consuming Selectivity – broad coverage difficult without a team of observers Reflexivity – event may proceed differently because it is being observed
Participant observation	Given your involvement in the case under study you are not a passive observer and are likely to have a direct role in the case. This may give you a chance to view the case from the 'inside' and give a more 'accurate' portrayal of people's experiences and feelings	Same as above for direct observations Insightful into interpersonal behaviour and motives	Cost – hours needed by human observers Same as above for direct observations Bias due to participant observer's manipulation of events

(Continued)

Table 6.2   (Continued)

Source of evidence	Social work examples	Strengths	Weaknesses
Physical artefacts	Looking at children's drawings, family photos, posters, art, etc. Also possibly to look at what technical equipment is used in casework and how and why this impacts on cases, e.g. computer usage, electronic recording, the impact of the 'paperless office'	Insightful into cultural features Insightful into technical operations	Selectivity Availability

Adapted from Yin (2009 : 102)

Some important considerations

The section above provides general guidance about case study work and you are reminded to look for specific guidance about producing a case study in your course programme. It is unlikely you will be expected or have the time or resources to use all the possible sources and opportunities to 'trawl' for data as outlined above. I have deliberately used the term 'trawl' here as this is a term you will find used in social research, the analogy here being in its simplest terms to fishing, with the goal for the researcher being the collection of as much potentially useful information as you can gather up. As it implies, the researcher trawls below the surface to gather data and by casting their net widely can pull in lots of different bits of information. This is good in terms of producing comprehensive and varied sources and for a range of comparative sources which can be used to compare and test our ideas, potentially making the findings more rigorous and valid.

The case study is sometimes described as 'an authentic anecdote'. This is a helpful description in that it acknowledges the need for a case study plan which is flexible in structure in order to be able to capture a complete picture of the case under scrutiny, and also recognises and values that people involved in the case are able where possible to tell their own stories and views in their own ways. Case study, at its best, invites personal narratives which capture the 'lived experiences' of those involved in the case and which we are prepared to reflect on and learn from.

A social work case study report can be divided into several key parts. These will vary from programme to programme but will be likely to include elements of:

- The brief context and background to the case.
- An analysis and report on the services and interventions involved in the case.
- The case as seen from the view of the recipients of your services.
- Critical analysis of social work values, theories and approaches.
- Critical self-reflection – what 'I' did and how and why I did it.
- Links to social work professional requirements (PCF and HCPC).

- Consideration of risk.
- Understanding of and commitment to anti-oppressive practice.

However, as ethical professional social workers we need to take care in how we undertake our case study. We owe a duty of care to our service users, carers and colleagues and must be sensitive to people's personal feelings, experiences and circumstances. Our primary aim has to be to do no harm as a result of our investigative work or reporting of the case. Thus managing confidentiality and ensuring anonymity need to be at the forefront of your plans and actions. So, you must take advice from your programme and practice educator about what form of study is considered appropriate for each case and how you should go about your work.

Evidencing your Work: Observing and Shadowing Others

Observing or shadowing an experienced worker – whether this is a social worker or other person – is a really valuable way of learning from others about professional practice.

For our purposes here we will distinguish between observing and shadowing, with observing being something we can and should all be doing in our general approach to learning in practice and which can be both formal (you are asked to observe something or someone) and informal observation (as part of a more eclectic and iterative approach to learning). Shadowing, by contrast, is more usually and properly something pre-arranged, with a more specific outcome and agreed with others (notably, with service users and carers consulted and consenting).

Whether you are observing or shadowing, such activities allow you the opportunity to watch someone going about their daily work, perhaps dealing with routine agency work (answering phone calls, discussing tricky cases, preparing and attending meetings) or dealing with particularly challenging and difficult situations (dealing with emergencies, coping with hostility or breaking bad news).

You can learn a lot from these situations, which you can adapt and use later in your own work and can be described as a form of reflective practice by proxy. Here, instead of reflecting on your own practice, as an observer you draw on someone else's experience to reflect and think about what went well and what went less well. You can decide which bits of the activity or actions you will take and use. It may sometimes seem as if an experienced worker who can communicate effectively and genuinely engage with service users, carers and other staff has arrived at this point in their career fully formed and that the things they do are just natural and spontaneous. Don't be kidded! Good workers have usually had to work very hard at their practice, and where they are now is often the product of sometimes less successful and difficult exchanges and encounters over the years. The key is as active learners they have committed to improve their practice and as a result have reflected, learned, adapted and changed the way they work.

Good practitioners are also good reflectors and thinkers who are willing to look at *what* they do, *how* they do it and *why*. They seek to do things better and are always learning. Sometimes this is from having to think on their feet in a situation (reflection *in* practice) or after an event or incident (reflection *on* practice).

Points to Consider

Shadowing – watching and seeing

Early in your placement you may well go out with your practice educator and other staff as part of your introduction to the service and its work. This hasn't been arranged to simply fill your time. It is a learning opportunity which you should grasp fully.

Task: think about a home visit you are going to with your practice educator to see a family, perhaps for a routine review visit to see how things are going. Think about:

- What the meeting is for.
- What you observe happening.
- What you hear.
- How the people you observe behave and talk.
- How the visit begins and ends.

You may only have a passive role in the visit. But, *you do* have a role and should be attentive and alert. Don't, simply be a passenger! Also consider:

- Was your presence explained to others present? It should have been.
- The person being observed may ask you how you thought the visit went.

Remember, your practice educator will be concentrating hard and may not be able to 'see' everything that happens during the visit. You may be asked to comment on what you observed happening during the visit. So, although you may not have said anything during the visit, you do have a real and relevant role to play.

Shadowing other people

Even if you have previously worked in a social work setting, you may not have had the opportunity to enjoy dedicated time to observe and reflect upon the work being undertaken by qualified and experienced workers.

To maximise your learning from shadowing, undertaken you should be clear about what you want to achieve, including identifying particular information you would like to obtain from these activities. These may include:

- What is the nature of the work of this agency?
- Which service user group(s) do they work with?
- What are the roles and functions of the staff? What is the structure of the team?
- How is the work supervised and line-managed? What is the worker's role and what responsibilities do they hold?
- What kind of workload do they have?
- Is there a particular approach or social work theory that informs their practice?

- What policies and procedures govern the work?
- How do these relate to current legislation?
- What is discussed in team meetings (if they have them)?
- Do they work with other professionals and/or agencies?
- What are the rewards in being a social worker?

Points to Consider

Planning for your shadowing activity

The social worker or worker you shadow will probably not have time to answer all of these questions (plus any others of your own!). So, you will therefore need to consider:

- Which questions are best answered by the worker you are shadowing?
- What information can you obtain simply by other means (e.g. talking to other workers, looking at policy documents, annual reports)?

Practical things to do before shadowing

Check any particular rules and procedures you need to be aware of and comply with (e.g. dress codes). Identify any particular issues the social worker you will be shadowing needs to be made aware of and which may impact on the shadowing activities, e.g. you have another appointment which may restrict whether you can stay for the whole activity.

During shadowing activities

Think carefully about what you want from your shadowing experience. Some useful questions to consider may be:

- What is the work of the service?
- Which service users, carers, groups and communities does the service work with?
- What are the social worker's roles and responsibilities?
- What essential skills, knowledge, values and attributes does the social worker think it important to develop?
- What are the roles and functions of other staff and professionals involved with the agency?
- What is the structure of the organisation, service and team?
- How is the work managed and supervised?
- What laws and policies are relevant to the work of the service?

Finally, think about what the person – who may not know you – may ask you about yourself and prepare for this (e.g. why you want to come into social work, what is your work experience, areas of interest).

Points to Consider

Evidencing shadowing experiences in your reflective log

Summarise the activity you have been observing during shadowing.

- What happened? What was the activity for?
- Briefly outline the role of the social worker or other worker you have been shadowing.
- Think about what have you learned from your shadowing experience.
- How could you use your shadowing to evidence the PCF or HCPC requirements?

Remember, the person being shadowed, whether this is a social worker or someone else, will probably form an impression of you based upon the following areas:

- Punctuality: Did you arrive on time and show some understanding of time management in general?
- Presentation: Were you courteous and professional towards the social worker, their colleagues and service users?
- Motivation: Did you come prepared with questions to ask and through the day demonstrate an eagerness to learn from the experience?
- Communication skills: Were you able to communicate clearly?
- Confidentiality: During discussions did you show a grasp of confidentiality issues?
- Anti-oppressive and anti-discriminatory practice: Did you act in a manner that showed that you understood the importance of these principles in social work?

Evidencing your Work: Direct Observation of your Practice

Just as you ought to find observation of others a valuable learning opportunity, you need to be aware that each day you are on placement you are being observed as part of the assessment process undertaken by your practice educator. Direct observation is an accepted part of social work practice learning. Your practice educator should as part of your contract of learning discuss how you will be observed and assessed on your placement.

Direct observation means you will be observed by your practice educator (or someone acting on their behalf) undertaking a pre-planned task (e.g. meeting and interviewing a service user; presenting at a meeting; facilitating a group). This form of observational assessment can be *formative* (i.e. it is something which is ongoing through the duration of your placement and part of quick, immediate developmental feedback) or *summative* (i.e. it forms part of the formal assessment of your practice learning and placement and is typically drawn from accumulated feedback and observations based on several different activities). It could be both formative *and* summative. However, it will be part of your assessed practice.

You will be able to draw on the feedback received during your placement to evidence and demonstrate your practice. It is recommended you keep a record of this feedback and comment so you can draw on it to show to your practice educator or to include in your placement portfolio. Your practice educator can advise you about this in supervision.

Direct observations vary in number and structure across courses, but generally have some common features. Direct observation reports typically include:

A contribution from you:

- A brief summary of the intervention and activity which is to be observed.
- The context and background to the intervention.
- Your preparation and planning for the activity.
- The planned goals and outcomes for your intervention.
- How you will demonstrate the relevant PCF domains.
- How you will meet the HCPC Guidance on conduct and ethics for students.

A contribution from the observer:

- How the activity went.
- How well you achieved your stated goals and outcomes.
- How well your planning worked.
- How well you responded to unanticipated or unplanned events.
- How well you met your requirements for the PCF and HCPC.
- Identifying areas for development?.

A contribution from others present:

- Feedback from service users, carers and others.

More from you:

- Your response to the feedback.
- Your reflections on the intervention and activity.

Note: Remember, you need to think about getting consent for your observer to be present and for you to take away any written feedback. This also ought to include some consideration or statement about confidentiality. Check this with your practice educator before the observation starts.

Indirect observation of your practice

Indirect observation of your practice may be undertaken from a range of different sources (e.g. in feedback from service users, carers, staff or others) and may occur in both formal and informal situations and circumstances. It may also take different forms, with both verbal and written feedback and comment being considered acceptable and useful.

Indirect observation and feedback is a standard form of information gathering about your work on placement. Practice educators will be grateful to be able to draw on feedback from a range of sources in order to make a more holistic, rounded and comprehensive assessment of your practice. However, it is good practice for you to know that this form of information gathering is part of your placement and your practice educator should discuss this with you. If this doesn't happen raise it during your supervision.

Points to Consider

360° feedback

Use Figure 6.2 below to help you gather feedback on your practice from a range of sources.

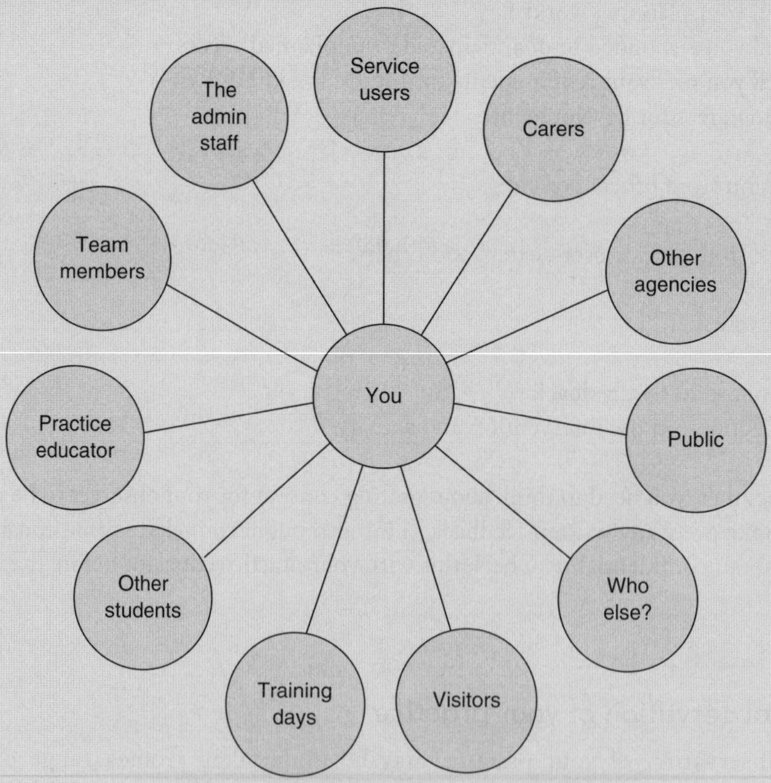

The circles are arranged around a central circle labeled "You", connected by lines to surrounding circles: Service users, Carers, Other agencies, Public, Who else?, Visitors, Training days, Other students, Practice educator, Team members, The admin staff.

Figure 6.2   Useful sources of 360° feedback on your practice

Evidencing your Work: Training and Development Days, Professional Forums, Presentations and Other Events

As part of your development on placement you may have the opportunity to attend training events, development days, briefings, etc. These are valuable in themselves for the concentrated information, knowledge and skills you may be able to gain but also as an opportunity to meet people away from the pressured environment of the duty rota and busy team rooms.

Sometimes experienced staff use training and development days to step back from their day-to-day work and find a moment in a busy schedule for a bit of calm and to be able to think about their work in a different way.

You should approach these days as a great opportunity to gain new knowledge and skills. Make sure you make time to listen to expert presenters and participants as they share and exchange ideas, or discuss practice experiences, dilemmas and challenges in their daily work. Good workers use these days to not only 'sound off' but also share approaches and solutions that work.

As a student, you can also use these events to ask questions, meet new people and introduce yourself to potentially useful people (e.g. people who seem to know what they are doing, and have resources you and your service users may benefit from on another occasion). You may even be able to identify your next placement opportunity, so this is a time to impress!

Checklist

Attending training, development days, policy briefings, professional forums and other events:

☐ Seek approval to go on the event and then book yourself a place (this seems obvious but occasionally is forgotten).
☐ Know when the event is; where it is; parking and lunch arrangements.
☐ Find out something about the presenters and audience.
☐ Stay for the day – if you leave early it will look like you aren't interested enough. Not good and always gets back to your practice educator! Explain your imminent exit. If you really need to leave early let the presenters know and anyone else you think relevant.
☐ Make notes (you will forget). Grab any useful handouts or freebies.
☐ Use the event to sound people out and perhaps make some useful contacts.
☐ Be interested and alert.
☐ Share your learning by feeding back to the team, service users and carers.
☐ If there is a certificate of attendance, take one! Good for your current and future CPD (Continuing Professional Development) and evidence portfolio.

In addition to attending and participating in events organised and presented by other people, placements also throw up opportunities for you to do some interesting and worthwhile activities which enhance the work of the placement agency and the lives of the people they serve and support. The list of potential activities is long but examples of this could include making presentations to the placement team about an area of practice you have researched or have some previous experience of; producing information leaflets for the agency; undertaking a survey for the agency about an area of practice or service they are interested in reviewing or developing.

There are some fairly obvious tasks here – some practical, some applied. First, make sure you have recorded this event in your diary; keep and be ready to produce any certificate of attendance; keep any materials you have produced or had a direct hand in producing (e.g. PowerPoint slides, handouts, leaflets, questionnaires, films).

Perhaps more importantly, find ways of applying your new information and incorporating your new knowledge into your practice, direct work and assignment and portfolio work. Discuss the things you find and discover in supervision and in conversations with colleagues and other students.

Summary

This part of the book seeks to link the expectations and requirements of your practice learning with some of the key tasks and activities social workers are involved in during their day-to-day work. We have included some examples of things you may do which can be used to demonstrate and evidence your practice and development. This is the beginning of your journey to becoming a qualified worker and there are lots of other areas to discover and develop. Keep active and alert.

7

Introducing Risk in the Context of Social Work Practice Learning

With Dawn Whitaker

Overview and Learning Outcomes

This chapter will cover:

- Social work practice and risk.
- Definitions of 'risk' in the context of social work.
- Social work practice learning and working with risk in the context of social work practice.

By the end of Chapter 7 you will be able to:

- Demonstrate awareness of some of the key issues that surround risk in social work practice.
- Explore ideas of risk in relation to social work and your practice learning.

Introduction to Chapter 7

Risk assessment and risk management are increasingly acknowledged to have become a key focus for social work in the 21st century. This part of the book introduces the topic of risk in relation to social work as an important and inherent element of social work practice. Inevitably (and properly) you will find yourself dealing with risk in various ways during your placements and practice learning. However, just to reassure you, work will be supported by your practice educator, who as your supervisor also has a professional interest in what you do and is also committed to delivering a good quality service. In addition, your practice educator will also have the added incentive that she or he will have ultimate responsibility for all your casework during your placement, so you shouldn't be too surprised when discussion of risk forms an important part of your supervision discussions.

It is important to note that as a student in training you should receive clear supervision and support with regard to your practice. However, you do have to take individual responsibility for your own work and practice; for how you work as part of a team or as a co-worker in relation to risk (e.g. how you communicate information, check concerns with your practice educator) and how you ensure that you make an effective and professional contribution to assessing and managing risk. However, the emphasis in your placement and practice learning ought to be more towards *a shared contribution to managing risk* rather than having a *lone or lead responsibility*. Thus, your practice learning placement should offer you a graduated introduction to social work practice and working with risk issues. This may begin with relatively straightforward tasks and activities and move to more complex work as the placement progresses and as and when your practice educator feels you are ready to take on more complex levels of work.

→ Look at: **Chapter 2 The New Professional Capabilities Framework and Revised Placement Structure**.

Social Work and the Risk Society

Aaron Beck is generally credited with having coined the term 'risk society' and has described risk consciousness, security and protection as a key driver of individual and collective approaches to daily living. This view is hard to challenge. Frank Furedi (2006) has written extensively on the 'culture of fear' that seems to affect our daily lives in relation to risk. In fact, when we stop to think about it, virtually any discussion of modern life in the western world does seem to be permeated by considerations of risk. This includes health (weight, exercise, smoking, diet), the foods we eat (fats, sugar, salt, salmonella, BSE), jobs and lifestyles (work–life balance, leisure pursuits, stress), relationships and much, much more.

Such external societal preoccupations about risk have had a profound impact on social work today. Stalker plots the changing emphasis on risk in health and social welfare in the post-1945 era as shifting from one 'based on optimistic ideas of improvement and rehabilitation' through to notions of risk which have 'superseded that of welfare', influenced by the collapse of welfare and the growth of neoliberal ideas about welfare and care provision (Stalker, 2003: 216). Nigel Parton (2011) has analysed changing trends in language and policy associated with assessment of risk in children and families social work and has identified a creeping change of emphasis in policy from a narrow focus on risk as dangerousness to a much more all-embracing attention on 'risk' and 'safeguarding'. This trend has impacted on social work to the extent that Horlick-Jones has suggested that social work is now 'saturated' by the language and techniques of risk (2005).

The task of this chapter is to provide you with an introductory understanding of the ideas of risk in relation to social work and to help you to relate risk to your social work practice learning.

Working with Risk on your Placement

As we indicated in Chapters 2 and 3, your first and final placements will differ in their focus, with increasingly complex casework emerging as your experience, knowledge and skills develop. This graduated exposure to more complex casework will not only be a feature within each placement but also across each placement. The College of Social Work has indicated how practice educators should plan, identify and allocate work that involves risk-related elements and features which you ought to undertake during your placements. This is set out below.

First placement

Your first social work placement should introduce you to core social work knowledge, skills and values, as outlined within the PCF. At this stage, you will be expected to demonstrate an awareness of risk as it relates to general practice:

- With guidance, to demonstrate an holistic approach to the identification of needs, circumstances, rights, strengths and risks (PCF 7).
- With guidance, to identify the factors that may create or exacerbate risk to individuals, their families or carers, to the public or professionals, including yourself (PCF 7) (TCSW, 2012c: 2).

Second and final placement

Your final social work placement should aim to build upon your primary practice learning experience and prepare you to undertake statutory social work intervention. This will involve opportunities to engage in more complex work, including formal processes of risk assessment and management relevant to social work. At this stage, you will be expected to demonstrate:

- An ability to understand forms of harm, their impact on people, and implications for practice (PCF 5, 7).
- Working with formal processes for considering risk and safeguarding as it relates to particular areas of practice, e.g. child protection, mental health and/or vulnerable adults (PCF 7, 8).
- Outcomes of formal assessment processes, including analysis of risk/recommendations in line with organisational policy and procedures (PCF 6, 7, 8) (TCSW, 2012c: 6–11).

As the College indicates, there is an emphasis in the first placement on developing skills and knowledge of *risk awareness* and provision of appropriate and adequate *guidance* to help you practise and learn. This experience and guidance is overseen and provided principally by your practice educator and the other experienced and skilled staff you will be working alongside. In your second and final placement, the task is to *build upon* your first placement experience and work on *more complex work*. Again, your practice educator and the staff you work alongside will be expected to instruct, guide and support you to develop your professional practice. Thus, your final placement is in some ways a final stepping stone towards your professional qualification.

What is Risk?

Before proceeding to look at risk in the context of your practice learning, we need to consider what we mean by risk and how ideas of risk impact on social work. However, defining risk is not straightforward. Have a look at the exercise below.

PLACEMENT ACTIVITY
Defining risk 1

Consider the following definitions and statements about risk:

A situation involving exposure to danger. (Oxford Dictionaries, 2013)

The possibility that a given course of action will not achieve its desired and intended outcome but instead some undesired and undesirable situation will develop. (Alaszewski, 1998: 22)

- What are your initial impressions of risk from the above definitions?
- Is all risk negative, undesirable and something to be prevented?

Traditionally the notion of 'risk' within health and social care has been perceived in largely negative terms, most often with reference to the probability of an adverse outcome occurring (Skills for Care, 2011: 1). However, should risk always be viewed as a negative force? Try the exercise below.

PLACEMENT ACTIVITY
Defining risk 2

Having considered the definitions of risk offered in the exercise above, now look at the additional definitions offered below:

The possibility of beneficial and harmful outcomes and the likelihood of their occurrence in a stated timescale. (Alberg et al., 1996: 9)

An occasion when one or more consequences (events, outcomes and so on) could occur. Critically (a) those consequences that may be harmful and/or beneficial and (b) either the number and/or the extent of those consequences and/or their likelihood is uncertain and/or unknown. (Carson and Bain, 2008: 242)

The purpose of risk analysis and management is to open up opportunity and to enable progress to be made with greater certainty. (Disability Rights Commission, 2005: 3–4)

- What are the key features we need to think about in trying to define and understand risk?
- How do these definitions differ from the first set offered in the exercise above?
- How might our ideas about risk impact on our goals of social work practice?

Risk and Social Work Process

In Chapter 6 we set out and considered the key features of 'social work process', namely:

ASsessment > **P**lanning > **I**ntervention > **R**eview & **E**valuation

As you may recall, in our earlier discussions we suggested that social work process perhaps more accurately ought to be seen as cyclical rather than linear (Figure 7.1).

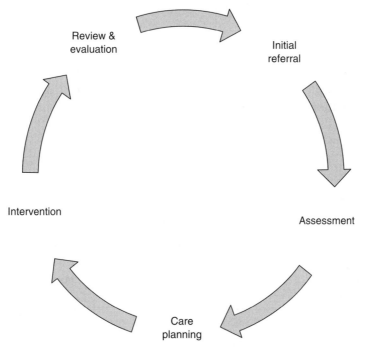

Figure 7.1   Social work process

In relation to risk assessment and risk management we can identify several activities which help us to locate risk within the stages of social work process. Let us begin by identifying the stages of risk assessment and risk management. These are:

- Identify any risks.
- Assess and rate the risks.
- Prioritise the risks to be addressed.
- Plan your intervention to manage the risks.
- Deliver and oversee the intervention plan.
- Monitor and review; adjust the plan and intervention.

In terms of risk four main elements should guide our approach to sound risk practice. These are:

- Risk assessment and management is a systematic process which features identifying, evaluating and addressing potential and actual risk. It is active and not static or passive. It requires practitioners to be alert and vigilant.
- Risk should be managed through a well-designed programme that minimises negative risk exposure and moves identified risks from the 'likely' and 'harmful' categories, to the 'unlikely' and 'beneficial'.
- Effective risk management should support positive risk outcomes and seek to promote the well-being of service users, carers, communities and others (including colleagues and ourselves).

- Risk taking must be responsible and defensible. As social workers we ought to be goal/change oriented; thorough, prepared, flexible, ready and alert. Risk taking is much too important to be based on guesswork or hope.

Thus, a basic principle here is to minimise the likelihood of adverse events and maximise the possibility of producing the best possible outcome in the circumstances.

Table 7.1 maps the basic stages of risk assessment and management onto our model of social work process.

Table 7.1 Mapping risk assessment and management onto the social work process

Social work process	Risk assessment and management
• **Assessment**	• Identify risk • Assess and rate the risks
• **Planning**	• Prioritise the risk issues • Plan your intervention
• **Intervention**	• Risk management intervention
• **Review and evaluation**	• Monitor and review; adjust the plan and intervention

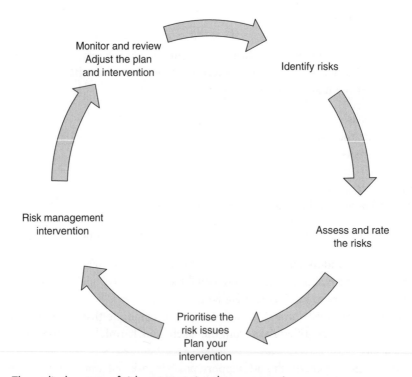

Figure 7.2   The cyclical process of risk assessment and management

As we proposed in our discussion of the structure of social work process, we can also characterise the process of effective risk assessment and management as cyclical and each of the constituent stages as interconnected and interdependent (Figure 7.2).

Again, as with the cycle of social work process, social work practitioners may themselves have to engage with risk issues at different stages of the risk cycle and have to revisit sections (e.g monitoring and reviewing, re-assessment) numerous times during an intervention, as risky situations can change quickly and without much prior warning.

Points to Consider

As social work students on placement you should not be asked to have sole responsibilty for assessing and managing risk in the course of your practice. However, you will be expected to contribute and support social work interventions where risk is present or may arise.

This does not mean you are expected to be an expert practitioner at this point but does indicate you should be keen to improve your experience, skills and knowledge and in turn be committed to work towards developing expertise in order to become a better practitioner. On placement, this means you need to be:

- As thorough as you can be in your knowledge and background of a case.
- As knowledgeable as you can be of relevant social work theories, approaches and research.
- Observant and alert in your day-to-day practice.
- Willing to ask questions and check details in order to clarify, confirm and update what is known (or, what we think we know).
- Willing to bring back information, findings and questions to your practice educator to check things out.
- Willing to act on advice and help given.
- A good record keeper.

These are offered as general points to reflect on. On placement you will find you will probably be able to add to this list. You have the benefit of an experienced practice educator to help you here, so we recommend you use supervision to discuss risk. Clarify your role and contribution to promoting safe and effective practice, drawing on the experience and specialist knowledge and skills of your practice educator.

Identifying and Assessing Risk Using Case Examples

In order to consider how well we might be able to assess and manage risk complete the case example below. This has been adapted from several similar real cases and is sufficiently complex to test even an experienced practitioner. Your principal task here is to see how well you can identify potential risk issues. Good quality information gathering is the basis of a good quality assessment. The better our information gathering, the better our knowledge of the case, and from this it is more likely we will produce a sound and comprehensive assessment. From this we can devise a plan which helps us to prioritise our work and deliver a timely intervention.

Have a go and see what you find. Perhaps ask another student to repeat the exercise and compare notes. This collaborative approach is sensible and one you should take into your field-based practice education.

PLACEMENT ACTIVITY
A complex case scenario

Barry is 59 and lives on his own in a small block of flats. Barry has recently been diagnosed with a rapidly developing form of early onset dementia. This is increasingly affecting Barry's memory and daily living skills.

The condition leaves him feeling frustrated, and frightened by the changes in his health and loss of independence.

In the last six weeks there have been two small fires at the flat both of which resulted in the block being evacuated. In the last incident Barry was admitted to hospital having collapsed in the lift. This story featured in the local paper. The tenants group wants Barry to leave. The housing association is very concerned.

Barry is also a heavy drinker, smokes heavily and neglects himself. He has also been diagnosed as diabetic. Budgeting is a problem and he regularly runs out of money before his next payment day. He has rent arrears.

You are Barry's social worker and have been asked to attend a hospital pre-discharge meeting. Also at the meeting are Barry, his brother Michael, Barry's new consultant (psychiatrist), a diabetic nurse and a psychiatric nurse (from the memory clinic).

Barry *is* considered to have mental capacity in terms of the decisions regarding his accommodation and care, and has stated that he intends to return home without support. Barry's brother Michael thinks Barry should return home, but should be compelled to have support. There are differing views across the professionals.

Tasks

- What do you assess are Barry's care needs? E.g. dementia care.
- What risks can you identify? E.g. fires.
- What strengths and assets can we draw on? E.g. Barry has lived independently quite successfully until recently. He has family around who may be able to offer support and/or advocate for him.
- How might the choices Barry makes (perhaps choices we don't necessarily agree with) impact on your risk assessment? E.g. Barry's declaration to refuse support.
- What might be included in your risk management plan? E.g. trying to engage with support services.

Now, consider Barry's case as a possible source for your placement portfolio of evidence for evidencing PCF 7:

... to demonstrate an holistic approach to the identification of needs, circumstances, rights, strengths and risks (PCF 7);

... to identify the factors that may create or exacerbate risk to individuals, their families or carers, to the public or professionals, including yourself (PCF 7). (TCSW, 2012c: 9–10)

At the end of this chapter: compare your own answers to the first part of the above activity to those of a small group of first-year social work students who also looked at this case.

Points to Consider

In relation to the Barry case, reflect on your findings to consider the following in terms of the decisions you made:

- Barry's rights
- The needs of Barry versus the needs of the community
- Care versus control
- Risk, choice and responsible risk taking
- Your personal feelings and your professional obligations
- Balancing Barry's needs with his personal strengths and the other assets available to him.

Further, here are some common questions to consider when assessing and managing risk in social work:

- What is the nature of the risk? Is it life-threatening or a minor inconvenience?
- What is the level of the risk? Is it high or low?
- Is there a risk to a child, young person or vulnerable adult?
- Is the individual able to judge the level of risk for him or herself? Does the individual have the mental capacity to make the decision themselves? Is it a subjective or objective definition of risk? Whose definition is being adopted?
- Is there agreement between those involved about the level of risk?
- What protection can people take for themselves against the risk?
- Are there risks associated with the proposed intervention? How are these weighted against those associated with non-intervention?

(Adapted from Kemshall and Pritchard, 1996, in Doel et al., 2011: 195–6)

Revisiting the case of Marcia, Patrick and their family

In Chapter 6 we looked at the case of Marcia, Patrick and their family. If you recall, you were allocated this case and one of your first tasks was to identify the presenting issues, support needs and concerns in the case scenario. In answering the question we posed, you may have identified a range of issues which had potential risk elements, e.g. the children's school attendance, reports on Marcia's presentation and behaviour, the absence of a key carer and support.

PLACEMENT ACTIVITY
Marcia and her family revisited

Case summary (a reminder)

Marcia is a 28-year-old mother with two children (Joel 5, Carrie 9). Her mother, Lillian – who is Marcia's main and consistent support – is concerned Marcia is 'not coping with the kids' and is 'stressed out'. Lillian is going to Antigua in one week to attend a family wedding and will be away for four to six weeks.

Lillian has tried to persuade Marcia to come to your office. Lillian reports that Marcia says she will ask for help when she needs it but not before.

Marcia recently separated from Patrick, her long-term partner and the father of Joel and Carrie. Patrick is described as a heavy 'social drinker'. There have been difficulties and domestic violence within the relationship. There are concerns about the finances of the family. However, at other times when Patrick is settled he has helped at home.

Marcia has a history of mental health problems (described as a 'bipolar illness' in case records). In the past, Marcia has self-harmed by cutting herself on her upper arms and has also made one suicide/para-suicide attempt using gas from a domestic gas fire in her home.

Marcia was 'admitted informally' for psychiatric treatment approximately 18 months ago. There is no recent record of contact with mental health services.

School rang social services about three weeks ago to pass on concerns about Joel and Carrie's progress. Both are coming to school late in the mornings and Joel has been quite disruptive in class. It was commented on that Marcia had been tearful a couple of times when bringing Joel and Carrie to school. You learn Joel and Carrie have been off school for the past fortnight.

Let us see if we can identify the risk issues present. Take your notes into one of your early supervision meetings with your practice educator. See what they think and compare your findings.

Risk issues: Marcia, Patrick and their family

Read the summary provided above and identify presenting and potential risks you think may need to be assessed and addressed in this scenario. Use Figure 7.3 below to note the risks.

In addition:

- Which risks do you think need to be addressed first? This will help inform your plan of work.
- What strengths and assets can we identify here?
- In an early supervision meeting, ask your practice educator to read the case and see what they think; compare your findings.

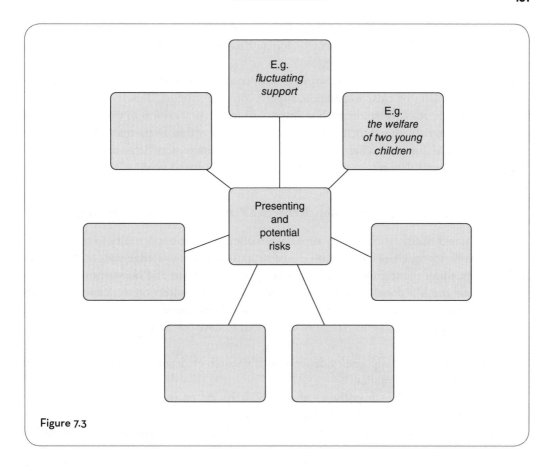

Figure 7.3

Risk and the Importance of Social Work Supervision

You will find the challenges, dilemmas and opportunities of managing risk are typically at the forefront of more complex social work practice. The organisation Skills for Care have identified several reasons for the prevailing emphasis on risk in social work and social care practice, notably:

- Individuals may make 'unwise decisions' for which services may be held responsible; some people may lack mental capacity to make a choice.
- Safeguarding duties 'require services to avoid exposing vulnerable people to unnecessary risks'.
- There may be 'undesirable and serious consequences' for individual workers or agencies 'if something goes wrong'.
- 'Negative' consequences may result in agencies being subject to inquiries and inspections by regulatory authorities, commissioners or contract managers. (Skills for Care, 2011: 4)

These features put social workers right at the heart of trying to be as effective as possible in terms of assessing and managing risks which may have negative outcomes and consequences for individuals and those around them.

However, as a student in training, working with complex cases and risk issues should only occur with provision of clear instruction, supervision and support. This is why supervision is such a valuable asset for students. It is important to use supervision to discuss and reflect upon your role in risk-related social work. This is reiterated within Department for Education recommendations for improving practice, notably that supervision helps social workers to 'minimise bias', 'articulate reasoning', 'implement evidenced-based practice' and 'manage their emotions' (DfE, 2011b: 84).

→ Look at: **Chapter 8 Using Supervision, Reflective Practice and Critical Thinking**.

In the context of risk, good quality supervision offers you the opportunity to talk through your casework, identify risks, issues and concerns, raise and acknowledge your own hunches and feelings; think about goal setting and make plans for actions and interventions.

Macdonald and Macdonald (2010) have written about child protection work and safeguarding and the importance in social work of 'intelligent risk management'. They suggest that in order to make 'good judgements', social workers need to have certain critical thinking skills:

1. An ability to critically appraise evidence – both research evidence and evidence in relation to children and their families.
2. An ability to formulate hypotheses about children's circumstances in ways that enable receptivity to new evidence (particularly contrary evidence).
3. A knowledge of what interventions are most likely to impact positively on identified problems.
4. An ability to set clear goals and indicators of change. (MacDonald and MacDonald, 2010: 1184)

These interconnected abilities and knowledge can be applied to any service or setting of work. Good supervision should offer you the opportunity to develop your skills and experience in relation to intelligent risk management with an experienced and knowledgeable practitioner.

The generic principles of good quality risk assessment are akin to those relevant within all social work assessment and management processes. These include:

- Minimising harm.
- Protecting.
- Maximising potential.
- Responsible risk taking.
- Transparent decision-making.
- Defensible practice.
- Improving care and quality of life.

Balancing Effective Risk Management with Humane Social Work Practice

As we have suggested, social work is a complex task that frequently involves workers having to balance multiple and conflicting perspectives and responsibilities. In risk-related social work, this often means trying to balance an individual's right of self-determination with the rights and protection of others. As we discussed in Chapter 1, social work has found itself the subject of high profile news reporting and genuine and understandable public concerns about some aspects of social work practice, notably in relation to child protection work. Recent tragedies and deaths have been key drivers in shaping recent responses to the reform of social work, and criticism of social work has swung the pendulum of frontline practice to being risk averse and cautious.

Karen Broadhurst et al. argue that social work should embrace the task of delivering effective risk management but also seek to deliver what they termed, 'the humane project of social work' (2010: 1047). The challenge for social work here becomes how to ensure *both* effective risk management *and* public protection, *and* to deliver this in an ethical *and* humane way. Dixon elaborates on the challenges and dilemmas that this can present for social workers:

> The skill that social workers must develop is the ability to work within a framework that considers risk, whilst not losing sight of the needs of the individual. In doing so, they should be open to applying a utilitarian position that considers public protection, whilst regularly re-evaluating the appropriateness of this position through consideration of service user autonomy. (Dixon, 2010: 2400)

Points to Consider

Balancing effective risk management and humane social work

What do service users and families want from us? We would suggest the following are important:

- Keep us safe.
- Remember effective risk management can be used to help us learn to manage things in a safer way.
- Listen to us and check out your judgements with us.
- Bear in mind that we may have experience of prolonged, excessive and unnecessary risk management in the past!
- Respect us and our views. We are often experts in our experiences.
- Include these views in your judgements.
- Involve independent advocacy if we can't represent ourselves.
- Remember we are the ones who suffer the consequences of poor judgements.

(Continued)

(*Continued*)

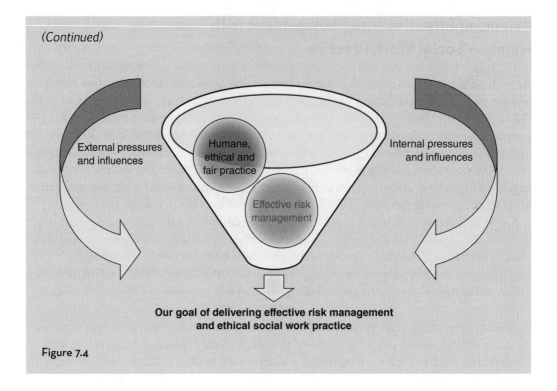

External pressures and influences

Humane, ethical and fair practice

Effective risk management

Internal pressures and influences

**Our goal of delivering effective risk management
and ethical social work practice**

Figure 7.4

All human activities carry a degree of risk and their success or failure depends on their effective management. Beneficial outcomes of effective risk management in social work include:

- To reduce harm and dissatisfaction.
- To provide valuable and valued support for individual families and communities.
- Improving quality of life.
- Ranking of risks supports targeted interventions and more explicit and justifiable decision-making.
- Reducing and preventing poor use of staff, time and money.

The elements of good risk assessment include:

- The assessment process should be user friendly and be inclusive, i.e. include users', carers' and others' relevant views.
- It should be systematic, recorded clearly, shared where appropriate and lead to a management plan based upon the information gained.
- The process should seek objective data and corroboration to support observations and reports.
- Subjective views, impressions and judgements should also be acknowledged and recorded.

- Should allow for new information to be included.
- Objective views recorded – with evidence.

Promoting Positive Risk Management

The language of risk has become increasingly unhelpful to the goal of positive risk management; terms such as risk 'assessment' and 'management' have been criticised for implying an unrealistic potential for risk eradication. In contrast, a more positive language of risk has begun to emerge – one aimed at enabling professionals and people who use services to think differently about 'risk'. This new approach intends to facilitate positive risk taking in practice by redefining the aim of risk intervention:

> 'Risk enablement', 'risk mitigation', and 'risk benefit assessments' are some suggestions for improving the way we talk about risk. (DH, 2010a: 15)

Concerns regarding the traditional language of risk are reinforced by the negative connotations often associated with assessment and diagnostic labels such as 'dementia', 'mental illness' and 'learning disability', as well as their associated risk descriptors, e.g. 'dangerous', or 'vulnerable'.

Positive risk management is founded upon balancing the positive benefits of 'taking risk, against the negative effects of attempting to avoid risk altogether' (DH, 2010a: 8). 'What matters is that we work with people to help them recognise risks', so as to 'develop a shared understanding of what can be done in terms of living their life as they would wish, whilst reducing the risk of harm they may experience' (ADASS, 2011: 16). This reflects growing service user, carer and professional momentum for a 'redefinition of society's approach to risk', and recognition that, in the right circumstances, risk can be beneficial (Better Regulation Commission, 2006: 3).

Nothing Ventured, Nothing Gained is a government publication founded upon recent research and ideas of best practice regarding positive risk management (DH, 2010a). Whilst the framework is designed for people with dementia its principles should inform our broad approach to social work practice. It proposes a four-step framework for assessing, enabling and managing risk in a positive and constructive way:

Step 1: Understanding the person's needs.

Step 2: Understanding the key risks for the person and others.

Step 3: Assessing the impact of risk.

Step 4: Risk enablement, management and planning. (DH, 2010a: 43)

The Department of Health asserts that this approach provides 'a way of thinking about what might make a person [family] vulnerable in certain situations, and what can be done to help manage risks', to produce the results that people want (DH, 2010a: 44).

We do not intend to take you through each step of the framework but offer this in order to make the point that, wherever possible, we should seek to promote positive outcomes that are identified and agreed with service users and carers. This approach to managing risk supports a *person-centred* approach to social work practice.

Remember, as we indicated in the introduction to this chapter, you will not be expected to manage complex risk in your practice learning but you will have a contributing role to assessing and managing risk. Your practice educator is an essential person in this regard and you should use supervision to talk through your casework.

Summary

You are expected to demonstrate evidence, notably in your final placement, that you are able to engage with complex cases and risk as part of assessing your capability and readiness for professional social work practice. This will include elements of risk-related social work. Notions of 'risk' are interwoven throughout each of the nine domains across the PCF.

This chapter is intended as an introduction to risk in relation to social work. You will have many opportunities in your course programme and practice learning to further develop your knowledge and skills about risk in social work practice.

The key message here is to be alert in your day-to-day practice; to think about your roles and activities; finally, and perhaps most importantly, as a social worker in training, to communicate effectively and regularly with your practice educator.

Student responses to Placement Activity (Barry)

Compare your answers to the Placement Activity featuring Barry earlier in this chapter.

Two small groups of first-year social work students looked at the Placement Activity featuring Barry. Compare your answers to the short notes below produced by the groups on Barry's case. The notes are headings they used to present their findings, views and questions to the class.

Barry

Barry's care needs and things to be followed up:

- Impact of dementia on daily living and self-care.
- Diabetes and impact on health plus challenges of treatment.
- Self-neglect and daily living.

- Not feeling well.
- Loss, fear and stresses of changes of health and loss of independence.
- Budgeting.
- Rent arrears and possible eviction.
- Social isolation.
- Barry's vulnerability.

The immediate risks we have identified:

- The fires and the safety of Barry and other residents.
- Lifestyle, ill health and now longer term health and wellbeing.
- Eviction.
- Impact of health problems on Barry.
- Barry's actions if he feels anger and frustration.
- Barry's understandable resistance to losing his independence and choice.
- Residents' and landlords' possible/probable feelings and frustration at Barry and services.

Strengths and assets we could draw on:

- Barry has lived independently and wants to retain his independence.
- His brother (Michael) is supportive.
- Barry has a home to return to and live in.
- We have an opportunity to identify and build on some specific and mutually shared goals, e.g. not being evicted.
- Other services are involved.
- We are committed and also have good, experienced colleagues to support and advise us.

Classroom discussion – What we are not so sure about and would want to find out more about:

- What is 'early onset' dementia?
- What is the impact of early onset dementia and Barry's prognosis?
- What will the other services offer?
- Is Barry's age a problem in terms of eligibility and continuity of who provides a service?
- How could we use supervision to work on this case?

8

Using Supervision, Reflective Practice and Critical Thinking

With Michaela Rogers

Overview and Learning Outcomes

This chapter will cover:

- Social work and supervision.
- Using reflection in social work.
- Critical thinking and active learning in social work.

By the end of Chapter 8 you will be able to:

- Describe different models and elements of effective supervision.
- Identify differing roles and responsibilities in relation to supervision.
- Link reflective practice and social work.
- Link critical thinking, social work practice and professional development.

Introduction to Chapter 8

This chapter is divided into three main sections, which aim to introduce you to supervision in social work; the value and use of reflection in social work practice; and finally, consideration of the application of critical thinking and active learning in social work.

Supervision and Social Work

Supervision is something which you will find forms a key part of your forthcoming practice learning and of your future development as a social worker, both in your initial qualifying social work education but also after you qualify and enter professional practice. Good quality supervision will lay the foundations for a solidly person-centred approach to your work but one which is simultaneously holistic and imbued with the principles of social work. Done well, supervision offers an opportunity to think not just about what you have been doing, but also how and why you have been practising the way you have, and perhaps most importantly how, as active learners, we can develop to become better practitioners.

Planned supervision is in essence special time set aside exclusively for you to focus on your work and your practice; giving you space within your busy day-to-day work to pause and critically reflect on your practice and actions as well as receive feedback on your work from an experienced practitioner. Numerous writers have commented on supervision in the context of social work (Adams, 2010; Shardlow and Doel, 2006; Thompson, 2009). Several recurrent features of supervision and the supervisory relationship are identified in these writings, notably management, administration, education and support. Thompson (2009) and Horwath and Morrison (1999) also include mediation as a feature of modern managerial and professional supervision tasks in social work and social care. We will look at these features in more detail below but it is useful at this point to consider why supervision is considered so important in social work. Neil Thompson (2002) very neatly summarises the importance of effective supervision as being the difference between:

- Success and failure.
- Stress and job satisfaction.
- Worry and reassurance.
- Good practice and excellent practice.

We should know which side of these continuums we would want to be on. Good students know this. So how do we get there?

What is Supervision?

Lomax et al. (2010) suggest that student supervision should be regular, planned and offer a student and practice educator the opportunity to discuss and reflect on the student's work on placement and relate this to their learning and development. Mark Doel (2009) suggests that it is useful to think of supervision in terms of a dialogue, over a series of formally arranged meetings, between two people often involved in the same range of professional tasks. Doel makes the point that this dialogue may take a different form according to the relative experience and seniority of the two people involved and is about developing *professional knowledge* and *practice*. A different emphasis in student supervision is that, as a student in professional training, you will be asked and expected at different points in your learning to examine your value-base and its appropriateness for the social work profession that you are entering.

Thus, discussions about values may occupy a more central place in the agenda, and proportionately more time, than during supervision for qualified workers. This is because we need to be crucially aware of our personal beliefs and attitudes, of our personal and professional values, and of our commitment to social work ethics and principles if we are to understand what drives what we do.

For our purposes, supervision can be said to have the following key elements or functions (see Figure 8.1).

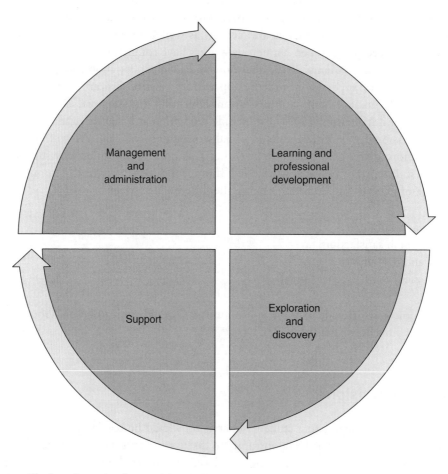

Figure 8.1   The key elements of supervision

- **Management and administration:** Supervision in the context of social work practice should report on your work and activities; ensure that standards of professional social work practice and organisational expectations and standards are maintained; clarify decision-making and accountability; locate student work in relation to ethical and professional standards of practice; and identify an action plan for work between supervision meetings. In the context of student supervision, it is also important to remember that your practice educator has the task of assessing your practice learning and overseeing the production of placement-related work which will form part of your assessment on placement.

- **Learning and professional development:** Supervision should offer the opportunity for a student to reflect on what has been learned from the work and tasks undertaken on placement; celebrate things that go well and reflect on what has worked well or less well; explore dilemmas which have proved difficult and challenging in the work; link this thinking and learning to where and how to improve on key social work skills, knowledge and values relevant to experience and stage of training. This aspect of supervision should also impart and exchange new knowledge and identify opportunities for training and further development.
- **Exploration and discovery:** Good supervision should also be a forum for discovery of things we do well and things we could do better; of hidden skills and talents we hadn't identified as assets in our work (e.g. language skills, how to communicate with smaller children); of attributes and attitudes we now see as valuable (e.g. being calm, not being intimidated by events). This activity can help identify areas which can be shared with other workers.
- **Support:** Social work is not easy. Working with people who are experiencing difficulties in their lives is emotionally demanding and stressful at times, but it can also be uplifting and rewarding. Supervision gives the opportunity to 'offload', which makes it more than just a means of support directly to the student but is also indirectly of benefit to those receiving the service by enabling individuals to remain work-focused and motivated. Similarly, good quality supervision should have a pastoral care element within it which enables you to share your own feelings and emotions which may be impacting on your practice and learning. However, it is important to remember that where someone needs professional support for personal difficulties, then supervision may not be appropriate for this and a practice educator may signpost you to specialist support services.

These elements of supervision are applicable to many different professional health and social care settings. In student supervision, each of these elements of supervision should be given due attention and time. Liz Beddoe (2010) has written about the strong incentive in contemporary social work and social care to link professional supervision to the need for managerial surveillance, particularly in the context of contemporary social work practice within a 'risk society'.

Look at: **Chapter 7 Introducing Risk.** →

Beddoe consulted a group of supervisors in order to review the practice of supervision in contemporary social work and concluded there was a sometimes difficult relationship between reflective and developmental supervision and line management and instruction. Within effective student supervision, management and instruction are important but should be accompanied by attention to learning and development. For example, your workload needs to be managed; you will need emotional and practical support; and you should have the opportunity to assess your professional development and identify future learning needs.

Peach and Horner (2007) suggest that the 'hallmark' of good quality student supervision goes beyond organisational concerns in order to promote and engender 'transformative learning'. Good student supervision should be characterised by its commitment to support the individual needs of a trainee social worker and by its contribution to supporting students to make the transformative journey into becoming a rounded and capable professional social worker.

⌨ Social work comment

A practice educator's views of having a student on placement:

> *I am a social worker on a busy Community Mental Health Team. Although my duties, training commitments and caseload are very demanding, for me the decision to commit to a social work student on placement has always been important and extremely positive.*
>
> *The chance to enable students and future social workers to develop their professional skills, and to support them in confronting the realities of the profession and social work role is vital. Not only is this important in continuing to contribute towards delivering consistent services in the future, but fundamental in providing quality support and positive outcomes for the service users we seek to support in their recovery.*
>
> *I often find the practice educator role demanding and challenging. This obviously varies depending on a student's level of previous experience, enthusiasm, expectations and capabilities; however I always enjoy the experience and find other professionals on the team also benefit from the student experience.*
>
> *Working as a practice educator enables me to keep up-to-date with theoretical perspectives, read new research articles and continue to evaluate the implications of relevant legislation. At times, answering questions and linking theories to case work can be challenging. However, I believe this is crucial to my own professional development as well the students. Reinforcing the necessary commitment that social workers must continue to develop and reflect on their own judgments and experiences in an open minded manner; as well as gaining a sound understanding of theory and its implications to practice. (Zoe, practice educator)*

Good supervision should take into account several things, including: the student's strengths (existing skills and prior experience); areas for development (learning needs); the student's learning style; the placement setting; and the wider context of practice.

The benefits of effective supervision in the context of student practice learning cannot be underestimated but these are dependent on the preparation, planning and participation of both the supervisor (the practice educator) *and* the supervisee (the student learner). Joyce Lishman (2007) describes six prerequisites for effective supervision. These are:

- A focus on learning.
- Regular and reliable meetings.
- Mutual trust.
- Awareness of issues of authority and responsibility.
- Support and opportunities to express feelings.
- That supervision should be anti-oppressive and anti-discriminatory in its principles, content and process.

> ## PLACEMENT ACTIVITY
> ### Supervision
>
> Having looked at what is meant by supervision, in preparing for your own supervision consider the following:
>
> - What is the purpose of supervision?
> - How does supervision differ from talking to colleagues?

Models and Types of Supervision

Discussion about student supervision often presupposes you and your practice educator sitting down at a pre-arranged time with a clear agenda about what you are going to talk about. This is a good model of providing supervision. However, as in almost all busy services, there will be occasions when this is not always possible and meetings have to be postponed or moved. On such occasions you may be able to have discussions instead with other team members, rather than your practice educator. All of this activity is a form of supervision as well. However, it is never enough to *only* have this sort of supervision because although it is immediate it tends to be situation-specific and relatively non-reflective.

Sometimes, where there is more than one student on placement, it can be beneficial to have joint or group-based supervision. This may have a particular theme (for example, to discuss a particular intervention, method or technique). Such sessions lend themselves to simulation methods, such as role-play. These sessions can be a good place to share experiences and feelings about the placement; it is quite likely that you will discover that other students on placement with you are having similar experiences and feelings (positive and negative). Group supervision also presents an opportunity to exchange useful ideas and strategies to develop your learning.

A number of different types of supervision can be identified which are relevant to student practice learning.

Formal supervision

Formal supervision has administrative, educational and supportive functions. Formal supervision, as the term suggests, is something that happens on a regular basis and at a mutually pre-arranged time. It is generally undertaken on a one-to-one basis between the student and practice educator. However, it should always be a two-way process and it is the responsibility of both parties to contribute to setting the agenda and participating in the meeting. Formal supervision often involves reflection *on* practice that has already taken place. As we identified above, a typical supervision session may include an update and review of recent work, discussion of progress, successes and barriers to progress. In turn, formal supervision may move on to discuss and agree further activities, plan, agree training and development, support, and so on.

Formal supervision should always take place in a quiet, private environment with no interruptions (where possible). There should be an agenda and one person should take responsibility for producing a record of the meeting. Both the practice educator and student should keep a copy of notes from the meetings.

Informal supervision

Informal supervision may potentially take place at any time and in a variety of settings, for example if a student needs immediate advice whilst participating on the duty rota or to clarify something having returned from a visit. Informal supervision in this sense is often opportunistic or reactive and might be initiated by either the practice educator or the student. Sometimes the need for informal supervision is driven by the degree of urgency or importance attached to the subject matter. We can describe this as supervision where the emphasis is on reflection *in* practice.

It is important to note that although the supervision is described as informal, the discussion may need to be acknowledged and revisited in the next formal supervision meeting. Additionally, it may be pertinent to record the outcome of the discussion or any decision made in the case files.

Group or peer supervision

Group or peer supervision can be formal or informal, planned or spontaneous. It can be between groups of practitioners, between groups of students or groups which are quite mixed. Group or peer supervision is a powerful tool and can be used as a way of sharing good practice, clarifying and developing roles and processes, problem solving, or as a forum for generating mutual support. Typical discussions may take the form of analysing a complex case, analysis of legislation and case law, or exploring the implications of a new policy or procedure. Group or peer supervision can provide valuable support and opportunities to trainee social workers and also promote mutual support for experienced workers as well. You may go on to experience this as a newly qualified social worker in your Assessed and Supported Year in Employment (ASYE).

→ Look at: **Chapter 10 Getting Ready for Professional Practice**.

Live supervision

Live supervision typically occurs when the practice educator is observing the student delivering a service or interacting with a service user or carer. It involves reflection *in* practice rather than reflection *on* practice and is often immediate.

This type of supervision can take place daily, depending on the placement team or agency. For example, the placement agency may operate a drop-in where you are asked to take a lead or you may be dealing with telephone queries. During the course of this work you may need to check or seek advice 'live' and 'in the moment' with your practice educator or another experienced worker. These are good learning opportunities.

Have a look at the following activity.

> ## PLACEMENT ACTIVITY
> ## Models of supervision
>
> Identify a minimum of two potential advantages and two potential disadvantages for each of the following models of supervision:
>
> - Formal supervision.
> - Informal supervision.
> - Group or peer supervision.
> - Live supervision.

Preparing for Supervision

Preparation is fundamental to successful supervision. Ideally, the main problem in supervision should be finding enough time to discuss all the issues and agenda items you both want to cover. However, as we have suggested previously, to make supervision work, all those involved must ensure supervision time is dedicated and focused time.

Dr Alison Ronan is a youth worker and academic at Manchester Metropolitan University who has taught extensively on supervision. Ronan proposes that supervision has to have a number of important features and stages if it is to work effectively as a forum for management, support and development. These features and stages are:

- Preparation.
- Establishing the supervision relationship.
- Developing the supervision relationship.
- Creating a working alliance.
- Endings.

Ronan also identifies a number of key themes which should run through supervision. These are:

- A consideration of practice which is located within an ethical and non-oppressive framework.
- Creating and maintaining an effective learning environment.
- Working with and within personally and professionally challenging situations and events.

> ## PLACEMENT ACTIVITY
> ## Getting ready for supervision – establishing the supervision relationship
>
> During the very early part of your placement you have your first supervision session. In preparing for this first session, consider the following:
>
> - Your practice educator may ask you about your hopes and fears about your forthcoming placement. What are these? Make some notes about this. Your answer will help the

practice educator (and you) get a sense of what you hope to get from your placement and identify what concerns you at this early stage of your placement.

- What ground rules and principles (if any) do you think it would be important to have in place if supervision is going to work?
- What mutual values do you think would help establish a good working relationship between the practice educator and yourself?
- What will be your commitment and contribution to making supervision work and to developing practice expertise?

 Social work comment

Supervision is always effective and rewarding (for me and the student) when BOTH of us prepare. I make sure that I read the minutes from our previous meeting and check that I've done ALL the things I've said I'll do. I expect the same from the student. Checking any previously agreed action is always considered early in the agenda at each supervision. The rest of the time allocated for supervision can get caught up with discussions about cases and ongoing work so one thing I've found to be really helpful (to me and the student) is for the student to email me a brief update on all her cases before our supervision meeting. This enables me to be really focused on the cases or work which could really benefit from deeper, more analytical discussion. (Practice educator)

It is important to remember that your placement agencies are likely to use different policies and procedures relating to supervision. This book does not attempt to accommodate all the particular types and approaches of supervision that you will encounter in your practice but identifies some key principles and features for ensuring effective supervision.

Points to Consider

Getting ready for supervision – things to do

Before each supervision session, there are several useful things you can do to improve the quality of your supervision. These are not tasks which necessarily take up much time in themselves but they do require some time to be set aside for thinking. This is time well spent, as not only will it make you look organised, but it will also ensure you make the points you want to make and contribute effectively to good supervision.
Things to do before your supervision meeting:

- Summarise your activities since the previous supervision meeting in relation to your allocated casework.
- Identify what you want to discuss in relation to things you are not sure about; questions you want to ask; risk issues; how best to proceed.
- Identify what has gone well, what less well? Reflect on your work.
- Think about what skills, theories and knowledge you have used ... or need to use.
- How do you feel? How has this impacted on your practice and learning? Think about how you would like to use supervision to explore these feelings and their potential impact on how you are working.

Barriers to Effective Supervision

Neil Thompson (2002) has identified some of the ways in which the effectiveness of supervision can be impeded. Such barriers include:

- Destructive processes (e.g. avoidance of problems, relationship dependency).
- 'Unfinished business' (e.g. previous issues within the supervisory relationship or matters left unaddressed from the last supervision).
- Personality clashes (or conflict of values, power dynamics).
- Imbalance of activities (e.g. supervision is too focused on workload management).
- 'Burn-out' or emotional exhaustion.

It is fair to acknowledge that whilst the above list of potential barriers to effective supervision may not be evident all the time, at least some of the features are likely to occur, to varying degrees, over the period of a placement. Some features may be momentary and pass without either person feeling the need or wish to draw attention to them. This is a question of judgement. However, if a problem persists and starts to impede effective and balanced supervision, there is a duty on both the supervisor and supervisee to identify the problem, address it and resolve it.

A good supervision relationship relies on both supervisor (your practice educator) and supervisee (you) taking responsibility for establishing and maintaining effective supervision. Therefore, it is important to seek to address problems or barriers appropriately and in a timely fashion. If there is a written supervision contract in place it may be useful to return to the terms of the contract. A good supervision contract should include principles for supervision which are mutually agreed and mutually binding (e.g. values of honesty, fairness and mutual respect; agreed ways of dealing with disagreements which may arise). A contract can help to facilitate 'healthy' supervision processes and offer procedures to resolve problems.

Social work comment

My tip for using supervision is to make sure you prepare so you can get the most out of it. I was fortunate to establish a good rapport very early on with my practice educator so difficult issues could be discussed openly and freely.

In getting ready for supervision I found it really useful to write out a summary of my cases and the main points and issues I wanted to discuss. Also write down any learning opportunities you would like to pursue – this may involve going to other agencies or training opportunities.

Make sure you have time to talk about personal issues and any issues you might be having on placement. Remember that your practice educator is there to help and support you to get the most out of your placement.

Always keep a copy of your supervision notes. (Charlotte, MA student)

The Value of Using a Contract in Supervision

A supervision contract or agreement is a commonly used tool for planning and preparing for supervision. Some contracts and agreements are written and formal; others verbal and informal. You may well experience one or both of these approaches during your different practice learning experience. Whatever the format, a supervision contract should encompass a set of jointly agreed principles and ground-rules for each participant to abide by. In this way, the production of a supervision contract is an explicit recognition of the principles, structure and features of the supervisory relationship. A supervision contract is very helpful and will enable you and your practice educator set out how you intend to work with each other over the period of the placement.

As previously mentioned, it is important to remember that the most effective supervision is a two-way process. The practice educator will have a number of activities and actions that she or he needs to ensure are completed, for example: overseeing and supporting your work and activities; assessing your progress and learning; planning learning activities.

As a trainee social worker you also ought to have items on the supervision agenda which you want to ensure are included: reporting work undertaken and receiving feedback, guidance and instruction; and having the opportunity to seek clarification, ask questions and discuss things you are not sure about or which concern you.

Specific time set aside for your supervision is important and should definitely be built into the contract of having a student on placement. Above all, good supervision should be your opportunity to think, reflect, learn and develop! If you do not have supervision on a regular basis, you are, in effect, being deprived of a key support to your learning and to the likely prospects of successfully completing your placement.

Using Reflection in Social Work

The terms 'reflection', 'reflective learning', 'reflective practice' and 'the reflective practitioner' are commonplace in social work literature. Don't worry if the idea of reflection feels rather abstract at the moment. Reflection will be a very useful skill for you to develop, and when approached and supported properly, will help you throughout your social work career.

Boud et al. suggest that reflection 'is an important human activity in which people recapture their experience, think about it, mull it over and evaluate it' (Boud et al., 1985: 20). Kydd (1996) adds a further dimension to this idea by proposing that professional development begins from a process of reflection on where things are, where we would like to get to and how we get there. In other words, Kydd acknowledges the need within reflection to look back, to consider the present and to form an action plan to facilitate moving forward. Additionally, Kydd clearly indicates that reflection in our professional working lives should have momentum and a focus which is about review, change and improvement in our social work practice.

Race and Brown (2007) in plain terms (often the best way) define learning and professional development as 'fitting new stuff into old stuff'. They suggest we do this by:

- Sorting out what is important.
- Identifying some fundamental principles.

- Improving our skills and knowledge.
- Getting rid of unhelpful things.
- Owning our learning and our practice.

In essence, reflective practice and supervision should be seen as instruments through which all social workers – whether trainees or seasoned practitioners – can develop their 'new stuff'.

The Reflective Practitioner

The term 'reflective practice' was used by Donald Schön (1983) to mean the practice of a worker who is able to:

- Use *knowledge* in their work.
- Be *sensitive* and *self-aware* in their work.
- *Evaluate* and *reframe* work done and incorporate this into future work.

For Schön, *knowledge* was not just factual data, but about the appropriate application of a *critical understanding* of a professional's knowledge base to the task in hand.

In practice placements, the student's task is to critically select from a mass of theoretical ideas and models, and *apply* these to practical tasks when working with individuals or groups. Your development as a reflective practitioner will be greatly aided in supervision by *discussion* of your knowledge base. This is a major reason why *supervision* is of vital importance, and why each student has an experienced and specialist practice educator.

Sensitivity and *self-awareness* are also important in developing as reflective practitioners. Shulman (1993: 64) asserts that:

> The capacity to be in touch with the service-user's feelings is related to the worker's ability to acknowledge his or her own. Before a worker can understand the power of emotions in the life of the client, it is necessary to discover its importance in the worker's own experience.

Now have a go at the practice activity below.

PLACEMENT ACTIVITY
Values, reflection and supervision

Developing a value-led and anti-oppressive approach to practice

Our values and attitudes should and do influence the way we think and act. To be able to manage how our values and attitudes impact on the way we work we need to be aware of our personal feelings and beliefs. Begin this process by answering the questions below:

(Continued)

(Continued)

- What personal values and beliefs are most important to you? Put them in order of impor-tance and reflect on why they are important for you.
- Think of examples (from relatively ordinary everyday situations*) of how your personal values and beliefs have influenced your attitudes, responses and behaviour to others?

* Examples could perhaps include your attitudes and responses to smokers, swearing, lit-tering and so on.

Note: these may not turn out to be particularly easy questions to consider and often there isn't a definitive or fixed answer. However, exploration of your personal belief systems and values informs your thinking and in turn your approach to social work. This should always remain an important aspect of your learning and development.

Remember, if we agree that social work is a moral, ethical and emotional activity, then the need for the sort of self-awareness both Schön and Shulman identify may be considered as funda-mental to the development of capable social work practitioners. As social workers, we typically find ourselves on a daily basis meeting people who have complex problems or who may be in crisis; we seek to be effective but humane in our actions; we seek to balance safeguarding and managing risks with empowering people.

As we suggested earlier, social work supervision should seek to explore how our values and feelings impact on our approach and practice. This involves reflection. In this way we will better understand what influences our work and it will help us maximise direction and action which promotes and demonstrates social work values. In turn, developing qualities and skills of reflection should also help us minimise the effect of subjective feelings and emotions which may impact negatively on our practice. Your practice learning setting is the ideal opportunity to test out the use and value of reflection and of reflective practice. Student placements offer the opportunity to reflect upon your practice in several areas, including:

- Developing as a confident and assertive practitioner.
- Improving decision-making and problem solving.
- Developing and maintaining professional boundaries and relationships.
- Addressing power inequalities.
- Developing anti-oppressive and anti-discriminatory practice.
- Managing conflicts, tensions and dilemmas.

These activities rely on your ability to assess and analyse – skills which link to Schön's third feature of reflective practice, *evaluation* and *reframing*. This points to the need for workers to be able to:

- Stand back after a particular activity.
- Assess what worked and what didn't.

- Ask why this was the case.
- Set about viewing the work differently.
- Decide upon a new or modified approach.

Schön's work was influential in challenging narrow 'technical-rational' approaches to social work. Put simply, the 'technical-rational' approach advocated that all problems would respond to the same treatment or intervention in the same way. Schön highlighted the limits of a technical-rational approach to adapt to complex, variable and diverse situations which require competent instinctive and flexible responses.

Schön discussed the potential of intuition and reflection to take place in different contexts of time and space. This makes a distinction between *reflection-in-action* (in the moment) and *reflection-on-action* (after the moment).

Schön described the concept of *reflection-in-action* as the process by which we intuitively (and often unwittingly) use our knowledge in our daily practice. In this regard:

> … our knowing is ordinarily tacit, implicit in our patterns of action and in our feel for the stuff with which we are dealing, it seems right to say that our knowing is in our action. (Schön, 2002: 50)

Boud et al. (1985: 20) describes *reflection-on-action* as a process where we seek to 'recapture [our] experience, think about it, mull it over and evaluate it'. So, what do we need to do and be in order to be a reflective practitioner? In planning for this work, let us consider Kolb's (1984) reflective cycle of learning.

Kolb's cycle of learning

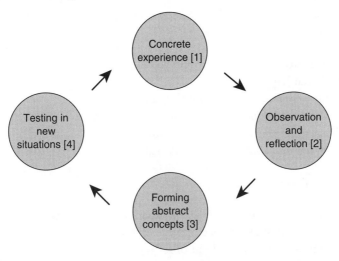

Figure 8.2   Kolb's cycle of learning in the context of social work supervision and reflective practice

In the context of social work supervision, and reflective practice, these parts of the reflective cycle can be translated into the following activities:

- At 1 the supervisor (practice educator) will probably introduce his or her own observations and introduce feedback from other contributors.
- At 2 the supervisee (student) will feedback events and feelings.
- At 3 the supervisee (student) will be encouraged to draw on theory and previous experiences in order to explain and analyse their work.
- At 4 the supervisor (practice educator) will introduce new information and skills where relevant to help the student choose new ways to approach the work.

You may have already noticed that several of the activities you have been asked to complete have involved elements of reflection and then go on to invite you to think about ways of changing how you might do things in the future.

Supervision in social work is often used as a vehicle for reflection. However, reflection is something which you need to ensure takes place before, during, after and between supervision sessions.

As a tool for learning, reflective practice is circular and constantly evolving as depicted in Kolb's cycle of learning. Activity leads to description > which leads to reflection > which leads to reconsideration > which leads to planning > which leads to new or revised activities > which leads to new descriptions ... and so on.

Gibbs's model of reflection

Gibbs's (1988) model of reflection develops Kolb's learning cycle and can be useful for reflecting on specific experiences or pieces of work that you have undertaken. Gibbs's model (Figure 8.3) also embeds Schön's advocacy of the concepts of self-awareness and sensitivity (in the stages of 'feelings' and 'evaluation') and evaluation and reframing ('evaluation', 'analysis', 'conclusion' and 'action plan') as essential to good practice.

- **Action plan** – If it arose again, what would you do?
- **Description** – What happened?
- **Feelings** – What were you thinking and feeling?
- **Evaluation** – What was good and bad about the experience?
- **Analysis** – What sense can you make of the situation?
- **Conclusion** – What else could have been done?

Thus, effective reflection requires:

- Being specific and accurate in *describing* the experience or work you have done.
- *Reflecting* critically on that experience or piece of work.
- *Reconsidering* your approach in the light of reflections.
- *Making fresh plans* for future work.
- *Acting* afresh.

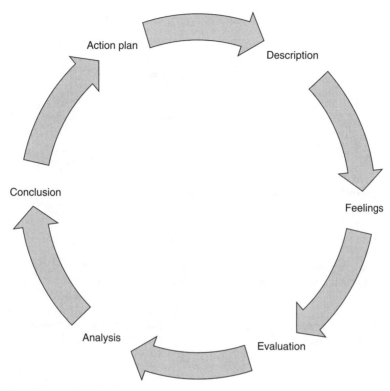

Figure 8.3   The Gibbs model of reflection

Schön (1983) raised a cautionary note in his work *The Reflective Practitioner* – he identified the danger of 'overlearning'. This concept results in a tendency of practitioners to be complacent and practise in a routine and uncritical way. It cannot be emphasised enough that the foundations for good practice involve being alert, open and receptive to the learning that can be gained from new experiences and reflective practice.

PLACEMENT ACTIVITY
Be a SWOT!

Before your first supervision session with your practice educator, you should complete a SWOT (**S**trengths, **W**eaknesses, **O**pportunities and **T**hreats) analysis. This can be very useful during your early supervision sessions, helping you identify some of the strengths and assets you bring to the placement, and also of identifying your learning needs, personal fears/hopes and aligning each of these with the placement opportunities that have been identified for you. Here are some examples of things you could include in your personal SWOT analysis:

(Continued)

(Continued)

Strengths	Weaknesses
I get along with most people. *I am a fairly calm person and do not get easily flustered.* *I have worked with the police and am knowledgeable about their policies and procedures.*	*I am worried that I will become too attached to the children that I will work with.* *I am not confident in using IT.* *I am sensitive to criticism.*
Opportunities	**Threats**
I hope to develop my knowledge of child development for the younger age group. *I hope to work in a multi-disciplinary team of social workers, health visitors and midwives.*	*I am scared by the thought of being responsible for making big decisions.* *The thought of a high caseload makes me nervous of failing, and although I set high standards for myself, maybe I can be too unrealistic.*

Now draw the diagram out and have a go yourself. Identify your own:

- Strengths.
- Weaknesses.
- Opportunities.
- Threats.

Social work comment

On reflective practice and working with students:

It is not uncommon for students to start placements with lots of thoughts and feelings about what they perceive to be the opportunities that placement will offer, or they have worries about what the placement won't do for them. Asking a student to compete a SWOT analysis at the first supervision session helps them to really pinpoint their hopes and fears and we can then plan to address these together. More importantly I find this a valuable and positive exercise as it enables me to emphasise their strengths and remind the student that they bring to the placement a wealth of personal, work or voluntary experiences and with that a range of skills and knowledge which they can utilise and build on through the placement period. (Practice educator)

Using a Reflective Log

A reflective log, diary or journal is a very positive resource to use in your placement and practice learning. However, this is not the sort of record which describes 'what I did today', but is used to note your personal observations, feelings and value-statements about the things that you experience on your placement. If completed every week or following some form of intervention, especially in advance of a supervision session, the journal can keep you alert to your own development and assist you not only in evaluating learning from your first placement, but also in identifying areas for you to develop in your final placement. Yes, your practice educator has a key role in assessing your practice-based learning but the task of identifying your further learning needs is also yours. It could be argued this task is primarily yours.

 Social work comment

On using a reflective log:

> *I found using a reflective log really useful. It helped me remember what I had been doing at the beginning of the placement. It was interesting looking back as I'd completely forgotten some things I'd done and then when I came to look again I was either impressed by things I'd done or looked now and thought I can't believe I did that. You don't always appreciate how much you change in a placement. (MA student)*

It is important to use a tool like a reflective journal positively. It is not just about identifying gaps in your understanding or pointing to aspects of your practice that you feel need to be changed or reframed. It is also a place you can record successes and own your achievements. We all need to know what we are good at and if your practice educator tells you 'well done', or (better still) if a service user or carer thanks you for your help, make sure you record this in your journal. Subjective views and feelings as well as facts have a legitimate place in your journal entries.

Your practice educator will seek to test and assess your skills, knowledge and attitudes through the lens of the work that you undertake on placement as well as to analyse the potential you show for further development. At the same time, you (as the learner) will be expected to increase your ability to assess your own learning and performance and contribute to understanding your future development needs.

Checklist

A possible list of headings you could use in a reflective journal:

☐ Key dates or events.
☐ Brief details of work undertaken.
☐ Skills and knowledge I have used or drawn on.

(Continued)

(Continued)

☐ New skills or knowledge I think I have developed.
☐ Values identified in my work.
☐ Theories applicable to my work (which could be divided into three levels: general approaches; applicable models; methods used or drawn upon).
☐ Notes linking my practice to the PCF.
☐ Legislation used/applicable.
☐ Reflections/issues/dilemmas to discuss with my practice educator.
☐ My feelings, attitudes and opinions.

Brockbank and McGill (2006) offer a simple tripartite model for asking yourself questions which can develop your reflective thinking. These three questions are: what, how and where.

What:

- were you trying to achieve?
- were the crucial interventions?
- worked well and what worked less well?
- affected the activity/interview/meeting?
- do you think was happening and when?
- will you do differently next time as a result of this experience?

How:

- do you now feel about the activity/interview/meeting?
- far do you think you achieved your aims?

Where:

- do you go from here?
- are you doing ok?
- can you learn and improve?

Knott and Scragg (2007: 53) suggest that there are three stages to writing a reflective journal:

Stage 1 – **reflecting** on the issue or piece of work completed. This should be written in an unstructured manner so that it is spontaneous and natural.

Stage 2 – **analyse** your written account and ask yourself:

- What is going on?
- What assumptions am I making?
- What does this tell me about my beliefs?
- Can I look at this in another way?

Stage 3 – **action.** Ask yourself the following questions:

- What action can I take?
- Would I respond differently if this happened again?
- What have I learnt about the beliefs that I hold about myself?

Points to Consider

Early into your placement identify a piece of work you have recently completed. Reflect on the work using the Knott and Scragg stages, drawing also on the list of questions Brockbank and McGill offer.

Critical Thinking and Active Learning

Thinking critically: What is 'critical'?

Brechin (2000: 26) defines 'being critical' in the context of social work and social care practice as an 'open-minded, reflective appraisal that takes account of different perspectives, experiences and assumptions'. In simple terms, being critical involves purposeful and focused reasoning and consideration of experience or observation. Critical thinking has been described as:

> ... the intellectually disciplined process of actively and skilfully conceptualizing, applying, analyzing, synthesizing, and/or evaluating information gathered from, or generated by, observation, experience, reflection, reasoning, or communication, as a guide to belief or action. (Scriven and Paul, 1987)

Thinking critically: Reflexivity

Adams et al. (2002: 3) state that:

> Critical thinking leads to critical action, forming critical practice ... critical practice is a cycle ... part of a reflexive cycle. Reflexivity means being in a circular process in which social workers 'put themselves in the picture' by thinking and acting with the people they are serving so that their understandings and actions inevitably are changed by their experiences with others. As part of the same process, they influence and change others and their social worlds.

Thus, critical thinking, reflection and action conflate to form practice which, at a deeper level, encompasses a reflexive approach. Reflexivity involves: knowing yourself; understanding how your background, presence and behaviour affect others; alertness to how your value-base and world views reflect upon your choices, actions and behaviour; and being alert to how this all affects others and how the background, values, presence and behaviour of others affects you.

At this point you may be thinking that reflection, critical reflection and reflexivity all amount to the same thing, and it is important to point out that many academics use the terms interchangeably. The difference, as outlined by some (Fook, 2002; Webb, 2006), is that reflection (or reflective practice) is at the narrow, shallow end of the continuum and that critical reflection and reflexivity are at the opposite end and represent processes that are much deeper and broader, concerned with wider sociopolitical conditions.

In relation to a critically reflective approach, Thompson and Thompson (2008: 155) distinguish between *critical depth* and *critical breadth*:

> **Critical depth**: this involves being able to identify underlying arguments and assumptions (which may be false, distorted or otherwise inappropriate). It is geared towards making sure that (i) our own thinking is not flawed and thereby potentially dangerously misleading; and (ii) we are not seduced by the flawed thinking of others.
>
> **Critical breadth**: professional practice can easily become 'atomistic' – that is, too individually focused and thus neglectful of the wider social and political context of our practice (and indeed of the lives of the people we serve). Critically reflective practice therefore takes account of power relations and related processes of discrimination, stigmatization and exclusion.

Jones (2009: 98) suggests that reflexivity moves on from reflective practice in that it requires you to evaluate yourself within your social work practice from 'a personal involvement perspective and recognises that practitioners are subject to change and continuity through the impact of that interchange'. Further to that, reflexivity requires you to frame this analysis on a micro basis, in terms of your self-identity and social location, and on a macro level, in relation to preexisting social, political and cultural conditions. Reflexivity connects with critical thinking and reasoning as essential in terms of your analysis of self, your practice and the ability to locate these within several dynamic contexts.

Webb (2006) suggests that the ability to be reflexive relates to the evaluation of your social work practice as a moral and ethical activity. In addition, Thompson and Thompson (2008) contest that reflection should always contain a critical perspective to ensure attention to anti-oppressive and anti-discriminatory practice (which is, obviously, interwoven with ethical and moral issues in social work).

Thinking critically: Power

Each situation, individual or family that you work with is unique, and a high degree of criticality will enable you to make sense of and manage the complexities of managing diverse caseloads and prioritising competing demands whilst achieving and maintaining high quality practice. This is not an easy task when you are working with service users who may be affected by structural inequality and injustice, and who have very little power or control over their life course. Everyday situations are complicated when in the line of duty you are required to manage dilemmas with strong elements of power inequality (both overt and nuanced), for example, work which is based upon safeguarding children whilst trying to promote family relationships.

In relation to power inequality, Jan Fook (2002: 157) comments that:

> … a critical reflective approach should allow … workers to interact with and respond to power dynamics in situations in a much more flexible, differentiated and therefore effective way. By making less 'blanket' assumptions about power, the critically reflective practitioner should be able to engage with the specific power dynamics of situations in more relevant and effective ways.

Your ability to be critical and reflexive will enable sound decision-making, even if the outcomes are not those desired by the service user or carer. You will be able to support your judgements, be accountable and defend your position.

Throughout both your practice placements and subsequently when you advance to practise as a professional social worker, there will be a continuous focus on the necessity for your practice to be anti-oppressive and anti-discriminatory. Importantly, you need to recognise gaps in your own knowledge and understanding and have a willingness to learn from service users and carers. Achieving this requires a high degree of critical self-awareness and reflection.

Service User and Carer Perspectives in Critical Reflective Practice

As a trainee social worker you will be working with practice educators, social work and social care practitioners, practitioners from other disciplines (health, education, police, etc.) and most importantly, service users and carers.

Working with service users and/or carers will provide you with numerous opportunities for critical reflection in terms of evaluating your practice and for framing it within the wider sociopolitical context. For example, working with parents with disabilities can increase your awareness of the impact of structural oppression and discrimination that people with disabilities regularly face. This in turn can alert you to many areas for critical analysis, including:

- The construction and use of language.
- The impact of stereotyping and labelling.
- The impact of having normative/non-normative identities.

In addition, the ability to locate yourself and evaluate your role (as an agent of the state) is vital to your understanding of how service users and carers experience social work interventions. In particular, it is crucial that you consider the use of language, as it has historical and cultural implications which are bound with issues of power. Think about:

- How you address service users (think about differences in age – would you call an older person by their first name?).
- How you relate information to people (think about differences in age, communication disorders, issues linked to literacy).
- Cultural difference and language barriers (think about Euro-centric assumptions and be concerned to use qualified interpreters where language is a barrier to communication).

These are just a few examples, and your work with service users and carers will give ample and regular opportunity for reflection at a deeper level, applying a critical lens to some fundamental aspects of social work practice. The significance of language relates to power issues which in turn link to anti-discriminatory and anti-oppressive practice. When working alongside qualified and experienced practitioners you may hear or read things which you accept as part of the language or culture of that team or agency. However, you should seek to develop and maintain a critical and questioning mind and be prepared to appropriately challenge oppressive and discriminatory language.

To conclude, during your practice placements, service users and carers should be given the opportunity to provide feedback on their contact with you and your intervention in their lives; this feedback should be viewed as something to reflect upon which can improve or validate your practice.

In terms of your personal and professional development, critical reflection can help you to demonstrate your commitment to anti-oppressive practice; respect for individuals (service users and carers); practise in an empowering way, which recognises and seeks to reddress and rebalance power differences. These are important aspects of social work practice.

Active Learning and Social Work

It is widely accepted that adult learners achieve more when they learn by doing. Simply put, this is active learning and enables you (the student) to better recall and understand what you have achieved or undertaken. In addition, active learning methods require you to make sense of your own learning and development; you develop and ascribe your own meanings and conceptualisations to what you have learnt. Maclean and Caffrey (2009) suggest there are some basic principles to adult learning which link to active learning. These include:

- The law of exercise (we learn by doing).
- The law of association (learning needs a foundation which can be built upon, new facts or information can be associated with existing knowledge).
- The need to know motivation (what? why? how? approach to undertaking an activity).

- The need to be self-directing (taking responsibility for our own learning).
- Readiness to learn (recognising the importance and value of learning).
- Learning empowerment (building confidence).
- Positive learning (receipt of positive reinforcement and constructive feedback).

It is useful as a learner to understand our individual motivations and techniques for learning; don't forget, none of these principles are of value without the ability to reflect.

Whilst you are on placement, active methods in teaching and learning should ensure that you receive constructive feedback with encouragement and direction to meet any identified learning needs or gaps in knowledge. It may be that you are encouraged to address your learning needs by actively working with others (colleagues and other social work students on placement). Active methods rely on a continuous dialogue between you (the student) and your practice educator. Active methods should assist you to develop your critical thinking skills, which in turn enable you to become more sophisticated and effective in your ability to analyse, problem solve and evaluate. These are critical (and fundamental) skills of good practice in professional social work.

Surface and Deep Approaches to Learning

The surface approach to learning focuses on acquiring and memorising information. However, this is at a level which is uncritical, unquestioning and thus there is no need for reflection.

A deep approach to learning requires the student to have the capacity for critical thinking as new ideas require analysis, deconstructing and linking to existing knowledge. Deep learning enables you to apply your learning in new and different contexts. This is of vital importance as you will need to show that the skills and knowledge that you acquire throughout your placements equate to transferable skills and knowledge that are of value in different social work contexts.

A deep approach to learning is expected and required within the professional placement environment; it is this which connects to critical reflection, the application of theory to practice; and a deep approach can be nurtured and developed as an aid to learning.

Honey and Mumford (1982) have identified four different learning styles relating to how we learn and develop new knowledge and skills. These are: *activist, reflector, theorist* and *pragmatist*. You may have already come across Honey and Mumford's learning style questionnaires, which may be found on the internet and you can try for yourself.

Maclean and Caffrey (2009) have linked the four different learning styles (activist, reflector, theorist, pragmatist) identified by Honey and Mumford to Kolb's experiential learning theory, as shown in Figure 8.4.

In reality most people have a mix of learning styles and so you might find yourself comfortable at more than one stage of Kolb's cycle.

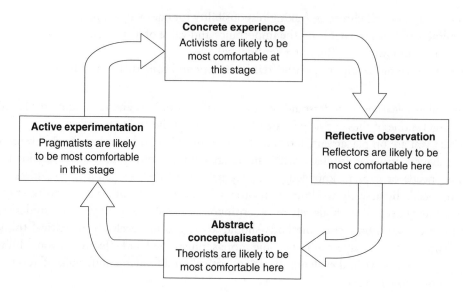

Figure 8.4   Linking Honey and Mumford's four learning styles to Kolb's cycle of learning

Understanding yourself forms an important element of critical reflection and reflexivity as you need to be able to plan for change and take action; this is clearly interwoven with your learning and development. Furthermore, every day we are presented with opportunities to learn and we should try to recognise and exploit these when they present themselves.

Thompson and Thompson (2008: 167) have summarised seven areas of continuous professional development, which form the basis for critically reflective practice:

- **Thinking:** draw on your analytic powers and your professional knowledge.
- **Critical thinking:** evaluate the influence of sociopolitical factors and the significance of arguments and assumptions attached to presenting situations and the lives of service users.
- **Being self-aware:** recognise the impact that we have on others and the impact they have on us. Be socially aware of wider sociopolitical issues.
- **Capitalise on learning:** critical reflection and continuous learning are connected at a foundational level.
- **Supporting others:** in our learning and practice.
- **Being professional:** draw on professional knowledge and a professional value-base and practise professional accountability.
- **Making practice work:** try to ensure our work is effective and rewarding.

Developing in these areas is not an easy task, but if you make use of the resources and opportunities available to you, including formal and informal supervision, you will be able to give yourself effective tools to develop as a critically reflective social work practitioner.

Managing Feelings and Looking after Yourself

So far this chapter has explored the value of supervision, the need for critically reflective practice and the benefits of self-awareness in relation to your status as an adult learner. However, you can only progress as a competent and reflective practitioner if you balance the development and care-taking of your professional identity with the emotional strains of the social work task. All practitioners have emotional responses to the work that they do and the people that they work with. There is no doubt that working with complexity, uncertainty and risk in, sometimes, bureaucratic and over-stretched organisations can be emotionally and mentally demanding and you will need to develop strategies for managing this and taking care of your emotional and physical self.

Ruch (2007) discusses how reflective practice, within the context of supervision, can be facilitated and promoted using Bion's (1962) theory of containment. In this sense containment refers to how difficult thoughts and feelings brought about by practice can be managed (or contained) within the therapeutic relationship which develops between the supervisor and the supervisee. Ruch (2007: 659) states that:

> Practitioners need to work within safe containing contexts characterized by: clear organizational and professional boundaries; multifaceted reflective forums; collaborative and communicative working practices; and open and 'contextually connected' managers.

Your ability to keep emotionally and physically healthy does not solely rely on your organisation's provision of support and guidance; you will need to commit to engaging with these processes. So, in order to allow the therapeutic relationship to unfold in supervision you will need to be honest, share your emotions (and do so in good time – don't let negative feelings fester) and engage in a discussion about how to manage or use these feelings.

Look at: **Chapter 9 Understanding Problem Solving**.   →

This does not mean that you should not have an emotional response or that you should be switched off at an emotional level, but that you must keep a clear perspective about your role, remit and responsibilities. In his discussion Agass (2002) reinforces the message that supervision and reflection are essential to managing your feelings and being alert to your emotional health needs. Developing and maintaining an appropriate set of professional boundaries (or working to your agency's policy) also assists in the process of taking care of yourself.

Summary

This chapter has introduced you to supervision in social work, the value and use of reflection in social work practice and consideration of the application of critical thinking and active learning in social work. These three elements can and ought to be viewed individually but are really used to best effect when brought together.

Really getting the best from supervision, reflective practice and critical approaches to learning requires a certain leap of faith until you begin to experience and use these for yourself. The key here is to have a go and see how it works for you and, perhaps most importantly, whether good supervision, effective reflective practice and active critical thinking improve service delivery.

This chapter has introduced you to the concept of reflection and argued for its intrinsic value in social work education *and* practice. You have been offered models for encouraging and supporting your development as a reflective practitioner. We hope you find them useful in your forthcoming placement.

9

Understanding Problem Solving

With Donna O'Neill

Overview and Learning Outcomes

This chapter will cover:

- Problems and problem solving on placement.
- Preventative strategies to help you on placement.

By the end of Chapter 9 you will be able to:

- Devise useful strategies and approaches to deal with difficulties and problems that may arise on placement.

Introduction to Chapter 9

Social work students often report that their placement is an exciting event they are really looking forward to starting. This is good, but it can also sometimes feel a daunting prospect. All of a sudden, you are leaving the classroom and now have to try to put what you have learned in class into practice.

As well as starting your placement, you will find yourself busy trying to quickly orientate yourself to the geographical setting of the placement and the layout of buildings and offices (large or small, labyrinthine, cramped or cosy, depending on your point of view). In addition, there are also new colleagues to meet, names and faces to remember as well as having to get to grips with new administrative processes and formal and informal organisational cultures. Managing all of this takes time and can absorb a lot of emotional energy.

There are also internal adjustments and experiences that can come to the fore on placement which may provide extra stresses you may not have immediately anticipated. As social workers in training, you need to be able to apply to practice the relevant social work skills and knowledge you have learned about on your course; you are also subject to assessment on placement and inevitably this will involve being observed in terms of your actual practice and also scrutinised and questioned with regard to your professional ethics and ability to be a social worker.

Social work training places special emphasis on exploring how our personal values, experiences and history inform and influence our practice. A willingness to examine our feelings and beliefs is really important if we are to understand how and why we act the way we do; to reflect on this and in doing so learn to better manage our 'self' in order to respond more effectively and professionally to the needs of those with whom we work. Whilst this form of exploration may not be deeply personal or introspective, it can at times be uncomfortable and challenging.

This chapter offers suggestions as to what you, as a student, can do to minimise difficulties and problems should they arise during your placement, address them where they occur and finally move on and learn from these as part of your professional learning and development.

Preventative Work and Problem Solving

Before we begin, perhaps the very first thing to note here is that the majority of placements are successful and pass off without major difficulty, with students enjoying their time on placement and completing this with a real sense of achievement.

Most general anxieties, day-to-day problems and difficulties can be addressed quickly and effectively by communicating how you feel with your practice educator or tutor. It may seem fairly obvious, but talking to someone when things become difficult or simply go wrong is essential, and also eminently sensible and practical. We encourage service users and carers to talk to us about their problems, so in turn we ought to embrace this in our own practice.

What do we mean by **TALK**

T – Tell your practice educator or tutor how you are feeling.

A – Accept that we are all different and therefore we see things differently.

L – Listen and consider the views and perspectives of others.

K – Knowing and recognising a problem affecting you and your work is the first step to resolving it.

In preparing to discuss your concerns with your practice educator, tutor or someone else you trust, you need to try to manage this in a professional and measured way. This is one aspect of being a professional worker. This means not denying how you feel or how something has impacted on you and in turn allowing yourself to express this but ensuring you try to do this in a balanced, calm and measured way and at an appropriate time. The person you speak to will be able to give you the attention you need and respect you better for this.

To present and share your concerns it may help you to make some notes about:

- Who you think you need to talk to.
- What you want to say and the way you want to say it.

- What you think has been happening.
- How this has been impacting on you personally.
- How this has left you feeling.
- Some possible solutions and clarity about your willingness to resolve this in a professional way.

Give some consideration to trying to identify a preferred setting (e.g. in the privacy of supervision or during a one-to-one conversation) and time (e.g. ideally when you are less likely to be disturbed) to raise your concerns. This means you can begin to exercise some control over how to tackle a problem or issue you would like to raise and have a safe space where you can express yourself in the way you want to. This also offers the opportunity to receive some comment or feedback without the need for the discussion to be interrupted or completed over a few different meetings. Of course, this level of planning is not always possible and may not suit every occasion or problem. Real life sometimes simply doesn't allow for a great plan or choreographed response. However, remember, the way you conduct yourself is important. You are on placement and you are being assessed in part on the basis of your capability to conduct yourself as a professional social worker.

Conversations about problems and difficulties can sometimes usefully be had first with your tutor, as talking issues through with someone outside the placement can help you contextualise your feelings and explore how you can address the problem, formulate a plan and seek to resolve it. It is sometimes tempting to discuss how you are feeling with friends, family and allies. However, you need to be careful about what you say and to whom, as, once disclosed, whatever you have said cannot be 'un-said' and once said is no longer within your control as to who else may be told 'in confidence' or 'off the record'. Caution and care are important here. You need to be aware of your professional and your personal boundaries. If you choose to share feelings, useful criteria to judge with whom you ought to share should include trust, confidentiality and mutual respect. Good quality professional supervision and support will incorporate such principles in the supervision contract you and your practice educator commit to, as well as including provision for managing critical feedback, disagreement and addressing problems. So, make sure you fully understand how these features will work in practice.

Look at: **Chapter 8 Using Supervision, Reflective Practice and Critical Thinking.** →

Attitudes and approaches

It is important to remember that as an adult learner you must take responsibility for your own learning. There are obvious professional behaviours it is important to demonstrate whilst on placement: being on time, being organised and reliable, embracing the learning opportunities provided on placement. However, as an active learner, committed to developing your experience and learning, you should also seek to adopt healthy attitudes to practice learning. Many of these are similar to the features and qualities we discussed in Chapter 3 about the contribution and commitment you need to bring to practice learning in order to make your placement successful.

Look at: **Chapter 3 Planning and Beginning your Placement.** →

We can identify a number of helpful traits and attitudes which will help you address most difficulties, barriers and problems as they arise on placement. These include being:

- Committed to learn from difficulties, challenges and problems as well as successes.
- Willing to engage with problems and be committed to resolving them in a professional manner.
- Willing to explore and acknowledge how your own feelings or behaviour may be blocking resolution of a problem (e.g. possible feelings of anger, hurt or upset and actions which are defensive, resistant or disengaged).
- Willing to act on fresh approaches which contribute to positive change (e.g. being willing to listen, making your own points without becoming personal, acknowledging the feelings and views of others, genuinely seeking a resolution to the problem).

PLACEMENT ACTIVITY
Using problem-solving approaches to evidence the PCF and good practice

Consider how a positive approach to addressing difficulties, challenges and problems on placement could be a source of useful evidence of your learning and development. Make a note of some examples of positive qualities, attitudes and behaviours that would suggest you are able to operate as a professional worker. Relate these to PCFs 1 and 2, and HCPC Guidance 3:

PCF 1: **Professionalism** – Identify and behave as a professional social worker, committed to professional development.

Social workers are members of an internationally recognised profession, a title protected in UK law. Social workers demonstrate professional commitment by taking responsibility for their conduct, practice and learning, with support through supervision. As representatives of the social work profession they safeguard its reputation and are accountable to the professional regulator.

PCF 2: **Values and ethics** – Apply social work ethical principles and values to guide professional practice.

Social workers have an obligation to conduct themselves ethically and to engage in ethical decision-making, including through partnership with people who use their services. Social workers are knowledgeable about the value-base of their profession, its ethical standards and relevant law.

Notes

HCPC 3: You should keep high standards of personal conduct.

- You should be aware that conduct outside of your programme may affect whether or not you are allowed to complete your programme or register with [the HCPC].
- You should be polite with service users, your colleagues and the programme team.
- You should make sure that your personal appearance is appropriate for your placement environment.
- You should follow your education provider's or placement provider's policy on attendance.

A Commitment to Problem Solving

A frequently used practice approach recommended in social work relates to what is generally termed the *'problem-solving'* (or similarly, 'solution-focused') approach to social work practice. We do not intend to go into detail here about problem solving as a specific social work technique or approach, but it will be very helpful both in your direct work with service users and carers and also in the way you conduct your own practice and professional business.

As the International Federation of Social Workers (IFSW), in defining the purpose of social work, notes:

> The social work profession promotes social change, problem solving in human relationships and the empowerment and liberation of people to enhance well-being. Utilising theories of human behaviour and social systems, social work intervenes at the points where people interact with their environments. Principles of human rights and social justice are fundamental to social work. (IFSW, 2000a)

The value of 'problem solving' as an approach is that it is positive in its outlook and seeks to build on strengths and assets to solve problems; it asserts that positive change is possible and is a worthy goal of social work. Problem solving also implicitly accepts and acknowledges that in the course of our day-to-day work, problems will arise and are likely to be of sufficient number and significance to merit a strategy to address and challenge this.

A problem-solving approach can be seen to include several steps. These include the need to:

- Identify with honesty and accuracy, the problem or problems and the obstacles to resolving these (including yourself).
- Assess the impact of the problem(s). What is it stopping you from doing or achieving? How does it affect others?
- Identify and evaluate the range of actions and activities which may help reduce or resolve the problem.
- Devise a plan of action. In plain terms, *how* you will address the problem.
- If possible, make a contingency or back-up plan just in case things don't go as planned or as you had hoped.
- Implement your chosen plan.
- Evaluate how well your intervention has worked.
- If it has worked, good! We now have a useful strategy to use again. If not, review your intervention and try again. Maybe seek some further advice from someone you trust and you think can be helpful.

> ## PLACEMENT ACTIVITY
> ## Problem solving – building on past successes
>
> A good strategy for learning about problem solving is to draw on our previous experience. Identify a problem or challenging situation from your previous work or personal experience.
>
> - Describe in detail and as accurately as possible the problem or problems.
> - How did this impact on you and on others?
> - Describe your strategies and plans to address the problem(s). How did you decide which one to follow?
> - How did you implement your plan?
> - How successful was the action you took?
> - What worked well? What worked less well?
> - On further reflection, would you now do things differently?
> - What can you take from this experience and use to apply to other problems?
>
> Having completed the above activity, the task of drawing on a previous problem or challenging situation may have prompted you to reflect on how this situation left you feeling and how these feelings impacted on your response and actions at the time.
>   How might you try to manage things differently in the future if something arises during your placement?

Common Placement Difficulties, Challenges and Problems

The placement arena is the key practice setting for the assessment of students and their capability to function as professional social work practitioners. Given all the ingredients that make up placements, it is therefore not entirely surprising that, on occasions, things do go wrong. Below are some of the more common difficulties, challenges and problems that arise on placement and some strategies to address them.

Managing the urge for fight or flight

Social work placements bring with them some inevitable level of pressure, anxiety and stress. This is normal. However, if we feel under undue pressure this can lead to us also feeling overwhelmed and anxious. This can manifest itself in several ways, e.g. becoming angry and irritable or perhaps withdrawn or avoidant. This is sometimes referred to as 'fight or flight'. This is a natural response to a difficult or challenging situation. Some students, when they feel things are going wrong, may internalise their feelings, pretend things are not happening or avoid or accept something in the hope the problem will go away. It is often surprising the lengths we are willing to go to avoid confrontations or deal with discomfort and distress. By contrast, other people become quite irritable and openly hostile in responding to problems. Neither is particularly helpful for you in your training, for your future practice or for your own wellbeing.

Much better to try to acknowledge we are all vulnerable to stress and to commit, before your placement begins, to use the TALK and problem-solving strategies outlined above to begin to address the pressures of placement. If you do feel under stress, talk to your practice educator or tutor about this.

Social work comment

I was really unhappy on placement and really didn't want to go in each day. I didn't tell anyone about it and found the work really stressful. I went off sick and then had to give up the placement. It was only then I was able to tell my tutor that I'd a lot of things going on at home and I had been really down. I wish I had sorted things earlier. But I took some time out, got myself together and got another placement. It was a hard time but I feel much better now. (BA student)

The work and pace of the placement

We all work at different paces but generally like to think of ourselves as keeping busy. Often students are very keen to begin their placement and 'escape' from the university; to try to apply their new learning and to do practical, 'real' social work practice. However, after a few weeks some students begin to feel that their placement is too quiet and they have too little to do; or too busy and very rushed; or the allocation of work does not seem to be building and is rather uneven with some weeks busy, some quiet.

All these features are quite common in student placements and there can be several reasons for this happening. First, remember, you are on placement to learn rather than simply be another member of staff or pair of hands. The reason you are on placement is to experience practice and to have the opportunity to learn about social work in real time. This means being able to observe, pause and reflect on what is happening around you and become familiar with new people, new work and new activities and experiences. For this, you need time. Your practice educator knows this and will be trying to ensure you have some protected time to think about the work you intend to do and reflect afterwards on how things went and how to do these things better next time (which is why in social work we value the opportunity for reflection and supervision).

However, pacing of work is something which can be a genuine concern for students, generating a mixed range of feelings and responses. If you feel you are being given too little direct work with service users and carers then it can feel as if you are being seen as not experienced enough, not reliable and not trusted. Similarly, if you are so busy you feel you have no spare time at all, then you may feel used as an extra pair of hands and not valued as a social worker in training.

On a practical level, in the ebb and flow of work of the placement agency, it may sometimes simply be the case that work is not coming in at a sufficient pace to allocate suitable cases to you at a steady rate across the placement, or work can be fast paced and you are given work fairly early into the placement. Your practice educator will be aware of this. However, if you have concerns you should raise this with him or her in supervision. This is reasonable; this is exactly what supervision is for (as a two-way process) and shows you are interested and keen to gain experience and learn.

How some teams behave

Coming to a service you do not know is a new experience and takes some adjustment. Services and teams are unique in terms of staff profiles, experience and how they interact and function on a day-to-day basis. Offices and team rooms can be very quiet or very noisy environments. Some teams are very used to having social work students and have both formal and informal ways of bringing new people into their agency and practice. However, for some agencies having a social work student is a newer experience so you may have to take the lead to introduce yourself to workers, volunteers and others who may not be as familiar with social work and social work approaches. Each team is quite unique and individual in the way it operates. Each student on placement is also unique and individual. Typically, getting to know each other just takes time, but generally passes off without major difficulty. As a student on placement, you are, in a sense, now an 'insider' (at least for a temporary period of time) but also still an 'outsider' (as you have only a temporary status and presence). As a student, like any traveller to a new place, you will experience new things, new ideas, local customs and cultures. Hopefully, these will be positive experiences.

However, occasionally and notably during periods of great stress, crisis or change (not unusual features of social work), teams and individual staff can behave in ways which do not sit easily with the professional values, ethics and standards of social work. It is fair to say that no profession or agency (or worker come to that) is immune from this and social work and social care are no different. The manifestation of this behaviour in individuals and teams will vary, fluctuate and may or may not be a consistent presentation or feature. However, teams can do many things we had not necessarily anticipated or expected to see; e.g. people don't get on with each other, staff squabble, cliques form, staff and team seem generally unhappy, unsettled and more. Teams, just like people, can be subject to stresses and difficulties which are problematic and unsettling. This may be the result of a range of factors, e.g. history, the impending prospect of cutbacks and redundancies, recent critical events or disciplinary matters. Some of these things you may be aware of, some not. These features of teams may have become the norm for how they go about their daily business, to the point where it has become largely unremarkable to staff. However, this may be something quite new for you and something you may well have to learn to adjust to, despite it leaving you curious, uncertain and perhaps even disappointed with the placement. It is quite reasonable and appropriate to share these feelings in supervision. Remember, part of your professional learning is to analyse the context of organisations (PCF 8).

Points to Consider

Consider again PCF 8: Contexts and organisations

Engage with, inform and adapt to changing contexts that shape practice. Operate effectively within own organisational frameworks and contribute to the development of services and organisations. Operate effectively within multi-agency and inter-professional settings.

Social workers are informed about and proactively responsive to the challenges and opportunities that come with changing social contexts and constructs. They fulfil this responsibility in accordance with their professional values and ethics, both as individual professionals and as members of the organisation in which they work. They collaborate, inform and are informed by their work with others, inter-professionally and with communities.

However, there are other situations – thankfully relatively few in our experience – where individuals use derogatory or offensive language, are aggressive or inappropriate. This is not acceptable (especially where there is some possible impact on service users, carers, colleagues or professional practice) and, given the emphasis in social work on values and ethics, it is valid and proper for you to question and challenge such statements either directly or to discuss this in supervision. Similarly, you can discuss concerns with your tutor. Agencies will have policies and procedures in place to which you can refer and relate to the standards and expectations of the service and staff. One thing we would suggest is that at the beginning of your placement you make the time to discuss the context of the agency and talk to your practice educator about the culture of the team and service you are entering. This can be a very helpful conversation and help avoid some of the pitfalls we have discussed above. Again, use the strategies we recommended earlier to plan how you will do this and how you might respond where further situations arise.

Interpersonal relationships and boundaries

Related to the discussion above, during your placement you will meet and work with a range of different people. These will include your practice educator, other team members, other agencies and service users and carers. Social work is a profession and as such requires professional boundaries to be understood and used in your daily work. It is important to be aware that you are expected to work with people in a professional way and develop appropriate and sustainable working relationships. Boundaries can help us manage our personal feelings. The particular challenge in social work is that we ought to be trying to be effective in our jobs but also humane in the way we work. Acceptance of people and respect are part of our values. Being warm and approachable is appropriate and important in terms of engaging with people and establishing some rapport. However, you should take care to:

- Be aware of your professional expectations.
- Not simply mimic and copy the behaviour of others.
- Be clear about personal boundaries and the expectations and requirements of the placement agency.
- Be prepared to reflect on your actions and feelings about others.
- Be prepared to explain your actions.
- Be willing to step back when in doubt and talk with your practice educator.

If you suspect or know you have perhaps blurred or crossed boundaries in terms of working relationships, either with a colleague or service user, you must take action to correct this. This is important for you as a trainee professional but may also have implications for other colleagues and potentially vulnerable service users and carers. Seek out guidance and advice from your practice educator or tutor.

Recognising diversity and difference – valuing and being valued

A key part of value-led and ethical social work is a commitment to anti-discriminatory and anti-oppressive practice. As we discussed in earlier chapters, anti-oppressive practice finds it roots in humanism and values of social justice and acceptance. It recognises the existence of social divisions in terms of race, age, gender, sexuality, disability and social class; of societal and structural inequality and of imbalances of rights and power. Social work as an activity is tasked to challenge discrimination and oppression and, in doing so, promote justice and rights. However, it would be naïve and flawed to suppose that social work, social workers and settings for the provision of social work and social care are free from discrimination and oppression. Practice educators and students must recognise the potential for issues of power differentials, inequality and discrimination and oppression to occur. The form of this may vary in presentation and degree, but, as Neil Thompson (2006, 2009) asserts, there can be no middle ground in terms of how we address this, i.e. we choose to be either part of the solution or part of the problem. Thus, perhaps the first task is to acknowledge the presence of discrimination and oppression in our work; be committed to recognising and addressing it; and seek ways to amend and improve problems.

Realistically, you cannot address every possible presentation of discriminatory or oppressive language and behaviour you may encounter. However, there are some common points to recommend in seeking to address and redress such problems:

- Don't be pressured to remain dissatisfied or unhappy with a problem or situation. You have a right to be treated with respect and fairness.
- If you feel confident and able, raise the issues that concern you in an appropriate way and at an appropriate time and place. Decide who you ought to talk to about this. Plan what you want to say and how. Commit yourself to seeking some resolution and way forward.
- Seek advice and support if you want to talk things through first. Decide who is the most appropriate person to talk with; this may be with your practice educator, tutor, course student representative or student union.
- Read your education provider's and placement agency's policies and procedures relating to student placements and their commitment to equal opportunities, diversity and difference, raising concerns and making complaints. These documents usually also contain useful advice and guidance about how to take forward a complaint or grievance.

 Social work comment

Power inequalities and practice learning:

Teaching about power inequalities during the social work course often revolves around the social worker–service user relationship. On placement, power inequality may also be a characteristic of the organisation (especially in hierarchical organisations), or may need to be navigated when multi-agency working.

Within child protection, it is important to remember that multi-agency working is partnership working, and every agency has equal responsibility to safeguard children and families. It may be that during your placement you will be seen as someone in a position of power (particularly when working within a statutory organisation) or as someone at the bottom of the pile (perhaps because of 'student' status), or even both of these at different times! It's easy to get frustrated, and I found it useful to remember that power inequalities are transient and change over time. However, when I needed to challenge things I gave careful thought about how to proceed. This was useful and it worked! (Charlotte, MA student)

Social work comment

Sharing uncertainties in the context of assessment:

I learned on both my placements that as a social worker you are constantly challenged to contain emotions and carry uncertainties, whilst striving to maintain a positive attitude and a solution-focused approach. For example in my first placement involving advocacy work with looked after children, I was reported to have a strong accent that made it difficult to be understood or communicate with the children I was advocating for. This gave me some anxiety about how this might be fed back to my practice educator.

The solution was to discuss the issue with my tutor and my practice educator. But this can be sometimes easier said than done in certain situations. Nevertheless, the situation made me aware once again that social work practice is made up of power relationships and as a student I was in an unequal power relationship with my practice educator when I knew that I was being assessed by them.

I have to say that the issue of language barrier became an uncertainty and was not really resolved until I started my second placement where my differences were positively valued as my role included interpreting and working cases with a service user group that understood and trusted me more.

But overall, I think the placement system is not only valuable, but also absolutely essential because it is only through a placement that one can start gaining the work experience that social workers need to become true practitioners. I think the real challenge is to learn to apply the relevant theories and skills in our practice rather than simply learning theories. (Pierre, MA student)

Working effectively with your practice educator

As a student you will be working closely with your practice educator throughout your placement. You will be meeting in formal supervision and also experience informal supervision during your placement.

The placement learning agreement or placement contract offers both the student and practice educator an opportunity to define the boundaries of their new relationship and set out exactly what they expect from one another. As we have suggested above, it is really important this document is not neglected and continues to be a live working document throughout the placement. It is your opportunity to set out some of your aspirations for the placement, the expectations of you during the placement and also how to resolve potential disagreements or problems.

→ Look at: **Chapter 3 Planning and Beginning your Placement, and Chapter 8 Using Supervision, Reflective Practice and Critical Thinking.**

The practice learning agreement is also the point of reference to use when things begin to go wrong or issues are raised. On occasion it will be necessary for additional action plans to be put in place to address very specific areas which have arisen since the start of the placement and not covered in the original agreement. Typically, such action plans set out the issues which are impacting upon the progress and completion of the placement. This could include aspects of your work or the work of the practice educator or new issues in the placement setting which are affecting the placement, such as the absence of sufficient work, or funding issues.

Another point to consider is the working relationship between the practice educator and yourself. Generally, you will find you work well together through the duration of the placement. However, the relationship between the practice educator and yourself is not an equal one. You are being assessed on placement and are also under more scrutiny, examination and probing about the values and beliefs informing your practice. This is something which is worth acknowledging between the practice educator and yourself. You may disagree on things – this is common – but you must also strive to find ways of working together. Like most working relationships, it is good to be able to get on well together, but not essential; and ultimately you don't even have to like each other, you just have to work together! However, if you really cannot resolve an issue you should contact your tutor for advice and support.

Suspension or Termination of Placements

Occasionally, placements do run into more serious difficulties. This is not the norm, but it does happen. Where a problem arises and a placement has to be halted for a time or terminated (e.g. an agency closes due to loss of funding or there are staffing difficulties) then students will generally be found new placements, although this may take time to organise.

Where a student does not pass their placement or the placement is terminated for unprofessional or unacceptable conduct you should meet with your university tutor as soon as possible to seek guidance and support. All courses and programmes have internal procedures for addressing failed placements, or the breakdown or termination of a placement for other reasons. Remember, you can also seek independent advice from your student union.

Social work comment

When things go wrong …

I had an instinct very early into placement that it was not going to work. The most important thing is to make sure you can show your efforts to make things work. Stay in contact with your practice educator (especially if an off-site practice educator) and your university tutor. I was in daily contact at one point.

Be professional about the issues at placement and try to be as upfront and clear as possible. Make sure you follow your university's procedures – this might include difficult meetings so prepare well and take a log of work you have been completing.

If issues cannot be resolved, make sure you think through the implications of starting a new placement again – financial and academic if you have a dissertation to complete.

For me personally, changing placement ended up being the best thing I did. Remember that it is your learning experience at stake here – and your future practice as a social worker. (Charlotte, MA student)

Summary

Most social work placements go well and pass off largely without major incident. However, our strong advice is that investing time in your supervision contract and practice learning agreement is time well spent. If you do have concerns or difficulties then TALK will help you to plan and think about how to respond to some common difficulties and challenges. Most can be overcome using the guidance on offer and drawing on the support of your practice educator, tutor and your own good judgement.

10

Getting Ready for Professional Practice

Overview and Learning Outcomes

This chapter will cover:

- Completing your course, looking for jobs, thinking about a career.
- An outline of the Assessed and Supported Year in Employment (ASYE) and beyond.
- Looking after yourself.

By the end of Chapter 10 you will be able to:

- Plan better for your future career.
- Identify the key elements and features of the ASYE.

Introduction to Chapter 10

This chapter will begin by looking at the period following your final placement and as you complete your studies, introduce you to job seeking and the recently introduced Assessed and Supported Year in Employment (ASYE) for social workers. The chapter concludes by considering how to look after yourself now and in the future.

Coming to the End of your Course of Study

The end of the second and final placement and completing your course of study is a demanding time for students. Many things seem to come together at the same time and all need to be managed. In relation to your placement, you will find yourself trying to ensure that all your case records and files are up-to-date; you have arranged the handover, transfer or closure of casework; you have told people you are leaving; and in the process of saying your goodbyes to service users, carers and colleagues.

Look at: **Chapter 3 Planning and Beginning your Placement.** →

At this point you are also trying to gather together all the evidence for your practice educator so she or he can write their final placement report. To add to this, in the university, you are trying to meet the final academic deadlines for assignments, projects and dissertations to ensure you can be considered for your degree and professional qualifications. So, no pressure really!

Without doubt this is a testing time. However, there are things we can do to help us cope better and manage these tasks. Here are a few recommendations:

- **Be organised** – Make a list of all (not just some) of the things you need to do and the order you need to do them so as to meet the correct deadlines.
- **Multi-task** – You are now someone who has progressed through the requirements of completing an intensive social work course with all its reading, assignments, placements, practice learning, assessments and additional bewildering administration and bureaucracy. You are already a walking, talking, achieving, multi-tasker. You could not have got this far in your professional training without earning this particular badge of achievement. So, use these skills you have developed to good effect. You can definitely do this!
- **Keep your practice educator informed** about how things are progressing with placement-related matters and the production of all the necessary collected evidence of your practice learning. Your practice educator will want to help you to finish on time if possible. (They may have set aside specific time to write your placement report and may have a forthcoming break, holiday or other events planned after the date of your final placement.) So, it is imperative you let your practice educator know if work you are required to produce may be delayed. They may be able to help and advise you about what to do to get back on track.
- **Seek advice and support from your tutor** – In all my years of teaching I have yet to meet a student who was not in need of support and guidance (and even the odd prompt) to get across the final finishing line. This is normal. Your tutor will be familiar with the pressures around the end of placement and your course. They have considerable experience of helping people deal with this and genuinely want to help you to succeed.
- **Seek support from other students** – Other students will know exactly how you are feeling and so can generally empathise about this part of your student experience. It's good to talk. However, whilst it may be good to vent and share, take care to be judicious about the quality of advice and suggestions being offered around. Generally, this is good natured and sensible. However, third party information and statements about university regulations, course requirements, what is OK and what is not (however plausible and convincing they may sound) need to be verified. Check things with your tutor.
- **Try to work a normal business day** – I am not really confident this is truly achievable in the world of the final-year student social worker. However, I do think it useful to take breaks;

try to be methodical in your work and ensure you eat meals at regular points; get some decent sleep and begin and end each day with a plan of work. Tiredness and stress feed each other, so look after yourself!

- **Take a break from any paid work** – Inevitably, nowadays, many students have part-time paid jobs to supplement their income during their studies. However, if you can (and I appreciate this may be very difficult depending on your circumstances), I do recommend to students try to take a break from this in order to complete their studies and produce the best academic work possible. You only do your social work course once and it is important to try to leave feeling good about what you have achieved.
- **Have something to look forward to** – It is good to have something positive to think about doing when you have ended your placement and completed your course. This can vary in scope or immediacy but may typically include a get-together with friends from your course or planning for the graduation ceremony. Simpler pleasures like returning piles of books to the library, a lie-in or relaxing day are good things to have in your thoughts and can keep you going.

Preparing to Apply for Posts – Reflecting on your Placement and Practice Learning

By the end of your course of social work training you will have completed blocks of academic teaching and undertaken a total of 170 days of practice learning plus 30 days of skills development. The College of Social Work has set out guidance on the assessment of students and placements:

> Assessment of students' performance and learning on placement is likely to form a substantial part of the final assessment using the PCF, since in most programmes the end of the placement will be very close to the end of the programme. (TCSW, 2012b: 55)

Thus, it is clear that your placements and practice learning (notably, the final placement) are considered of significant importance in the final assessment of your readiness to be a qualified social worker. They also offer key resources and preparation for your forthcoming job applications. As we highlighted earlier in this book, according to TCSW the final placement should provide the opportunity for you to demonstrate your readiness to meet the statutory elements of the role of a qualified social worker. This should include:

- Formal assessment processes considering risk and/or safeguarding for child protection, for practice in mental health or with vulnerable adults (see PCF 7, 8).
- Opportunities to reflect on, discuss and analyse appropriate use of authority (see PCF 7, 6).
- Application and understanding of legal frameworks relevant for social work practice (see PCF 5, 8).

- Organisational policies and decisions and their impact on service delivery to service users (see PCF 8).
- The demands of a high pressured environment, where time and competing interests have to be managed effectively (see PCF 1).
- Multi-agency working, including planning interventions with other agencies, and analysing and managing tensions (see PCF 7, 8).
- Presentation of outcomes of formal assessment processes, including analysis of risk/ recommendations in line with organisational policy/procedure at, e.g., panels/meetings/ courts (see PCF 6, 7, 8).
- Use of formal agency recording for assessment/risk (see PCF 1).

PCF domains – quick reference

1. **Professionalism** – Identify and behave as a professional social worker, committed to professional development.
2. **Values and ethics** – Apply social work ethical principles and values to guide professional practice.
3. **Diversity** – Recognise diversity and apply anti-discriminatory and anti-oppressive principles in practice.
4. **Rights, justice and economic wellbeing** – Advance human rights and promote social justice and economic wellbeing.
5. **Knowledge** – Apply knowledge of social sciences, law and social work practice theory.
6. **Critical reflection and analysis** – Apply critical reflection and analysis to inform and provide a rationale for professional decision-making.
7. **Intervention and skills** – Use judgement and authority to intervene with individuals, families and communities to promote independence, provide support and prevent harm, neglect and abuse.
8. **Contexts and organisations** – Engage with, inform and adapt to changing contexts that shape practice. Operate effectively within own organisational frameworks and contribute to the development of services and organisations. Operate effectively within multi-agency and inter-professional settings.
9. **Professional leadership** – Take responsibility for the professional learning and development of others through supervision, mentoring, assessing, research, teaching, leadership (TCSW, 2012a: 1–3).

The activities outlined in the list above describe and indicate the higher level range of work expected of the final placement and also of a prospective qualified social worker.

Given you will be asked to evidence these features (by meeting the relevant criteria of the PCF for your final placement) so your final practice placement and collection of evidence (typically presented as a portfolio of work) will be a valuable source of material to help in your job applications. Keep a copy of your work provided during your course.

PLACEMENT ACTIVITY
Reflections on placements and practice learning

Having completed your placements and begun to think about your future career pathway, this activity invites you to reflect on each of your social work placements and consider what you have gained in terms of experience and learning. This information will help you gather material for your forthcoming job applications.

First placement (70 days)

- Setting.
- Service user group(s).
- Main work, role and activities.
- Training undertaken.
- Other agencies you had contact with or visited as part of widening your experience.
- Application of your academic learning to practice and professional development.
- Examples of translating values and ethics into practice.
- Dilemmas and challenges during the placement.
- Successful aspects of the placement.
- What did you learn about what being a good social worker entails?
- What did you need to develop during your second placement?

Second and final placement (100 days)

- Setting.
- Service user group(s).
- Main work, role and activities.
- Training undertaken.
- Other agencies you had contact with or visited as part of widening your experience.
- Application of your academic learning to practice and professional development.
- Examples of translating values and ethics into practice.
- Dilemmas and challenges during the placement.
- Successful aspects of the placement.
- What did you learn about what being a good social worker entails?
- What did you need to develop further following your second and final placement?

Skills development (30 days)

- List and reflect on your skills development days here.

Remember:

- In Chapter 8, we suggested you start a reflective log on placement to record your reflections, thoughts and feelings about each day of the placement. If you did this, go back to the log and see if there are any additional points of learning you can add to your notes.

- In Chapter 3, we also encouraged you to design your own curriculum vitae (CV) to build up a record of your education, training and experience for future jobs or courses. If you did this, you can draw on it as a source of additional information. Some agencies and employers may be willing to accept CVs if you get in touch with them enquiring about jobs, etc. So, keep this up-to-date.

Applying for a Post

Having graduated you are now entitled to register with the HCPC as a fully qualified professional social worker and use this title. You will want to start applying for social work posts. Although you may have developed specific or specialist areas of interest, one of the very good things about a social work qualification is that it is a generic qualification, which means you can consider a career in any area of practice and across a wide range of services and settings. Also, with a generic qualification, if you take a post in one sector, you are not bound or tied to that setting and can change in order to gain further experience or follow another career path.

Applying for a social work post marks the opportunity to draw together all your education and learning, practice experience and personal qualities that are relevant to making your application. This merits time and attention. Your application form is your first opportunity to impress a prospective employer. The first goal here is to be short-listed for the post. The comments which follow are offered as suggestions and you should adapt these to your particular application.

Preparing your application

Once you are clear what is required to meet the minimum standard for the post you are interested in you need to prepare your application. In addition to providing standard information about personal details, qualifications, names of referees, etc., the following items need careful thought in preparing your application and the 'Personal Statement' you are likely to be asked to complete:

- Knowledge.
- Skills.
- Values and ethics.
- Attributes and qualities.
- Recent placement and practice learning.
- Experience – work related.
- Experience – personal.
- Special interests and assets.
- Personal interests.

PLACEMENT ACTIVITY
Applying for social work posts

To help you plan your application and personal statement, make a detailed list of what you could include from the list below:

- Knowledge, e.g. law and policy (which ...), social work theory and methods (which ...), research interests, specialist subject areas.
- Skills, e.g. assessment, working with risk, managing complex casework, communication and engagement, critical analysis and thinking, second language skills.
- Values and ethics, e.g. honesty, respect, commitment to your professional ethical standards and codes, clarity about what being a professional social worker entails.
- Attributes and qualities, e.g. tenacity commitment, resilience, willing to engage with complex work.
- Experience – work related.
- Experience – personal.
- Special interests and assets, e.g. specialist subject areas you studied during your course, research areas, training courses you attended previously or during your recent course and placements, holding a full clean driving licence.
- Personal interests, e.g. relevant interests and hobbies (with the suggestion you have a life outside work).

This list is offered as a guide and you ought to decide for yourself what to include or omit.

Remember: a cleanly presented and well-organised application form makes the right impression from the start and is an absolute must! Proofread your form, check your spelling and grammar.

Interviewing the Interviewers

The first thing to say if you are invited for interview is very well done, as this is no easy feat! If you have not been short-listed then certainly do not lose heart. Ask for feedback and perhaps seek expert advice from your university's careers advice service or ask a friendly tutor or practice educator for some tips. Producing a good job application takes time, effort and patience.

It is not the intention here to try to give guidance about preparing for interviews.

However, as part of being interviewed we would like to encourage you to take any opportunity offered to ask legitimate, appropriate questions about the post and the organisation you may be going to work for. Again, it is important to stress that what you ask about is for you to decide and, perhaps as importantly, *when* you may choose to ask certain questions (e.g. details of pay and conditions are perhaps better discussed after you are offered a position). If there is time for you to ask something at the interview then it is very likely this will be towards the end. This means there is probably only a very brief time available (given the interview schedule) so try to keep things appropriate and to the point.

You may choose to ask clarifying questions about:

- The role.
- Job prospects.
- Support and supervision.
- Access to training.

These are legitimate areas of enquiry. As a social worker, you will have an interest in arrangements to help you in your first year of practice and support for Continuing Professional Development. Thus, the agency's commitment to support newly qualified social workers is a legitimate question to raise. Good employers should want to support you in your development as a professional worker.

The Assessed and Supported Year in Employment

As we discussed in Chapter 1, social work has undergone considerable reform and change. The previous regulatory functions of the now defunct General Social Care Council (GSCC) have now passed to the Health and Care Professions Council (HCPC). The College of Social Work (TCSW) has been founded to support the profession. Social work education has been reviewed to meet the College of Social Work's Professional Capabilities Framework for Social Workers (TCSW, 2012b) and the HCPC Standards of Proficiency for Social Workers (2012b).

The new PCF introduced in 2012 is intended to be the single framework for social workers to use to plan their careers and professional development. It takes you from initial training through your career after qualification. The award of your degree and social work qualification is the point at which you will be eligible to register with the HCPC and from that point be entitled to call yourself a social worker.

The Social Work Task Force (SWTF) was established in 2009 to identify ways of strengthening the social work profession. The Task Force reported on the very challenging working environments facing social workers, fluctuating levels of supervision and support and the burden of overly bureaucratic systems which reduce opportunities for direct face-to-face work with service users and carers. In its final report in December 2009, the SWTF reiterated many of the previous research and anecdotal views of many aspects of social work. It concluded that:

> ... the current mix of practical and professional support to frontline social workers is inconsistent and sometimes inadequate. To be effective, social workers need appropriate technology and equipment, secure access to supervision and robust sources of research and information – and enough time to make good use of all of these resources. (DCSF, 2009b: 6)

Over several years, there has been growing concern about the transition from initial social work qualification into professional practice. The Children's Workforce Development Council (CWDC) reported that newly qualified workers entering statutory children's services faced high demand for services, complex and challenging casework and often high caseloads (CWDC, 2008).

The Local Government Association (2009), representing local authorities in England, found 60% of children's services reporting retention difficulties with social workers. A study by Curtis et al. (2010) estimated that the average period of time a social worker remains in the profession in the UK is no more than eight years. Webb and Carpenter (2011) have observed that while some staff turnover within an organisation is inevitable, in the longer term it is costly and can be disruptive and damaging to service provision, impacting on efficiency, effectiveness and morale.

In response to these difficulties and in an attempt to bolster recruitment and retention, the CWDC introduced the Newly Qualified Social Worker (NQSW) pilot programme as a three-year project (beginning in 2008) to deliver a programme of supervision, training and development to newly qualified social workers during their first year of employment in children's social care services. From September 2012, the NQSW programme was replaced by the Assessed and Supported Year in Employment (ASYE) for social workers in England. The ASYE programme expands on the previous scheme and applies to social workers operating in services for children and adults and is designed to be used in all settings where a qualified and registered social worker is employed, from local authorities through to employers in the voluntary, private and independent sectors.

INFORMATION POINT

Review of the NQSW scheme (2008–2011)

The Department for Education commissioned a national review of the NQSW scheme over the first three years of the programme from 2008 to 2011, covering three cohorts of NQSWs. The report concluded that overall the NQSW scheme had helped newly qualified workers improve their skills, competence and confidence as child and family social workers during their first year of practice. Support and training in reflective supervision was appreciated by an increasingly large majority of NQSWs and thought to contribute to their learning. However, the review also concluded that links between the NQSW scheme and other post-qualifying training had not been fully developed and the initial requirement to evidence achievement through a portfolio or record of achievement was a source of dissatisfaction for many. Finally, there was no evidence that the programme had improved job satisfaction, although it should be noted that the proportion of satisfied NQSWs was high (DfE, 2012).

Just when you may have thought the days of portfolio and assessment were perhaps behind you, after qualifying as a social worker you will be required to complete a further assessed and supported year in employment as a social worker. The ASYE is a one-year programme and similarly to the NQSW which it replaces, seeks to promote the provision of extra support during your first year of practice. It is a product of the revised national review of the training and development for registered social workers, originally initiated by the SWRB and now steered by the College of Social Work.

The programme emphasises the development of skills and knowledge but also that you are required to demonstrate 'sufficiency' of your readiness for a career in social work. Both Skills for Care (leading the funding of schemes for workers in adult services settings) and the Department for Education (for workers in children and family services) suggest a relationship between the ASYE and future pay and progression in terms of your employment, but clarification of how this works actually seems to sit with the employer.

In May 2012, Skills for Care produced a short introductory document aimed at social work students, outlining the ASYE. It stated that:

> The ASYE is a year-long programme designed to help you to develop your capability and strengthen your professional confidence. Over the year it is expected that you will consolidate your learning from the degree and develop knowledge and experience in your employment setting. It will provide you with access to regular and focussed support and development and set out what is expected of you by the end of your first year in employment.

> The ASYE also includes an holistic assessment of an individual's abilities in their first year of employment as a qualified social worker. It introduces a consistent standard against which your knowledge and capability can be judged, which will be assessed against the Professional Capabilities Framework (PCF) developed by the Social Work Reform Board.

> All social workers who undertake the ASYE should benefit from:

> - reflective supervision – at least weekly for the first six weeks of employment, then at least fortnightly for the remainder of the first six months, and a minimum of monthly thereafter
> - workload – normally over the course of the year 90% of what is expected of a confident social worker in the same role in their second or third year of employment, weighted over the course of the year by things such as case complexity, risk and growing proficiency
> - their personal development plan
> - protected time for personal development, which normally equates to 10% over the course of the year.

> The overall aim is to provide you with additional support in your first year of employment to improve your confidence and capability, provide sector-wide consistency in what social workers know, understand and are able to do at the end of their first year in employment and support your own continuing professional development. (Skills for Care, 2012: 1–2)

The ASYE programme appears to include a range of sources for evidencing and demonstrating your practice. These will be familiar to you given your experience of placements and practice learning, typically including:

- Direct observation.
- Examples and products of work (reports, summaries, assessments, etc.).
- Supervision records.
- Critical reflection pieces.
- Service user feedback.

In producing your evidence, you will be expected to meet the requirements of the nine domains of the PCF at ASYE level. See Figure 10.1 below.

The ASYE and links to the PCF

As you can see from the PCF 'rainbow' you can plot your progress from the end of your qualifying training and entry into your own Assessed and Supported Year in Employment (see Figure 10.1).

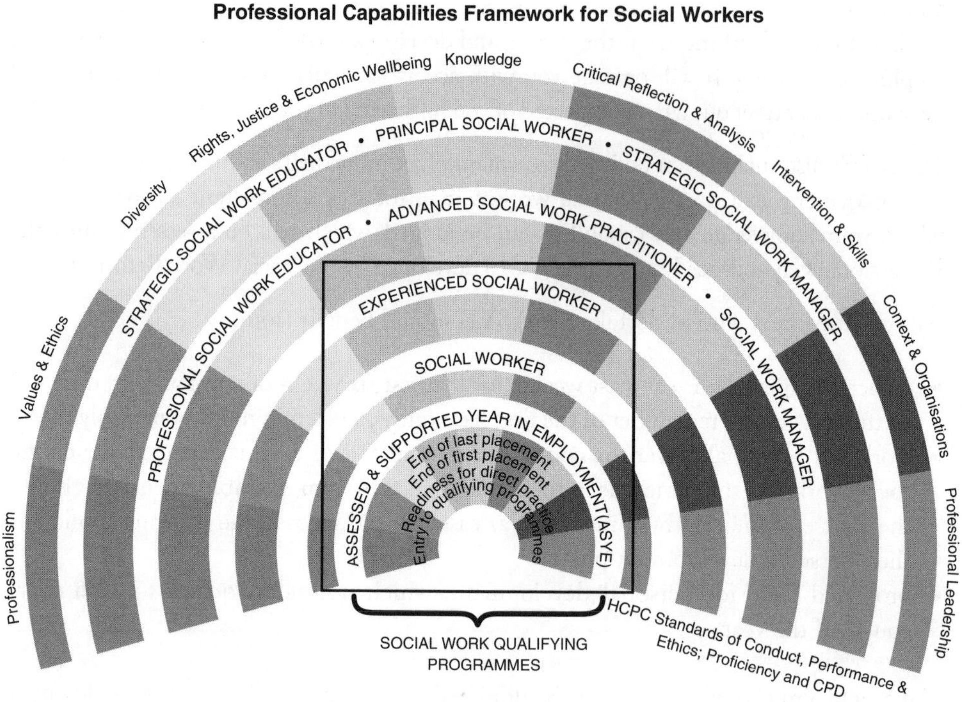

Professional Capabilities Framework for Social Workers

Figure 10.1   Extract from the PCF (TCSW, 2012a)

PCF domains – levels to be attained after your initial qualification

By the end of the ASYE social workers should have consistently demonstrated practice in a wider range of tasks and roles, and have become more effective in their interventions, thus building their own confidence, and earning the confidence of others. They will have more experience and skills in relation to a particular setting and user group, and have demonstrated ability to work effectively in more complex situations. They will seek support in supervision appropriately, whilst starting to exercise initiative and evaluate their own practice (taken from TCSW 2012e: 1).

Beyond ASYE

In order to remain on the HCPC register as a registered social worker, you will be required to renew your registration every two years and in doing so be prepared to show that you have kept up-to-date with your practice by maintaining a log or record of your Continuing Professional Development (CPD). ASYE can generally also be used to evidence your first block of evidence for CPD purposes.

Thus, ASYE can be used as part of accumulating your log or record of learning and development which you will need to have available when you re-register with the HCPC to retain your status as a registered social worker.

Registered Social Worker Status – The Pathway from ASYE through CPD and Beyond

Figure 10.3   The pathway from ASYE through CPD and future two-yearly registration

Figure 10.3 offers an outline of the new arrangements being introduced for social workers immediately after qualification. They will almost inevitably change and develop. So, it is important you keep an eye on the websites of the College of Social Work, Skills for Care and the Department for Education.

On a plus note, despite a rather convoluted organisational route planner for your early career path, we perhaps ought to be thankful there is at least some recognition and investment that endorses a commonly held view that the effectiveness of services, recruitment and retention and morale are all informed and improved by the provision of good quality support, supervision and some element of protection. The main body of recommendations supporting ASYE recognise this.

However investment in staff is something we ought to be able to expect of any decent employer.

Looking after Yourself

Social work is a demanding and stressful job. You need to look after yourself. To borrow Lynne Truss's title *Eats, Shoots & Leaves* (2003), I think the key message for a social worker is 'eat, sleep and take your leave'.

If you feel you are having difficulties and problems in your work, whether this is about workloads, management, lack of support, things you were promised which have not materialised, and more, then you need to respond to these promptly and in an appropriate way. Denial, pretence and acquiescence are not good for you and lead to low self-worth, low morale and a tendency to be anxious and stressed. Revisit Chapter 9 where we looked at dealing with problems which can arise on placement. Many of the features we identify are not unique to student placements and are frequently things we all face from time to time in our working lives. This does not make it OK. If things get really tough then seek advice from your management, human resources, from your union or professional association (see Chapter 9).

A Final Message

You have travelled a long way from those early days of beginning your course and getting ready for your first placement. I hope this book has been helpful. Good luck with your career and remember good social workers really do make a difference.

References

Adams, R. (2007) 'Reflective, critical and transformation practice', in W. Tovey (ed.) *The Post Qualifying Handbook for Social Workers*. London; Jessica Kingsley.

Adams, R. (2010) *The Short Guide to Social Work*. Bristol: Policy Press.

Adams, R., Dominelli, L. and Payne, M. (eds) (2002) *Critical Practice in Social Work*. Basingstoke: Palgrave Macmillan.

ADASS (Association of Directors of Adult Social Services) (2011) *Carers and Safeguarding Adults: Working Together to Improve Outcomes*. London: ADASS.

Agass, D. (2002) 'Countertransference, supervision and the reflective process', *Journal of Social Work Practice*, 16 (2): 125–34.

Akademikerförbundet SSR (2006) *An Ethical Code for Social Work Professionals*. Stockholm: Swedish Association of Graduates in Social Science, Personnel and Public Administration, Economics and Social Work.

Alaszewski, A. (1998) 'Risk in modern society', in A. Alaszewski, L. Harrison and J. Manthorpe (eds) *Risk, Health and Welfare: Policies, strategies and practice*. Buckingham: Open University Press. pp. 3–23.

Alberg, C., Hatfield, B. and Huxley, P. (eds) (1996) *Learning Materials on Mental Health: Risk assessment*. Manchester: University of Manchester/DH.

Aldridge, M. (1994) *Making Social Work News*. London: Routledge.

Asquith, S., Clark, C. and Waterhouse, L. (2005) *The Role of the Social Worker in the 21st Century: A literature review*. Edinburgh: 21st Century Social Work Review Group, The Scottish Executive.

Attlee, C. (1920) *The Social Worker*. London: Bell and Sons.

Audit Commission. Main website. Available at: www.audit-commission.gov.uk/

Australian Association of Social Workers. Main website. Available at: www.aasw.asn.au/

Baginsky, M., Moriarty, J., Manthorpe, J., Stevens, M., MacInnes, T. and Nagendran, T. (2010) *Social Workers' Workload Survey: Messages from the frontline findings from the 2009 survey and interviews with senior managers*. The Social Work Task Force. Available at: www.education. gov.uk/publications/eOrderingDownload/social%20workers%20workload%20survey%202009. pdf (accessed 22 November 2012).

Bailey, R. and Brake, M. (1975) *Radical Social Work*. London: Edward Arnold.

Banks, S. (2001) *Ethics and Values in Social Work*, 2nd edn. Basingstoke: Macmillan.

Barnard, A. (2006) 'Values, ethics and professionalization: A social work history', in A. Barnard, N. Horner and J. Wild (eds) *The Value Base of Social Work and Social Care: An active learning handbook*. Buckingham: Open University Press. pp. 5–24.

Barnardo's. Main website. Available at: www.barnardos.org.uk/

BASW (British Association of Social Workers). Main website. Available at: www.basw.co.uk/

BASW (British Association of Social Workers) (2012) *The Code of Ethics for Social Work: Statement of Principles.* Birmingham: BASW.

Beddoe, L. (2010) 'Surveillance or reflection: Professional supervision in the risk society', *British Journal of Social Work*, 40 (4): 1279–96.

Better Regulation Commission (2006) *Risk, Responsibility and Regulation: Whose risk is it anyway?* London: BRC.

Beveridge, W. (1942) *Report of the Inter-Departmental Committee on Social Insurance and Allied Services – the Beveridge Report.* Cm. 6404. London: HMSO.

Biestek, F.P. (1957) *The Casework Relationship.* Chicago: Loyola University Press.

Bion, W. (1962) *Learning from Experience.* London: Heinemann.

Birmingham Settlement. Main website. Available at: birminghamsettlement.org.uk/

Boud, D., Keogh, R. and Walker, D. (eds) (1985) *Reflection: Turning experience into learning.* London: Kogan Page.

Brechin, A. (2000) 'Introducing critical practice', in A. Brechin, H. Brown and M. Eby (eds) *Critical Practice in Health and Social Care.* London: Open University Press. pp. 25–47.

Broadhurst, K., Hall, C., Wastell, D., White, S. and Pithouse, A. (2010) 'Risk, instrumentalism and the humane project in social work: Identifying the informal logics of risk management in children's statutory services', *British Journal of Social Work*, 40 (4): 1046–64.

Brockbank, A. and McGill, I. (2006) *Facilitating Reflective Learning through Mentoring and Coaching.* London: Kogan Page.

Brody, S. (2009) Social workers deserve better treatment by the press. Available at: www.journalism.co.uk/news-commentary/-social-workers-deserve-better-treatment-by-the-press-/s6/a533768/ (accessed 1 March 2012).

Canadian Association of Social Workers. Main website. Available at: www.casw-acts.ca/

Care Quality Commission. Main website. Available at: www.cqc.org.uk/

Carey, M. and Foster, M. (2012) 'Social work, ideology, discourse and the limits of hegemony', *Journal of Social Work*, 13 (3) 248–66.

Carson, D. and Bain, A. (2008) *Professional Risk and Working with People: Decision-making in health, social care and criminal justice.* London: Jessica Kingsley.

Children's Rights Alliance for England (2013) *The State of Children's Rights in England: Review of government action on United Nations' recommendations for strengthening children's rights in the UK.* London: Children's Rights Alliance for England. Available at: www.crae.org.uk/assets/files/s%20Rights%202012.pdf (accessed 17 June 2013).

Citizens Advice. Main website. Available at: www.citizensadvice.org.uk/

Clark, L.C. (2000) *Social Work Ethics: Politics, principles and practices.* London: Macmillan.

Collins, S. and Wilkie, L. (2010) 'Anti-oppressive practice and social work students' portfolios in Scotland', *Social Work Education*, 29 (7): 760–77.

Coulshed, V. and Orme, J. (2006) *Social Work Practice.* Basingstoke: Palgrave Macmillan.

Cree, V. (2003) *Becoming a Social Worker.* London: Routledge.

Crisp, B.R., Anderson, M.T., Orme, J. and Lister, P.G. (2003) *Knowledge Review 01: Learning and teaching in social work education – assessment.* London: SCIE.

Curtis, L., Moriarty, J. and Netten, A. (2010) 'The expected working life of a social worker', *British Journal of Social Work*, 40 (5): 1628–43.

CWDC (Children's Workforce Development Council) (2008) *The State of the Children's Social Care Workforce*. Leeds: CWDC

Davies, M. (1994) *The Essential Social Worker*, 3rd edn. Aldershot: Arena.

DCSF (2009a) *Facing up to the Task. The interim report of the Social Work Task Force:* July. London: DCFS.

DCSF (2009b) *Building a Safe, Confident Future: The final report of the Social Work Task Force*. London: TSO.

DCSF and DH (2010) *Building a Safe and Confident Future: Implementing the recommendations of the Social Work Task Force*. London: DCSF.

DfE (2011a) *A Child-centred System: The government's response to the Munro Review of Child Protection*. London: DfE. Available at: media.education.gov.uk/assets/files/pdf/g/government%20response%20to%20munro%20-%20final.pdf (accessed 22 November 2012)

DfE (2011b) *The Munro Review of Child Protection: Final report: A child-centred system*. London: TSO. Available at: www.education.gov.uk/publications/eOrderingDownload/Munro-Review.pdf (accessed 22 November 2012).

DfE (2012) *Newly Qualified Social Worker Programme Final Evaluation Report (2008 to 2011)*. Research Report DFE-RR229, London: DfE.

DfE (2013) *Working Together to Safeguard Children: A guide to inter-agency working to safeguard and promote the welfare of children*. London: DfE. Available at: www.education.gov.uk/publications/eOrderingDownload/Working%20Together%202013.pdf (accessed 11 April 2013).

DfES (2003) *Every Child Matters*. London: TSO.

DH (2000a) *Framework for the Assessment of Children in Need and their Families*. London: HMSO.

DH (2000b) *Assessing Children in Need and their Families: Practice guidance*. London: TSO.

DH (2010) *Nothing Ventured, Nothing Gained: Risk guidance for people with dementia*. London: DH.

DH and DfES (2006) *Options for Excellence: Building the social care workforce of the future*. London: DH.

Disability Rights Commission (2005) *Whose Risk is it Anyway?* London: Disability Rights Commission.

Dixon, J. (2010) 'Social supervision, ethics and risk: An evaluation of how ethical frameworks might be applied within the social supervision process', *Journal of Social Work*, 40 (8): 2398–413.

Doel, M. (2009) *Social Work Placements: A traveller's guide*. London: Routledge.

Doel, M., Shardlow, S. and Johnson, G.P. (2011) *Contemporary Field Social Work: Integrating field and classroom experience*. London: Sage.

Dominelli, L. (2009) 'Anti-oppressive practice: The challenges of the twenty-first century', in R. Adams, L. Dominelli and M. Payne (eds) *Social Work: Themes, issues and debates*, 3rd edn. Basingstoke: Palgrave Macmillan. pp. 49–64.

DT (Department for Transport) (2007) *The Official Highway Code*. Norwich: Office of Public Sector Information.

Edmondson, D. and King, M. (forthcoming) 'The childcatchers: An exploration of the representation and discourses of social work in UK film and television drama from the 1960s to the present day'. Out for review.

Edmondson, D., Potter, A. and McLaughlin, H. (2013) 'Reflections of a higher specialist PQ student group on the Munro Recommendations for children's social workers.' *Practice*, 25 (3): 153–70.

FAST (Families and Schools Together). Main website. Available at: www.familiesandschools.org/

Ferguson, H. (2011) *Child Protection Practice.* Basingstoke: Palgrave Macmillan.

Ferguson, I. and Woodward, R. (2009) *Radical Social Work in Practice: Making a difference.* Bristol: Policy Press.

Fook, J. (2002) *Social Work: Critical theory and practice.* London: Sage.

Fook, J. and Gardner, F. (2007) *Practising Critical Reflection: A handbook* Maidenhead: Open University Press/McGraw-Hill Education.

Furedi, F (2006) *Culture of Fear Revisited.* London: Contiuum.

Galilee, J. (2005) *21st Century Social Work: Literature review on media representations of social work and social workers.* Edinburgh: 21st Century Social Work Review Group, Scottish Executive.

Garrett, P.M. (2012) 'Re-enchanting social work? The emerging "spirit" of social work in an age of economic crisis', *British Journal of Social Work,* doi:10.1093/bjsw/bcs146.

Gibbs, G. (1988) *Learning by Doing: A guide to teaching and learning methods.* Oxford: Oxford Further Education Unit, Oxford Brookes University.

Guardian (2012) Social care network blog. Available at: www.guardian.co.uk/social-care-network/social-life-blog/2012/feb/10/child-protection-social-worker-shoes (accessed 11 March 2013).

HCPC (Health and Care Professions Council). Main website. Available at: www.hpc-uk.org/

HCPC (Health and Care Professions Council) (2012a) *Guidance on Conduct and Ethics for Students.* London: HCPC.

HCPC (Health and Care Professions Council) (2012b) *Standards of Proficiency: Social workers in England.* London: HCPC.

Healy, K. (2012) *Social Work Methods and Skills: The essential foundations of Practice,* 1st edn. Basingstoke: Palgrave Macmillan.

Higham, P. (2006) *Social Work: Introducing professional practice.* London: Sage.

Holland, S. (2011) *Child and Family Assessment in Social Work Practice,* 2nd edn. London: Sage.

Home Department (1945) *Report by Sir Walter Monckton, KCMg, KCVO, MC, KC, on the Circumstances which led to the Boarding-out of Denis and Terence O'Neill at Bank Farm, Minsterley and the Steps taken to Supervise their Welfare.* London: HMSO.

Honey, P. and Mumford, A. (1982) *Manual of Learning Styles.* London: P. Honey.

Horlick-Jones, T. (2005) 'Informal logics of risk: Contingency and models of practical reasoning', *Journal of Risk Research,* 8 (3): 253–72.

Horwath, J. and Morrison, T. (1999) *Effective Staff Training in Social Care: From theory to practice.* London: Routledge.

Howe, D. (2008) *The Emotionally Intelligent Social Worker.* Basingstoke: Palgrave Macmillan.

Howe D. (2009) *A Brief Introduction to Social Work Theory.* Basingstoke: Palgrave: Macmillan.

Howes, N. (2010) 'Here to listen! Communicating with children and methods for communicating with children and young people as part of the assessment process', in J. Horwath (ed.) *The Child's World: The comprehensive guide to assessing children in need,* 2nd edn. London: Jessica Kingsley. pp.124–39.

IFSW (International Federation of Social Workers). Main website. Available at: ifsw.org/

IFSW (International Federation of Social Workers) (2000a) *Definition of Social Work.* Available at: http://ifsw.org/policies/definition-of-social-work/ (accessed: 11 February 2013).

IFSW (2000b) *Statement of Ethical Principles.* Available at: ifsw.org/policies/statement-of-ethical-principles/ (accessed 11 February 2013).

IFSW (2013) Our members Available at: http://ifsw.org/membership/our-members/ (accessed 13 June 2013).

INFED (The Encyclopaedia of Informal Education). Main website. Available at: www.infed.org/

International Federation of Settlements. Main website. Available at: www.ifsnetwork.org/

Jones, C., Ferguson, I., Lavalette M. and Penketh, L. (2004) *Social Work and Social Justice: A manifesto for a new engaged practice.* Available at: www.liv.ac.uk/sspsw/manifesto/Manifesto.htm (accessed 13 May 2010).

Jones, S. (2009) *Critical Learning for Social Work Students.* Exeter: Learning Matters.

Jordan, B. (2004) 'Emancipatory social work: Opportunity or oxymoron?', *British Journal of Social Work*, 34 (1): 5–19.

Jordan, B. (2006) *Social Policy for the Twenty-First Century: Big issues, new perspectives.* Cambridge: Polity Press.

Knight, P. (2006) 'The local practices of assessment', *Assessment and Evaluation in Higher Education*, 31 (4): 435–52 in TCSW (2012d) Understanding what is meant by Holistic Assessment. P.4.

Knott, C. and Scragg, T. (2007) *Reflective Practice in Social Work*, 2nd edn. Exeter: Learning Matters.

Kolb, D.A. (1984) *Experiential Learning: Experience as the source of learning and development.* Englewood Cliffs, NJ: Prentice Hall.

Kydd, L. (1996) *Professional Development for Educational Management.* Buckingham: Open University Press.

Laming, H. (2009) *The Protection of Children in England: A progress report.* London: TSO.

Leskošek, V. (2009) 'Introduction', in V. Leskošek (ed.) *Theories and Methods of Social Work: Exploring different perspectives.* Ljubljana: Faculty of Social Work, University of Ljubljana. pp. 1–5.

Levy, C.S. (1976) *Social Work Ethics.* New York: Human Sciences Press.

Lishman, J. (2007) *Handbook for Practice Learning in Social Work and Social Care Knowledge and Theory*, 2nd edn. London: Jessica Kingsley.

Local Government Association (2009) *Local Government Workforce Survey 2009 England.* London: LGA.

Lomax, R., Jones, K., Leigh, S. and Gay, C. (2010) *Surviving your Social Work Placement.* Basingstoke: Palgrave Macmillan.

Lymbery, M. (2005) *Social Work with Older People: Context, policy and practice.* London: Sage.

Macdonald, G. and Macdonald, K. (2010) 'Safeguarding: A case for intelligent risk management', *Journal of Social Work*, 40 (4): 1174–91.

McLaughlin, K. (2008) *Social Work, Politics and Society: From radicalism to orthodoxy.* Bristol: Policy Press.

Maclean, A. and Caffrey, B. (2009) *Developing a Practice Learning Curriculum: A guide for practice educators.* Rugeley: Kirwin Maclean Associates Ltd.

McLeod, A. (2008) *Listening to Children: A practitioner's guide.* London: Jessica Kingsley.

Manchester Settlement. Main website. Available at: www.manchestersettlement.org.uk/

Martin, R. (2010) *Social Work Assessment.* Exeter: Learning Matters.

Milner, J. and O'Byrne, P. (2002) *Assessment in Social Work*, 2nd edn. Basingstoke: Palgrave Macmillan.

Morgan, R. (2011) *Young Person's Guide to the Munro Review of Child Protection*. Office of the Children's Rights Director. Available at: www.rights4me.org/~/media/Library%20 Documents/Guides/GUIDE%20Childrens%20Guide%20to%20the%20review%20of%20 Child%20protection.pdf (accessed 21 November 2012).

Nobel Prize. Main website. Available at: www.nobelprize.org/

NSPCC. Main website. Available at: www.nspcc.org.uk/

Ofsted. Main website. Available at: www.ofsted.gov.uk/

Oxford Dictionaries (2013) Available at: oxforddictionaries.com/definition/english/risk?q=riskhttp:// (accessed 5 May 2013).

Parton, N. (2011) 'Child protection and safeguarding in England: Changing and competing conceptions of risk and their implications for social work', *British Journal of Social Work*, 41 (5): 854–75.

Payne, M. (1996) *What is Professional Social Work?* Birmingham: Venture Press.

Payne, M. (2005) *The Origins of Social Work: Continuity and change*. Basingstoke: Palgrave Macmillan.

Peach, J. and Horner, N. (2007) 'Using supervision: Support or surveillance?', in M. Lymbery and K. Postle (eds) *Social Work: A companion to learning*. London: Sage. pp. 228–39.

Pierson, J. (2011) *Understanding Social Work: History and context*. Maidenhead: Open University Press.

Pritchard, C. and Williams, R. (2010) 'Comparing possible "child-abuse-related-deaths" in England and Wales with the major developed countries 1974–2006: Signs of progress?', *British Journal of Social Work*, 40 (6): 1700–18.

QAA (Quality Assurance Agency for Higher Education) (2008) *Subject Benchmark Statement for Social Work*. Mansfield: QAA. Available at: www.qaa.ac.uk/Publications/ InformationAndGuidance/.../socialwork08.pdf (accessed 11 February 2012).

Race, P. and Brown, S. (2007) *The Lecturer's Toolkit: A practical guide to assessment, learning and teaching*, 3rd edn. London: Routledge.

Reamer, F.G. (1998) *The Evolution of Social Work Ethics*. Faculty Publications, Paper 170. Available at: digitalcommons.ric.edu/facultypublications/170 (accessed 17 March 2013).

Reamer F.G. (2003) *Social Work Values and Ethics*, 3rd edn. New York: Columbia University Press.

Ruch, G. (2007) 'Reflective practice in contemporary child-care social work: The role of containment', *British Journal of Social Work*, 37 (4): 659–80.

Schön, D. (1983) *The Reflective Practitioner: How professionals think in action*. London: Temple Smith.

Schön, D. (2002) 'From technical rationality to reflection-in-action', in R. Harrison, F. Reeve, A. Hanson, J. Clarke (eds) *Supporting Lifelong Learning. Volume 1 Perspectives on learning* London: Routledge Open University. pp. 40–61.

SCIE (Social Care Institute for Excellence). Main website. Available at: www.scie.org.uk/

Scriven, M and Paul, R. (1987) The Critical Thinking Community. Defining Critical Thinking. A statement by Michael Scriven and Richard Paul for the National Council for Excellence in Critical Thinking Instruction. Available at: www.criticalthinking.org/aboutCT/definingCT.cfm (accessed 6 June 2013).

Shardlow, S. and Doel, M. (2006) *Practice Learning and Teaching*, 2nd edn. Basingstoke: Palgrave.

Shardlow, S.M., Myers, S., Berry, A., Davis, C., Eckersley, T., Lawson, J., McLaughlin, H. and Rimmer, A. (2005) *Teaching and Assessing Assessment in Social Work Education within English Higher Education: Practice survey results and analysis*, Salford: Salford Centre for Social Work Research.

Shulman, L. (1993) *Interactional Supervision.* Washington, DC: NASW Press.

Simons, H. (2009) *Case Study Research in Practice.* London: Sage.

Skills for Care (2011) *Learning to Live with Risk: An introduction for service providers – full edition with notes on further reading.* Leeds: Skills for Care.

Skills for Care (2012) *The Assessed and Supported Year in Employment for Newly Qualified Workers.* Leeds: Skills for Care.

Smale, G., Tuson, G. and Statham, D. (2000) *Social Work and Social Problems: Working toward social inclusion and social change.* Basingstoke: Palgrave Macmillan.

Social Work Scotland. Main website. http://www.sssc.uk.com/

Social Workers Speak. Main website. Available at: www.socialworkersspeak.org/

Stake, R.E. (1995) *The Art of Case Study Research.* Thousand Oaks, CA: Sage.

Stalker, K. (2003) 'Managing risk and uncertainty in social work: A literature review', *Journal of Social Work*, 3 (2): 211–33.

Stark, R. (2008) *IFSW Statement on the 60th Anniversary of the Universal Declaration of Human Rights.* Available at: www.ifsw.org/p38001648.html (accessed 11 February 2012).

Stevens, M., Moriarty, J., Manthorpe, J., Hussein, S., Sharpe, E., Orme, J., Mcyntyre, G., Cavanagh, K., Green-Lister, P. and Crisp, B.R. (2012) 'Helping others or a rewarding career? Investigating student motivations to train as social workers in England', *Journal of Social Work*, 12 (1): 16–36.

Sutton, C. (1999) *Helping Families with Troubled Children.* Chichester: Wiley and Sons.

SWRB (Social Work Reform Board). Main website. Available at: www.education.gov.uk/swrb

SWRB (Social Work Reform Board) (2010) *Building a Safe and Confident Future: One year on – Progress report from the Social Work Reform Board.* London: DfE.

SWRB (Social Work Reform Board) (2012) *The Assessed and Supported Year in Employment for Newly Qualified Social Workers.* Available at: www.skillsforcare.org.uk/asye (accessed 10 April 2013).

TCSW (The College of Social Work). Main website. Available at: www.collegeofsocialwork.org/

TCSW (The College of Social Work) (2012a) *Domains within the PCF.* Version 1, 1 May. Available at: www.tcsw.org.uk/pcf.aspx (accessed 7 August 2012).

TCSW (The College of Social Work) (2012b) *Reforming Social Work Qualifying Education: The social work degree:* V 1.0, May. Available at: www.tcsw.org.uk/uploadedFiles/TheCollege/_CollegeLibrary/Reform_resources/ReformingSWQualifyingEducation(edref1)(1).pdf (accessed 2 July 2012).

TCSW (The College of Social Work) (2012c) *Student Social Worker Level Professional Capabilities.* Available at: http://www.tcsw.org.uk/uploadedFiles/TheCollege/_CollegeLibrary/Reform_resources/PCF5FullTableStudentLevels.pdf (Accessed 6 June 2013).

TCSW (The College of Social Work) (2012d) *Understanding What is Meant by Holistic Assessment* V1.0 May. Available at: http://www.tcsw.org.uk/uploadedFiles/TheCollege/_CollegeLibrary/Reform_resources/holistic-assessmentASYE1.pdf (accessed 6 June 2013).

TCSW (The College of Social Work) (2012e) *Understand What the Different Levels Mean.* Version 01/05/2012. Available at: www.tcsw.org.uk/uploadedFiles/PCFNOVUnderstanding-different-PCF-levels.pdf (Accessed 6 June 2013).

TCSW (The College of Social Work) (2012f) *Unfortunately it Will be Impossible to Eliminate Risk from Child Protection Work: The elimination of risk: an impossible ideal.* Available at: www.tcsw. org.uk/standard-2col-rhm-mediacentre.aspx?id=6442451146 (accessed 17 June 2013).

Thomas, G. (2011) 'A typology for the case study in social science following a review of definition, discourse and structure', *Qualitative Inquiry*, 17 (6): 511.

Thomas, N. (2005) *Social Work with Young People in Care.* Basingstoke: Palgrave Macmillan.

Thompson, N. (2000) *Understanding Social Work: Preparing for Practice.* Basingstoke: Macmillan.

Thompson, N. (2001) *Anti Discriminatory Practice*, 3rd edn. Basingstoke: Palgrave Macmillan.

Thompson, N. (2002) *People Skills.* Basingstoke: Palgrave Macmillan.

Thompson, N. (2006) *Anti Discriminatory Practice*, 4th edn. Basingstoke: Palgrave Macmillan.

Thompson, N. (2009) *Understanding Social Work: Preparing for practice.* Basingstoke: Palgrave Macmillan.

Thompson, S. and Thompson, N. (2008) *The Critically Reflective Practitioner.* Basingstoke: Palgrave Macmillan.

Tilling, J. (2009) 'Preparing for social work practice', in R. Adams, L. Dominelli and M. Payne (eds) *Social Work: Themes, issues and debates*, 3rd edn. Basingstoke: Palgrave Macmillan. pp. 355–69.

Toynbee Hall. Main website. Available at: www.toynbeehall.org.uk/

Trevithick, P. (2012) *Social Work Skills and Knowledge: A practice handbook* 3rd edn. Buckingham: Open University Press.

Truss, L. (2003) *Eats, Shoots & Leaves.* London: Profile Books Ltd.

UNICEF (2012) *A Summary of the UN Convention on the Rights of the Child.* Available at: www. unicef.org.uk/Documents/Publication-pdfs/betterlifeleaflet2012_press.pdf (accessed 21 November 2012).

United Nations Committee on the Rights of the Child (2008) *Committee on the Rights of the Child, Forty-ninth Session: Consideration of reports submitted by states parties under Article 44 of the Convention on the Rights of the Child, Concluding observations:United Kingdom of Great Britain and Northern Ireland.* Available at: www.crae.org.uk/protecting/socr.html (accessed 21 November 2012).

Watson, D. and West, J. (2006) *Social Work Process and Practice.* Basingstoke: Palgrave Macmillan.

Webb, C. and Carpenter, J. (2011) 'What can be done to promote the retention of social workers? A systematic review of interventions', *British Journal of Social Work*, 42 (7): 1235–55.

Webb, S.A. (2006) *Social Work in a Risk Society: Social and political perspectives.* Basingstoke: Palgrave Macmillan.

Whittington, C. (2007) *Assessment in Social Work: A guide for learning and teaching.* SCIE. Available at: www.scie.org.uk/publications/guides/guide18/files/guide18.pdf (accessed 2 February 2011).

Winter, K. (2011) *Building Relationships and Communicating with Young Children: A practical guide for social workers.* London: Routledge.

Workhouses. Main website. Available at: www.workhouses.org.uk/

Yin, R. (1994) *Case Study Research: Design and methods.* Thousand Oaks, CA: Sage.

Yin, R. (2009) *Case Study Research*, 4th edn. Thousand Oaks, CA: Sage.

Index